CW01629486

'The visitation of God'?

'The visitation of God'?

The potato and the great Irish famine

Austin Bourke

Edited for *Irish Historical Studies* by
Jacqueline Hill and Cormac Ó Gráda

THE LILLIPUT PRESS

Copyright © Austin Bourke 1993

All rights reserved. No part of this publication
may be reproduced in any form or by any means
without the prior permission of the publisher.

First published in 1993 by
THE LILLIPUT PRESS LTD
4 Rosemount Terrace, Arbour Hill,
Dublin 7, Ireland

A CIP record for this
book is available from
The British Library

ISBN 0 946640 93 9

Jacket design by Robert Ballagh
Set in 10 on 12 Guardi by
Diskon Technical Services Ltd of Dublin
Printed by Colour Books of Baldoyle Dublin

CONTENTS

Editors' foreword

Patrick Martin Austin Bourke was born on 10 May 1913, in Dungarvan, where his father was station-master for the Great Southern and Western Railway, and was educated at Ballyduff National School, Mount Sion CBS and at University College, Cork. He graduated from UCC in mathematics and mathematical physics in 1933, winning the Peel Memorial Prize for outstanding graduate of the year. He remained at UCC until 1938, lecturing, completing his M.Sc., and toying with the notion of an academic career in mathematics. Austin, the brilliant student, found time too for an amazing range of extra-curricular activities. He spent a year as president of the Students' Union, served as editor of the student newspaper, and played active roles in the student dramatic society and the hurling club. He also distinguished himself as a chess player, competing for Ireland at the Warsaw chess olympiad in 1935. Much later, in 1951, Austin would become Irish chess champion. Chess and classical music would remain lifelong loves.

Austin Bourke was a founder-member of the Irish Meteorological Service in 1939. After stints at Foynes, Rineanna, and Dublin Airport, he became assistant director of the service in 1948, and director in 1964, a position he held until his retirement in 1978. Early on, Austin developed a particular interest in agricultural meteorology, the field in which he was to become a world authority. From 1958 to 1962 he presided over the World Meteorological Organisation's commission for agricultural meteorology. In 1975 he was awarded the William F. Peterson gold medal for his work in the field of plant biometeorology.

As he recounts in the autobiographical memoir reproduced below, in 1955 Austin was seconded by the Meteorological Service to the Chilean government under a United Nations technical co-operation scheme. The Chilean potato crop had been badly ravaged by *phytophthora infestans*, or potato blight, and Austin's brief was to analyse meteorological links. The sojourn in Chile, 1955-6, turned his mind to aspects of Irish history, and so began Austin's lengthy researches on Ireland's involvement with the potato. These soon began to generate a flow of learned papers, but the culmination of this research was a Ph.D. from the National University of Ireland in 1967 for his thesis on 'The potato, blight, weather and the Irish famine'.

Obtaining the degree was never a career goal, since for Austin the pleasures of research (like those of playing chess) were truly their own reward. Yet the target of a Ph.D. provided some useful discipline and focus. Curiously, perhaps, the degree was awarded, not in history in Dublin, but in science in Cork. The bureaucratic reason for this was that he had had no formal training in history, but another reason is that

Austin's interdisciplinary brand of history was before its time. However, Kenneth Connell of Queen's University, Austin's external examiner, was very enthusiastic about the thesis. It is said that he deemed it worthy of a D. Sc.! The D.Sc. itself was to come in due course, in 1973. It came from the National University of Ireland, in recognition of Austin's contribution to science.

Remarkably, for many years Austin managed to combine his ambitious interdisciplinary historical researches with a successful professional career in meteorology. Since leaving the Meteorological Service Austin has kept up his professional and academic interests, publishing more papers and working on an EC project on the consequences of climatic change.

Austin's thesis, 'The potato, blight, weather and the Irish famine', was never published, yet it remains a brilliant and awe-inspiring piece of work. It combines great erudition, originality, and readability. It manages to be both objective and sensitive about a topic – the great famine – which popular accounts had tended to over-simplify and historians to shun. Before Bourke, serious Irish famine history was basically administrative history – the tragedy seen from the perspective of the politician, the medical practitioner, the emigration commissioner or the relieving officer. Bourke's shift of focus to the potato and plant disease and to their impact on the rural economy both before and during the famine opened the field for the economic historian. But Bourke's account of the potato in Ireland is not confined to the famine era; his treatment of the early history of the potato is simply the best there is, superseding that in Redcliffe Salaman's enduring classic, *The history and social influence of the potato* (Cambridge, 1949). The remarkable bibliography – reproduced here in updated form – speaks for the breadth of Bourke's scholarship. The thesis spawned a wide range of papers by Austin in scientific, historical, agricultural, and meteorological journals, both Irish and international. Most of these papers are included in this volume. Their subject-matter ranges from Irish potato consumption in the pre-famine heyday of the potato to the early spread and diagnosis of *phytophthora infestans*, the fateful potato blight – a disease unknown in Europe before the 1840s. The potato's role in the famine prompted Austin to estimate Irish crop yields before and after 1845 and to analyse the foreign grain trade before and during the famine. All these topics are at the core of current research into nineteenth-century Irish economic and social history, and this is evident in the number of citations of Austin's work in recent research. Whether in estimating the output of Irish agriculture before the famine, in assessing the regional impact of the blight, or in testing claims that Ireland produced enough food to feed its people in the late 1840s, or that a catastrophe such as the famine was on the cards in the 1830s and 1840s, modern economic historians simply cannot ignore the contributions of Austin Bourke.

For the most part Austin's historical studies have hitherto been known mainly to specialists. We believe that they deserve a wider audience, and hence this book. In addition to the key articles just noted, we have also included long sections of the thesis, previously unpublished, and two series of articles first published in *The Irish Times*. One debunks some over-simplistic interpretations of the great famine that were in the air in the 1960s (and perhaps are still). The other provides a spirited defence of Charles Trevelyan, the civil servant who controlled the purse-strings in Whitehall during the famine, and the main *bête noire* of traditional accounts of the tragedy. At the same time, Austin is no apologist for the doctrinaire policies pursued by ministers in the mid- and late 1840s. His work remains as fresh and scintillating as ever.

It is a great pleasure to honour Austin Bourke, a great scholar and a lovely man. Now in his eightieth year, *go maire se an cead!*

Cormac Ó Gráda,
University College, Dublin

I first heard Austin Bourke talk about the potato blight and the great famine at a lecture arranged by the Biology Society in Maynooth in 1983. Many things stand out about that occasion, but I was particularly struck (as a historian) by the sheer unfamiliarity of the sources used : weather charts, extracts from the *Gardeners' Chronicle*, contemporary continental journals published in Dutch, French, German. And then, the effortless mastery of the pre-famine potato varieties, and what each meant in the extraordinary potato-dominated economy that by the early 1800s had come to govern the lives of so many of the poorer classes in Ireland.

It was apparent, too, that years of grappling with the circumstances that combined to produce the terrible tragedy of the famine had not dented the speaker's humanity, or his sense of balance. It struck me as strange then that Austin Bourke's research was not better known, not simply by historians, but by the public at large: for his scholarship is worn lightly, and his work is highly readable.

In 1988, on the occasion of the fiftieth anniversary of *Irish Historical Studies*, the opportunity arose to acknowledge the importance of this work. Austin was invited to lecture on the famine at the journal's anniversary conference; and such was the impact of that lecture that the idea emerged of bringing out a selected edition of his writings as a permanent and accessible record of his famine research. The present volume represents our tribute to this outstanding scholar.

Inevitably, in the course of bringing this work to publication, *Irish Historical Studies* has built up many obligations to a great many people. For help with funding, we wish to acknowledge the contributions of

An Foras Talúntais, Agrolon (Seed Potato Specialists) Ltd. (Croydon), Seed Potato Promotions (Northern Ireland) Ltd., T. Rafferty (Ulster Bank, Maynooth), and above all the School of Irish Studies Foundation, whose generous grant has enabled publication to proceed. We also wish to record grateful thanks to Robert Ballagh, Margaret Crawford, Catherine Marshall, Mary Howard, Adrian Kelly, and of course to the Lilliput Press, who have produced the work to their usual high standard. For permission to reprint articles originally published elsewhere, we are grateful to the *Economic History Review*, *The Irish Times*, the *Journal of the Statistical and Social Inquiry Society of Ireland*, and *Nature*.

Jacqueline Hill,
St Patrick's College, Maynooth,
for Irish Historical Studies

NOTE ON STYLE

Spelling in original quotations has been left unchanged. All figures and tables retain their original numbering. *Irish Historical Studies* rules for citation, spellings and capitals etc. have been followed throughout.

Author's acknowledgments

Over the many years in which I have been collecting material on the potato crop, the blight epidemic and the weather during the years of the Irish famine I have amassed a great debt of gratitude to a wide range of people: to my wife Clodagh for unfailing support and encouragement; to my colleagues in the Irish Meteorological Service, and in particular to Mrs Lisa Shields; to my meteorological colleagues abroad, and in particular Professor H. H. Lamb; to the members of the Society of Irish Plant Pathologists, and to certain foreign plant pathologists, especially the late E. C. Large; to the staff of many libraries, at home and abroad.

My thanks are particularly extended to Dr Jacqueline Hill and Dr Cormac Ó Gráda, who have guided my tottering steps most unselfishly in recent years.

INTRODUCTION

Half a lifetime with potato blight*

In a preface to his classic book, *The history and social influence of the potato*, Dr Redcliffe Salaman felt it necessary to explain how his preoccupation with 'the otherwise inoffensive vegetable' had come about. Many of his friends regarded his studies with a pitying shake of the head and an indulgent smile, indicating that nothing, short of mental instability, could excuse a life-long obsession with so banal a subject.

I have met a very similar reaction to my own association over some forty years with an even narrower speciality, the course and history of potato blight, so I happily seize this opportunity to explain the chain of chance events which induced me to devote so much time to the pursuit of something which to other eyes might seem petty, if not downright potty.

Introduction to a life-long interest

As assistant director of the Meteorological Service it was part of my assigned duties, in the late 1940s, to encourage research and development in meteorology. This was far from easy, since my colleagues' noses were kept firmly pressed to the routine grindstone of transatlantic aviation meteorology; the best that one could hope to do was to link spare-time research projects with the hobbies and enthusiasms of individual meteorologists. For instance, the time of the rise of the mayfly in Irish lakes and rivers – and of the consequent stampede of fishermen to the local hotels – varies appreciably from season to season; an officer with an interest in angling might be willing to investigate whether the date could not be usefully forecast from environmental factors. Similarly a fan of radio and television might be induced to sacrifice part of his leisure to linking the quality of reception to the varying structure of the lower atmosphere. So, from year to year, a list of possible subjects for research was compiled and dangled before the staff, with the hooks so baited as to tempt persons of different temperaments.

Inevitably, tucked in among dozens of other potential ideas, there was listed a project for forecasting the seasonal onset and course of potato

* From *The Irish Meteorological Service: the first fifty years 1936-86*, ed. Lisa Shields (Dublin, 1987), pp 51-3.

blight. It is a disease of major economic impact in Ireland; that there is a broad relationship between its ravages and the seasonal weather has long been recognised. If one could establish a rational basis for forecasting the development of blight, growers could be advised on when and how often to apply fungicides, so as to contain the disease with the greatest efficiency and the least cost. The project was particularly promising since some progress on similar lines had been reported from the Netherlands and England. Nevertheless, none of my colleagues took up the theme.

Meanwhile, my director, Dr Doporto, gave one of his rare interviews to a newspaper reporter who, for one reason or another, got hold of the wrong end of the stick and announced in his article that the Meteorological Service would shortly begin a warning service on potato blight for Irish farmers. Faced with this development, Dr Doporto was adamant: 'You started this business, Mr Bourke. Now you must finish it.' I had been pitchforked into agricultural meteorology.

The task proved unexpectedly absorbing. The methods for forecasting the disease which had been empirically derived elsewhere were found to be less successful when transported to the Irish climate, and there was not available an adequate body of quantitative data on blight in past years to enable a domestic empirical model to be constructed. The only promising approach was to study the life cycle of the fungus and the results of laboratory research on the effects of temperature, humidity, etc. on different stages of its growth, and from the complex relationship between environment and disease to attempt to build up a simplified picture of the essential factors involved. By a lucky chance, I came early upon E. C. Large's fascinating book, *The advance of the fungi*, which proved to be a ready gateway to the rich pastures of nineteenth-century literature on plant diseases. With the guidance of Large and his forerunners, and with the help of the recent laboratory results of Crosier and others, it proved possible to establish a numerical model which permitted the use of routine meteorological observations to forecast the date of appearance each year of potato blight and the annual variations in its intensity. The new service of blight forecasts for Irish farmers was successfully launched, and the publication of several Technical Notes on the subject brought me into the position of being a domestic specialist on meteorological aspects of plant pathology. One of the great advantages of working in a very restricted field is that competition is reduced: in the kingdom of the blind, the one-eyed man is king.

The successful establishment of an Irish service of potato blight forecasts should have been the end of the matter, but it proved to be only the beginning. In 1953, the World Meteorological Organisation, through its commission for agricultural meteorology, decided to prepare a report on the forecasting from weather data of potato blight and other plant diseases and pests. In view of my recent activity in this field, I was appointed chairman of the international working group charged with preparing this review. As much of the relevant literature had already been surveyed here, it did not take unduly long to draft the required report, which was published by WMO over my name in 1955. From being a domestic specialist, I had been cast overnight in the role of international expert whose services, as luck would have it, were soon to be called upon.

Assignment in Chile

The potato had always been an important crop in Chile, and luckily one that long remained free from blight even though the disease was prevalent in most of its South American neighbours. Late in 1950 the first appearance of potato blight in the Chilean crop was confirmed in the laboratory. In the following year the disease caused disastrous damage to the crop and brought real distress to southern Chile. The distinguished German plant pathologist, Dr K. O. Mueller, was called in as an FAO expert; in his report to the government of Chile he suggested an investigation into the effect of climatic variations in different parts of the country and of weather conditions in different years, on the appearance and spread of blight. This might bring to light, he thought, clues as to the reasons for the severe attack of 1951, and could provide a basis on which to forecast the probable frequency of future attacks, and on which to make a rational choice of seed-producing areas. Coincidentally the government of Chile approached the UN for the services of an expert on the meteorological aspects of potato blight at the very moment when the report of the WMO working group was being published.

I went to Chile on a twelve-month assignment more as a conscript than as a volunteer. Indeed in the absence of external pressure I was highly unlikely to have been granted leave of absence from a Meteorological Service which was suffering from severe staff shortage: a later application to undertake a short-term mission in Turkey was rejected. When I arrived in Chile in October 1955, the disease had become quiescent, and my main concern, viewing the assignment as basically a piece of detective work, was that, after five years, the trail might be too cold to reveal the vital clues. The records were indeed sketchy in parts but, helped by a fresh outbreak of disease in 1956, it proved possible to piece the story together bit by bit, until at least the main lines were made clear.

What was of particular interest to an Irishman in Chile was the striking similarity with the Ireland of more than a hundred years earlier. The slight impact of blight when it first appeared in Chile in the late season of 1950 and the savage attack in the following year were an exact parallel to the course of the disease in Ireland in the successive years 1845-6. The survival of the feudal system in South America provided a living example of social conditions broadly similar to those of Ireland in the 1840s, even in the matter of absentee landlords; a master who spent his time in Santiago was normally farther removed from his estates than an Irish landlord in London or Paris. As regards climate and human temperament, Darwin had already noted a hundred years ago the analogy of the large island of Chiloé to Ireland, and conditions there had scarcely changed in the interim. As one stood by a blighted potato patch near Ancud and heard the cries of a distressed mother faced with the destruction of the main food of her large family, one had the eerie feeling of being transported through time and space to the Ireland of August 1846.

Equally striking were the differences. There was great distress in Chile when the potato crop failed, and much hunger and even local starvation, but nothing remotely resembling the Irish disaster of 1846-7. The Chileans were curious as to why the whole Irish nation had once been so dependent on a single crop, and one, in particular, of which the surplus in a good season could not be stored and carried over as reserve against later shortage; long familiarity with the facts had not dulled their astonishment at a historically unprecedented dependence on a non-cereal food crop. And why had so many died when blight came? I gave the traditional answers but, far from home, they did not seem entirely convincing.

Back in Ireland

Back in Ireland, these questions continued to nag. There were additional puzzling aspects the closer one looked into the matter. Potatoes to feed eight million people surely required an enormous acreage. How was this fitted, together with the ground needed for pasture and cereal crops, into the limited tillage land of Ireland? How was this vast acreage manured? What happened to the abandoned potato land after the famine? Why had potato blight wiped out the 1846 crop in Ireland while nowhere else, then or later, had it ever led to more than about a 50% loss? Was the weather in fact unique in the years of the great famine? Possibly the answers were buried in the rubble of time, but the satisfaction of following successfully a cold trail in Chile gave birth to the idea of picking up a still colder trail in Ireland.

There followed years of spare-time burrowing in Dublin libraries, the British Museum, the Colindale Newspaper Library, the French National Library, the Belgian Royal Library and indeed everywhere where clues to the first great European epidemic of potato blight might be found. The Royal Meteorological Society helped with a grant from its scientific activities fund, the Rockefeller Foundation contributed towards travel and subsistence costs, several (foreign!) airlines provided familiarisation flights and the civil service, thanks to Dr Thekla Beere, provided a short spell of special leave at a critical stage of the work. The picture finally took shape, first in an article published in *Nature* in 1964 and, three years later, in a Ph.D. thesis submitted to the National University of Ireland.

(My investigations over the years into the potato disease played some part in the award of a second doctorate in 1973, an honorary D.Sc. also from NUI.)

The disease in Iceland

Retirement from the Meteorological Service in 1978 brought leisure to travel and to ponder further meteorological aspects of plant pathology. A complication in assessing the effects of climatic change on agriculture is that one needs to take into consideration not just the direct consequences on growth and yield, but also the changes in the impact of diseases and pests. A visit to Iceland highlighted the effect of temperature fluctuations on the local potato crop. A distinct rise of air temperature in Iceland during the growing season in the 1930s and 1940s improved conditions on the one hand by lengthening the growing season, but also led to a series of severe blight attacks because conditions had become more favourable to the fungus. The plateau of warmth in these decades in Iceland was followed by the onset of cooling, gradual at first but sharper since 1960, to a level in the 1970s characterised by lower mean temperatures than any recorded for the earlier decades of this century. Simultaneously with the temperature fall, the impact of blight in Iceland gradually died down, so that in recent years the disease has been hard to detect.

Fungal spread: a re-appraisal

A return visit to South America threw fresh light on the importance of wind dispersion in the spread of plant diseases. Coffee leaf rust is a major disease of the coffee crop which has been known for more than a hundred years and is prevalent in India, Kenya and in other coffee-growing parts of Asia, Africa and Oceania. The coffee crops of the Americas, where the varieties in widest use are known to be highly vulnerable to the causal fungus, had been happily immune until 1970 when the disease was discovered in Brazil, borne there apparently by the wind across the South Atlantic from western Africa. The theory of transport of the infection by the prevailing winds was reinforced by the subsequent rapid spread of the disease from Bahia, where it first appeared, in the direction of Paraguay and Argentina.

This raised again a question which had arisen some twenty years earlier when the spread of potato blight in Europe in the epidemic year of 1845 had first been mapped. The spread of the disease from the initial infection in Flanders towards the north-east could readily be explained in terms of the usual prevailing winds; but were the wind patterns in that summer of 1845 consistent with a quite rapid spread also to the west and north-west? This problem was taken up in an EEC research project on 'The spread of potato blight in Europe in 1845-6 and the accompanying wind and weather patterns' undertaken by Professor H. H. Lamb of the University of East

Anglia and myself. It was established that there were frequent occasions when weather leading to sporulation of the fungus in July and August 1845 was accompanied by easterly or south-easterly winds.

The study also concerned itself with broader issues, such as the phytosanitary dangers of devoting great areas of land to a single crop (monoculture) and to the identification of the inherent vulnerability of the population as the prime cause of the disaster. It is hoped that the detailed analysis of the 1845-6 analogue, with its devastating social and economic consequences, may prove useful in interpreting and countering the threat of future plant disease epidemics, particularly in the Third World.

PART I

Agriculture and the potato before the famine

CHAPTER I

Towards the precipice: the potato in pre-famine Ireland*

'Of course', said the leader of the Gadarene swine,
Rushing furiously towards the sea,
'One knows
That the rest don't really want
To come over this steep place.
But what can one do?
I often wonder', he went on, panting,
'How we were manoeuvred
Into this position.'
(Richard Mallett, *Statesmanship*)

The questions of how and when the potato found its way into Ireland, where it later was to play a major role, are shrouded in mystery. It had been brought by the Spaniards from South America to Europe in 1565. Salaman argues plausibly that it made its appearance in Ireland 'some time during the last fifteen years of the sixteenth century'.[1] Its history in Ireland in the next fifty years or so is one of silence; scattered references begin to occur in the second half of the seventeenth century, and towards the end of that century, there was sufficient interest in the potato for speculation to arise as to how it originally came to Ireland. It was not until much later that efforts were made to assemble an integrated picture of the history of the potato in Europe. Payen and Chevallier concentrate on its history in France; McAdam, who was from Belfast, takes a wider target in what Wilde commended in the census of 1851 as a 'learned paper'.[2] Wilde himself made a contribution to the earlier history of the potato in Ireland, much of which was incorporated into the census of 1851.[3] In modern times, Davidson laid, as far as Ireland is concerned, much of the foundations on which Salaman built his monumental and comprehensive history of the potato.[4]

* From 'The potato, blight, weather and the Irish famine' (Ph.D. thesis, NUI, 1967), chap. 1.

TIME CHART OF THE POTATO IN IRELAND. 1700 – 1850

1700 – 1750 – 1800 – 1850

STAGE OF USE

RISE
In addition to its original role as a 'bulwark against famine', i.e., a crop which succeeded in wet sunless seasons when cereals failed, the potato gradually became the staple food of the poorest class in the winter half-year. For others, it supplemented a diet largely composed of grain and milk products.

APEX
The potato became the standard. and sometimes the only food, of increasing numbers over the greater part of the year. With the cultivation of improved varieties, it permeated all classes. At the time of Arthur Young's Irish tour, the potato was good and plentiful, normally supplemented by milk and often by oatmeal. A decline in conditions towards the end of the period was partially masked by the war-time agricultural boom.

FALL
The decline towards the famine, clearly visible from the end of the Napoleonic wars. Under pressure of shortage of land and manure, coupled with increase of population, inferior potato varieties, suitable only as cattle fodder, came into widespread use as human food.

MAJOR VARIETY

DISEASES AND CONSEQUENCES

WEATHER DAMAGE
No serious organic disease. Damage mainly due to weather hazards – severe drought, or waterlogging; occasionally high winds and salt spray. In some years, serious damage by frost. Cultivation in raised ridges gave improved drainage. Autumnal digging and pitting avoided major frost damage.

CURL
From about 1764, potato virus disease caused concern, first in Britain and later on the Continent. Led to –

(1) periodic renewal of seed. Rise of the Scottish seed potato trade,

(2) breeding of new varieties in the search for disease resistance; specialised varieties (early, heavy yielding, etc.) developed in England,

(3) unrestrained international exchanges of potatoes,

(4) a trend towards later planting.

TAINT
Dry rot serious in Britain and Ireland about 1830 and in Germany later. Intensified (2) and (3) above, led to a demand for the 'renewal of stock' from South America, and caused a thicker seeding rate using whole tubers. Widely confused with blight which followed close on its heels.

BLIGHT
First reported in Europe in 1845.

These writers have fairly thoroughly gleaned the early references to the potato in Ireland, and have indeed also harvested some ambiguous matter on 'roots', 'artichokes' and 'moist meals' which the more sceptical might classify as cockle. To the assembled facts and quotations little can be added, but the interpretations, often based on isolated references which seem rather slight to bear the weight of the inferences placed upon them, may sometimes be questioned. Thus, for instance, the rapidity with which the potato was adopted as the general food of the Irish people has been a matter of dispute for over a hundred years. Wilde, in his earlier studies, came to the conclusion that the potato was a major factor about the middle of the seventeenth century. He was challenged in this by Dr John Davy, and sufficiently modified his views as to admit that 'we have no proof that it was so extensively planted as to become a staple article of human food, or to displace corn to any great extent, until towards the end of the seventeenth century'.[5] Davidson reverted to the view of a rapid conquest of Ireland by the potato, and indeed he had little alternative in view of the authenticity and weight which he accorded to the 1606-7 entry in the *Montgomery manuscripts*; in this interpretation he was followed by Salaman. Again the view was strongly challenged, this time by Connell. Drake goes even further in deferring the move of the potato from a minor to a major role in Irish diet to about the middle of the eighteenth century.[6]

It is suggested, in broad agreement with the views of Connell and Drake, that the role of the potato in Ireland over the period 1600-1845 may be summarised as a series of progressive stages. In the following paragraphs, four such stages are differentiated; the dates shown are approximate only, since the successive stages progressively overlapped, and since the rate of progress and the final stage reached varied regionally, with the west and south leading the way and the north-east lagging.

The known facts about the potato, it is submitted, fit well into the scheme, and later it will be shown that the sequence of potato diseases, and the development of the main potato varieties, are consistent with this interpretation, which leads logically to the well-documented position of the potato on the eve of the famine. The relative chronology of potato progress, disease and varieties over the period 1700-1845 is summarised in the time-chart.

The history of the potato in Ireland

Stage 1 (1590-1675). *The potato as a supplementary food and as a stand-by against famine*

The first hundred years or so after the introduction of the potato to Ireland was one in which the new food came gradually into use, not, in normal years, as a *substitute* for, but as a *supplement* to other foods, mainly cereal. The most obvious and immediate advantage of the potato, to a people who must have regarded it initially with that lack of enthusiasm with which marked changes of diet have universally been greeted, was that it stood up so remarkably well to the rigours of a wet and sunless climate. Townley quotes 'an old writer' who characterised the potato as 'a plant, if possible, more tenacious of life than couch grass' and mentions that it had built up a high reputation – which had just been spectacularly destroyed – as a plant 'peculiarly exempt from blights and mildews'.[7] Before 1845 in Europe, the potato was, in fact, generally most abundant in wet seasons when the grain crop was poor in quality and quantity.[8] Except in the case where widespread floods led to waterlogging on low ground the lazy-bed 'mode of culture, rude and artificial as it was...protected the potato from excess moisture' and made it 'the most certain crop'.[9] On the other hand, cereal crops in Ireland suffered too often from lodging, failure to ripen, low yields, pre-harvest sprouting and high moisture content.[10] The potato thus made, in bad seasons, 'a most excellent substitute' for grain and 'very often preserved us from famine'. Wood-Martin confirms that the introduction of the potato 'stayed for a time the almost periodic famines'.[11]

It is to this extent only that we can agree with Davidson that climate played a vital role in winning acceptance for the potato in Ireland.[12] Climate and soil, *per se*, were well suited to the potato over much of north-west Europe, but the meteorological differential which favoured the potato against cereal crops in wet years operated most strongly in Ireland's humid climate.

It was precisely the reputation of the potato as 'the most certain of all crops', and as a 'palladium against famine' learned from Irish experience, which led to an agitation in the second half of the seventeenth century for the encouragement of the crop in England.[13] The relevant material has been given in full by Salaman and need only be summarised here.[14] A Mr Buckland from Somerset wrote to the Royal Society in 1662 urging that the cultivation of potatoes in England should be encouraged as a protection against famine. In the subsequent discussion at the Royal Society in the same year, Robert Boyle testified that the potato had kept thousands from starving in a time of famine in Ireland. John Beale continued the agitation from the same standpoint in 1663, and returned to the fray in 1672 and again in 1675, with fresh evidence that the potato relieved Ireland from recent famine 'when the corn crop failed them'. Houghton draws attention to the fact that it was not merely natural failures of the cereal crops in Ireland against which the potato gave protection but also the results of enemy action.[15] No doubt the rigours of war gave added impetus to the cultivation of the potato in Ireland in the seventeenth century, just as they did in Europe in successive wars in recent times. The role of the potato in making a people 'entirely independent of foreign nations for food' was approved by McAdam.[16]

The prime advantage of the potato as a prophylactic against hunger continued to be stressed for nearly two hundred years – until, in fact, blight turned it from a boast into a lamentation for things past.[17] Townley, in a similar vein, quotes from the earlier enthusiasm of Thomas Andrew Knight, Sir John Sinclair and J. C. Curwen, and adds his own quota of evidence that in the dreadful summer of 1799 in England the potato, deficient as it was due to waterlogging, came manfully to the rescue and earned a wider usage because of 'its conspicuous utility at this season'.[18] McAdam, writing from the comparative prosperity of oats-eating Ulster, attests that the potato 'is perfectly secure against those heavy late rains which so often destroy the [grain] hopes of farmers' and adds incautiously that it 'has placed us almost beyond the reach of those frightful famines which, in former times, so often devastated the land'. Even 'recent failures' did little to damage its reputation in this respect. It was considered to be 'as near as possible a certain crop when land is drained', and, in England, occasional failures did not lead to distress amongst the people.[19]

This last comment draws attention to a gradual change which had come about in Ireland in the part played by the potato as a defence against hunger. In the earlier years, the potato-cereal combination could act as a two-way safeguard against failure of either crop. Only if both lines of defence were broken down, as in 1739-40, did serious famine develop.[20] Even as late as 1816, Farran could claim that the potato, although small and wet, fared much better than grain, and played its part in staying famine.[21] But the reverse was no longer true; so many of the Irish people were on a total potato diet by the early nineteenth century that they had no further resource to fall back upon if it failed, and a deficiency in the potato crop led to famine even when cereals were abundant.[22] As Spear wrote in 1822:

> Potatoes are the grand nutrient principle and support of existence, and without this valuable vegetable, hundreds must daily fall into the grave. It forms the great barrier to the ravages of hunger, and indeed constitutes almost the only one.[23]

We may review briefly the evidence that, while Ireland was the pioneer, it was not the only European country in which the original stimulus to the cultivation of the potato was as a bulwark against food shortage. In Scotland, it was famine in the early 1740s that broke the prejudice against growing the crop.[24] 'The dread of the recurrence of a similar calamity led to the more general and extensive cultivation of what promised to be the most effectual remedy against such a visitation.'[25] In 1795-6, the British Board of Agriculture recommended an increased growth of potatoes as security against grain shortage, and parliament offered bounties for the same purpose. Sir John Sinclair, who had a leading hand in these moves, could claim that 'the introduction of potatoes is considered to be the greatest blessing that modern times has bestowed on this country' and one which had more than once saved its people from the miseries of famine.[26]

In Germany, Frederick the Great urged his people in 1745, during the latest of a series of grain famines, to grow potatoes as a guard against hunger. Nearly a hundred years later Pinkert testified to how well this 'noble vegetable', 'more certain than any other', had carried out its task in Germany, giving 'comparatively large produce when other crops fail'.[27] In the Low Countries, Mareska and Kickx, aghast at the first devastation by blight, recall the conviction that famine had become impossible with the general cultivation of the potato. 'It was based on long experience and on the observation that an excess of dryness or of wetness would give a good crop on one kind of land even if it damaged it on another.' In Switzerland potatoes were regarded with mistrust until the famine of 1771 made the people realise their value.[28]

The history of the potato in France has a special interest of its own.[29] Introduced prior to 1600, it was soon denounced by the savants as a solanum, and as such, poisonous and a probable cause of leprosy. Its culture was entirely abandoned, and its success in neighbouring lands aroused only the sarcasm of the French. Interest was not reawakened until the eve of the French Revolution, when during the food shortages of 1786, Parmentier staged a series of publicity stunts, including the placing of an armed guard on a plot of the valuable root, and the presentation to the king of a bouquet of potato flowers. Afterwards, with governmental encouragement, the potato acreage in France expanded sixteenfold between 1793 and 1815.

One is tempted to speculate on whether the French Revolution would have taken place if the potato had been widely enough grown there to blunt the edge of discontent due to poor grain harvests – if, in fact, the alternative to bread had not been cake but potatoes; whether, in the absence of the potato from Ireland, the rebellion of 1798 might not have received more widespread support (as William Drennan thought); to what extent rioting and revolution in Europe in the late 1840s was related to a diseased potato no longer standing squarely as a bastion against want.

Stage 2 (1675-1750). *The potato as the winter food of the poorer people*

It cannot have been long after the potato came into general use in Ireland before its second great advantage became clear to those with limited resources of land or money, *viz.* that food production per acre was far greater when the potato replaced grain crops. Further, it was available as human food without processing, whereas the miller had to be paid, in cash or kind, for converting oats to meal or wheat to flour. Yet the greater productivity of the potato was not a feature strongly stressed by the earlier authors, who were, of course, writing more for the well-to-do than the poor. Arthur Young mentions it in passing, but it is not until the nineteenth century, when the competition for land by a swollen population became intense, that the higher food value of the potato in terms of yield was developed at length.[30] The matter was discussed repeatedly in the evidence presented to the poor law inquiry.[31]

Confirmation that the potato had, by this period, developed from merely a useful standby to an important foodstuff for the poor is found in the references and quotations presented in detail by Davidson and Salaman. Here it will suffice to reproduce Leigh's comment in 1684; 'ye great support of ye poore sortes of people is thire potatoes' and Hale's comment, towards the end of the period, that in 1746 the potato was 'in a manner the food of the common people of Ireland'.

That in this period the potato was eaten only for a limited part of the year is clear from a number of sources. Petty, in a well-known paragraph, lists amongst the food of the Irish 'potatoes from August to May'. It is clearly this testimony that Dutton has in mind when he says that 'in the year 1672 potatoes seldom lasted longer than from August to May';[32] this he attributes to the poor keeping qualities of the varieties in use during the earlier period. A relevant factor may also have been the comparatively wider food range in normal seasons in the seventeenth century. Townsend says that 'formerly the use of them [potatoes] was limited to particular seasons, oatmeal having been used in spring and summer'.[33] Archbishop Boulter's famous letter on the food shortage of 1727 is precise: 'the winter subsistence of the poor is chiefly potatoes'; the letter is dated 24 February, and as he mentions that potato supplies had been exhausted nearly two months earlier than usual, this suggests that their use did not extend beyond April, at latest. McKay quotes an Irish poem written in the first half of the eighteenth century which represents the potato as in use 'from the first of August in the autumn until the feast of Patrick in the spring'.[34]

There are other points of interest in this poem, although it would, doubtless, be unwise to read too much into an ironical account of a fictitious battle presented as taking place in Tallaght, Co. Dublin, in 1705 between the supporters of the potato and of oatmeal. It does suggest that the potato had made a sufficient encroachment as a regular food as to cause resentment amongst grain producers. Other foods, including meat, are represented as accompanying the potato: it confirms other evidence that an important role throughout the land continued to be played, not only by grain, but also by dairy products, with frequent references to sour milk or bonnyclobber, which surely was related to the now fashionable yoghurt.

Two comments on cultural practices may be made before leaving this period. If the common crop of potatoes came into normal use as early as August (as Petty and the poem suggest, as against the phrases used by Boulter and Townsend), then the poorer classes must have planted their crops appreciably earlier than was the practice in the early nineteenth century. Indeed, if the potato varieties in general use did not keep much beyond March, they would have been forced to do so. There is evidence that this was, in fact, a period of earlier planting.[35] However, no maincrop variety was likely to be fully developed in August; the early white variety mentioned by Rye as being ready for use in June required to be planted in January, and was therefore confined to frost-free coastal nooks, nor indeed could a low-yielding early variety even have appealed much to the poor. The association of August with the beginning of the potato harvest was essentially a carry-over of the old feast of Lughnasa tradition which was more logically associated with the grain harvest. The strain of the transition in this earlier period may not have been too great where the potato planting took place in March-April, but, nearer the famine, when the people's crop was not fully ready until October, the tradition of eating new potatoes on 'Garlic Sunday' can, for most of the population, have represented no more than the ritual sampling of scarcely formed tubers. We shall return to this point later.[36]

In this period, also, it appears to have been largely the custom to leave the potatoes in the ground and dig them out as required during the winter months. Thus, the severe frost stated to have set in about Christmas 1739 found much of the potato crop still in the ground, so that it was either destroyed or became inaccessible; 'it was not understood or generally believed that the potato could be preserved in any other way than by allowing it to remain in the earth where it had grown'. No doubt, experiences of this kind taught the people to dig and pit their potatoes with an insulating layer of earth, or to keep them indoors for the winter; but the trend towards earlier harvesting was later intensified both by a desire to escape disease (see later under 'curl') and by the necessity, in the wheat-growing areas, to vacate ground for the winter-sown crop when this culture spread under the encouragement of bounties. Thus, 'the memorable frost in the winter of 1813-1814 did not in any way affect the food of man in this island'.[37]

Stage 3 (1750-1810). *The potato as the staple diet of small farmers over the greater part of the year, and as an important part of the diet of all classes*

A spectacular expansion – it may not be exaggerated to call it an explosion – took place in the culture of the potato in the earlier part of this period. Connell cites part of the evidence, including Young's comment that potato culture had increased twentyfold in the twenty years before his Irish tour.[38] To this we may add the opinion of M'Sweeny, in a paper read in 1830, that 'the vast increase of the potato culture, and the general use of this vegetable as the entire dependence of the peasantry, have been within the memory of the old persons of the present generation'. And again,

> it was not until towards the middle of the 18th century that it [the potato] assumed the importance of a general field-crop. From that period, until within the last few years, this vegetable went on increasing in variety and improving in quality.[39]

This phenomenon was indeed closely linked, as we shall see in more detail later, with the development of new and improved potato varieties, not only more appetising and nourishing, but also remaining fit for human food over a longer period of the year. As the Reverend Dr Maunsell writes:

> About fifty years ago we had but few kinds of potatoes in this kingdom, and it is probable that these few kinds only would have still continued, was it not for the ingenuity of some gentlemen who tried experiments on the seed of the apple of the potato, from whence arose the great variety of potatoes that we now have.

He goes on to sing a hymn of praise to the potato as 'the most fruitful root we have; its fructifying quality is visible in every cabbin you pass by. They produce good soldiers, good seamen, good citizens and good husbandmen.' He commended its greater use by 'the higher classes of life' as an encouragement to fecundity – 'Doctor Lloyd, whose eminence as a physician was very great, frequently recommended potatoes as a supper to those ladies whom providence had not blessed with children, and an heir has often been the consequence.'[40] Nor did they lack attractions for the unwed maiden; Henry wrote in 1771 that where 'the potato is most generally used as food, the admirable complexions of the wenches are so remarkably delicate as to excite in their superiors very friendly and flattering sensations'.[41]

Whatever the cause, there is no doubt that, from then until the outbreak of the famine, potatoes formed an important part of the food of all classes. As early as 1775, Twiss comments that even with the Irish gentry, 'potatoes form a standing dish at every meal'.[42] 'Of them, it has been justly stated', quotes a writer in the *Munster Farmers' Magazine*, 'that they are the luxury of the rich and the food of the poor; the chief cause of our population and our greatest security against famine.'[43] Later, during the corn laws controversy, the use of potatoes by the titled Irish aroused the ponderous humour of English protectionists. Sir Charles Knightley told a Northamptonshire audience that the late Lord Sydney

> had been invited by Mr Spring Rice's father-in-law, the late Earl of Limerick, to dine with him on Saturday, and by one of those mistakes which Irishmen sometimes make, the invitation was sent for the Saturday before that on which the dinner was intended. Accordingly, Lord Sydney went, when Lord Limerick said 'I am very glad to see you, though I did not expect to see you today, but I shall be very glad if you will dine with our family.' Accordingly they sat down to table, with the four daughters of the noble earl, and four covered dishes were placed on the table. 'What have you got there, my dear?' said Lord Limerick, addressing his eldest daughter, 'lift the cover and see.' The young lady, dutifully lifting the cover, replied 'Potatoes, papa.' 'Humph' said the noble lord, 'what have you got there?' The second daughter, lifting the next cover, replied 'Potatoes, papa.' 'What have you got?' (to the third). 'Potatoes, papa.' (It is impossible to describe the vivacity and point with which Sir Charles told the anecdote, nor the ludicrous effect it had upon the meeting.) That was really a fact, for the late Lord Sydney told him, so the

story was literally true – and in those days the potatoes were not Peeled (shouts of laughter).[44]

The remarkable spread in the popularity of the potato derived, in part, from its third and final advantage, *viz.* that, once improved varieties were available, it could, unlike other vegetables, be eaten frequently and in abundance without revolting the appetite. For the poorer classes, no doubt its very bulk was habit-forming. Foster, the *Times* correspondent, was told by 'an eminent surgeon' that he had established by dissection 'that a potato-fed peasant has a stomach of nearly twice the ordinary size', as a result of which 'he craves for the quantity'. Earlier, even before the legal opening of British armed forces to Irish Catholics, an export trade in potatoes, the first international commercial exchange on record, took place from Ireland 'to our garrisons of Gibraltar and Portmahon, and to some other parts'.[45] There is ample evidence that the Irish abroad – and not only the poorest – remained faithful to the potato even when other foods were freely available. The father of the Brontë girls, at Haworth parsonage, insisted that potatoes rather than meat should form their midday meal, 'with which they are said to have been perfectly satisfied ...The Reverend Patrick Brontë had grown to gigantic proportions on potatoes; he knew no reason why his children should fare differently.'[46]

That this loyalty was unique neither to the Irish nor the period may be illustrated by two quotations:

> Many of the natives of Dumfriesshire and Galloway, who have resided for many years in foreign countries, have been heard to declare that the recollection of the savoury 'beat potatoes' continued to haunt them with the most provoking pertinacity, even while indulging in the more refined luxuries of the East.

> The mere thought of them made his mouth water. Potatoes filled the stomach without seeming to overload it. They filled hunger like nothing else. They were the one food that prisoners never forgot and always yearned for.[47]

The second half of the eighteenth century was, without doubt, the golden age of the potato in Ireland: it had proved itself 'universally palatable, from the palace to the pig-sty'.[48] We quote from three writers, as cited by Davidson:

> Ireland is famed for its crops of potatoes...the culture of this plant has been longer and more universally practised there than with... any other European nation...the Irish have always, very judiciously, looked upon this article as an object of the greatest importance. (Mills, 1767)

> The potato has become the staple of their support and they have been the first people in Europe or, perhaps, in the world, that have led the example in an extensive improvement of it. (Irwin, 1764)

> In the latter [Ireland] it soon attained a perfection it had never known before, and it became part of the diet of the rich and the whole diet of the poor; nor was this all, it became an article of commerce and was soon known and admired in every part of Europe by the name of the Irish potatoe; a name which it deservedly

obtained, and maintains to this day, from the pre-eminence which the Irish nation has obtained in the method of cultivating it. (Birch, 1790)[49]

It was the excellent Irish varieties, developed in this epoch, that blazed the way for the full adoption of the potato as human food in Europe and North America. As late as 1812, there were complaints that many of the potato varieties used as food in England had been introduced from Ireland and, having been bred for a long growing season in the temperate Irish climate, were poorly adapted to withstand the early and late frosts of Britain. 'The Irish varieties, being excessively late, are almost always killed by the frost when in full blossom.'[50] Nowadays, the complaint could well be reversed – for the varieties in extensive use in Ireland today are either English or Scotch and take little advantage of the milder Irish climate.

For all the pre-eminence of Ireland in evolving an ideal potato for human use, it would seem that the English, who adopted it as livestock food as early as 1659, may have led the way in using it as animal fodder. There are no early references to such a use in Ireland; this may, of course, reflect no more than its restriction, in the initial period, to acting as a food of the poor and their unpublicised pigs. But it is not illogical that the British farmer, lacking Ireland's mild winter climate and abundant pasture, should have been moved first to try the new food on cattle. Once, however, the Irish 'gentlemen' became interested in the potato, it came into increasing use as livestock feed, as Arthur Young repeatedly testifies. According to the *Dublin Journal* of 10 April 1759, potatoes were in such plenty at that time that 'they would have been thrown to rot on the dunghill but for the accidental discovery in Limerick that cows fed on potatoes throve and quadrupled their milk yields'.[51] A comment in the *Munster Farmers' Magazine* adds plausibility to this chronology: 'of late years, they have been also much used as food for cattle which has increased the demand for them'.

By the turn of the century, potatoes were in the highest esteem as food for farm animals as well as for men:

> There is no article of husbandry, particularly for winter food, so profitable and essentially material to a farmer as potatoes. No other species of food (quantity and quality considered) can bear any competition with them. From the meanest hovel to the palace, they are in high estimation, and on no other bulbous root will cattle and sheep thrive so well and fatten so quickly.[52]

> If we advert to the endless variety of soils in which the potato thrives, to the universal knowledge of the mode of its cultivation, to its ameliorating properties, especially if planted in drills, to its undisputed fattening quality, to the superiority it possesses over every other vegetable production for cattle of keeping good for upwards of twelve months, to the ease and perfect safety with which it is kept in large quantities, and to its many other advantages, we should consider whether it should not in great measure supersede the use of many others.[53]

Thus, even to the end of the period, the keynote was one of untempered eulogy of the potato and of admiration for the foresight of the Irish in adopting and developing it; there was, as yet, no apparent realisation of the menace arising from the complete domination of the potato. Maunsell had noted that cottiers, forced to deal first with the tillage of their landlords, were getting later in planting their potatoes, but there are no signs that this led to more than isolated loss of yield. We have quoted a reference to the abundance of potatoes in 1759; forty years later it could still be said that in good seasons surplus potatoes were thrown away as useless. Later, Irish folk tradition was to hark back in guilt to the times of potato plenty when 'they left them stacked in heaps at the backs of ditches, piled them in the gaps of fences, used them as top-dressing, buried them or stacked them in fields and burned them'.[54]

The sinister trend towards monoculture went on steadily during the period. In the earlier years, as we have previously noted, the use of the potato by no means completely supplanted oats and other foods; this is further confirmed in the evidence of Pococke (1752), Varley (1770) and Young (1780).[55] The picture gradually changes, with the rye crop giving way to the potato in hill farms; and oats disappearing as part of the normal diet over a large part of the country.[56] By the end of the period, grain was no longer a normal part of the daily diet of the common people in the southern and western half of the country (approximately south of the line xy in figure 2). But these developments are recorded in contemporary writings without apparent regret or concern. Presumably, over the period 1790-1810, the false agricultural prosperity created by the Napoleonic Wars masked the first signs that the peak of the potato's golden age had already been passed.

Stage 4 (1810-45). *The decline towards the famine; inferior potato varieties and increasing distress*

There can be no doubt when the rude awakening of Irish agriculture occurred; it coincided with the end of the Napoleonic Wars. 'General despondency amongst the higher classes and extreme misery amongst the poor ensued.'[57]

But the dream of a potato utopia had begun to fade even before peace came. A new sombre undertone had begun to creep into the writings of the potato enthusiasts:

> If practical evidence were wanted to prove the extent to which the culture of the potato is calculated to increase and support the population of a country, Ireland most amply affords it, where population has increased amongst the Catholic poor with almost unprecedented rapidity, within the last 20 years, under the pressure of more distress and misery than has perhaps been felt in any other spot in Europe.[58]

Wakefield saw on his tour a far less cheery picture than Arthur Young had found thirty years earlier:

> The population of Ireland and the division of land have so much increased since Mr Young was there in the year 1779, that I am convinced that he

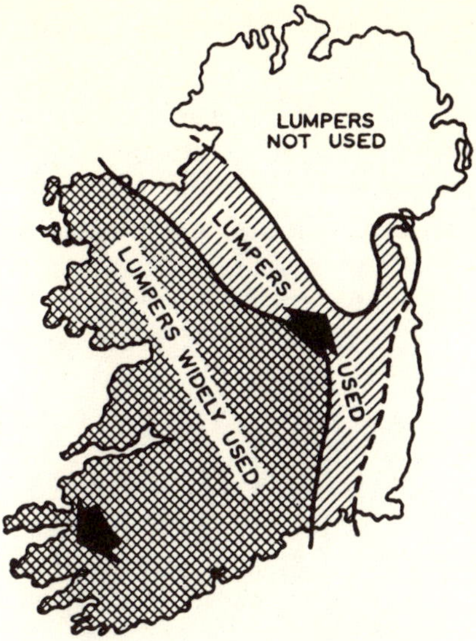

Fig. 1 Distribution of the Lumper Potato as Human Food, c.1835

The double-hatched area is that in which the lumper was well-established as the normal food of small farmers and labourers. The single-hatched area is that of mixed varieties, including the lumper. The unhatched area is that in which the lumper was not in use as human food. The dividing line is broken where the boundary is uncertain. Arrows illustrate where there is evidence of recent extension or intensification in the use of the lumper.

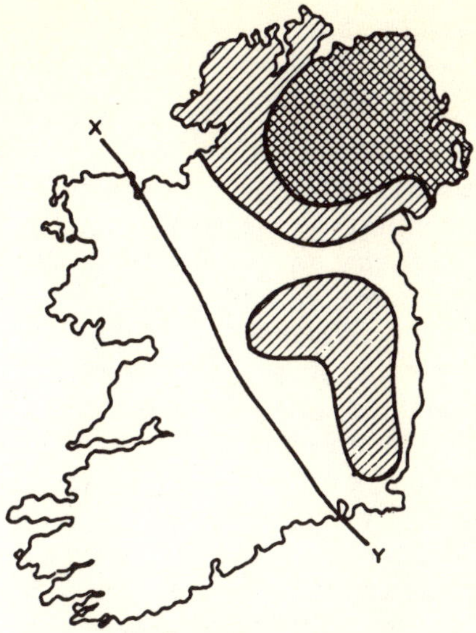

Fig. 2 Distribution of Oats-eating areas, c. 1835

The core of the oateating zone in the north-east is double-hatched. The single-hatched area is that in which oat products continued to form a part of the normal popular diet. The unhatched area to the north of the line XY is approximately that in which oats had ceased to form part of the normal diet within living memory.

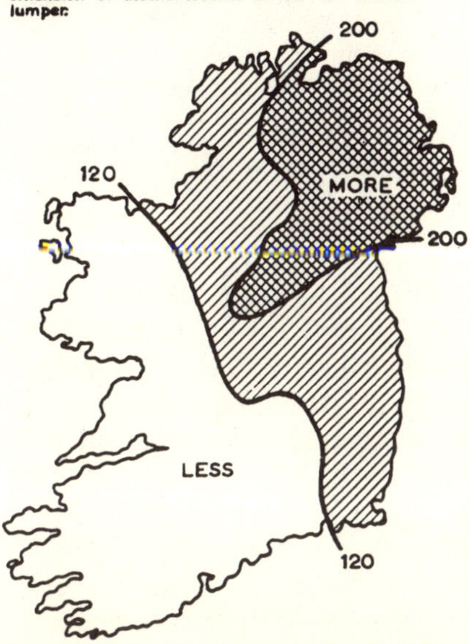

Fig. 3 Density of oats cultivation in 1847.

Isopleths indicate the number of acres under oats per 1000 acres of crops and pastures

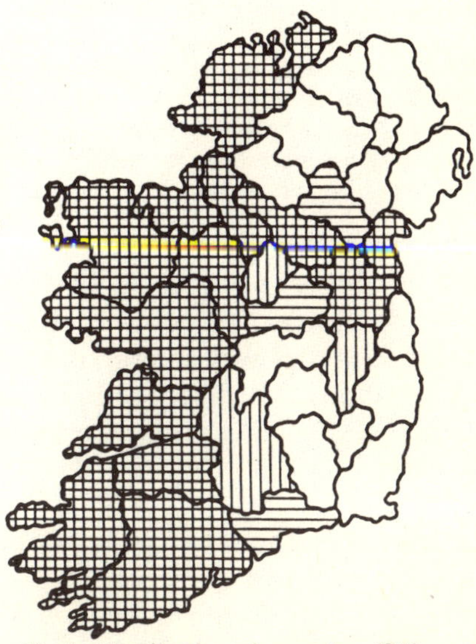

Fig. 4 Distribution of poverty, 1841 as shown by

POOR HOUSING ILLITERACY

would now change his statement of that invariable 'belly-full' of which he then spoke.[59]

The superb potato varieties which had sustained the earlier period had gone into a gradual decline by the end of the eighteenth century, and inferior varieties had begun to make their appearance as human food by the transition date (1810) which we have selected. The ill-famed precursor of the famine, the Lumper potato – 'a vile watery bulb, in which there is neither flavour nor nourishment'; 'not food sufficient for the very brute' – was first mentioned in County Clare in 1808; by 1835 (fig. 1) it had spread over a large part of the country.[60]

The disadvantages of a potato, as compared with a cereal, diet came more and more into the limelight as successive shortages caused distress and even local famine.[61] It was impossible to store and keep the potato in reserve from one year to another to guard against the bad years; the sheer bulk of the crop made it difficult to transport across land to an area of distress; a population living on the worst kinds of the cheapest food had no reserve to fall back upon when the potato failed.[62]

The strain of the potato economy on a swollen and underemployed population and the frantic scramble for land were obvious to the most casual observer by the 1820s. The more sanguine looked for a second miracle, to parallel the coming of the potato:

> The wants of the latter [the people] cannot possibly exceed the productive powers of the former [the land], under the guidance of that Providence that presides over it, and that, by a special foresight of the exigency to be met, multiplied food in Ireland *tenfold*, by the discovery of a single root, although, in all probability the instrument of this discovery – we believe Sir Walter Raleigh – did not see the design for which he was thus made the locum-tenens of the great and universal provider... Can any one doubt the adequacy of the same Providence to the discovery of another root, by which the present produce of the soil of Ireland might be multiplied tenfold more, if that were needful?[63]

The more practical and mobile fled from the sinking ship to a new shore, leaving a greater misery behind them. They were 'the energetic, the industrious, and the monied', who saw a poor future for their children in Ireland; as they went 'new tenants rapidly fill up the vacancies caused by emigration; and they continue, or else they make an effort, to pay the old rents by living more miserably than their predecessors could well submit to'.[64]

Men of compassion, like 'J.K.L.' (Bishop J. W. Doyle) and Sir John Sinclair, worked on the hopeless task of devising some scheme by which the potato might be preserved from one year to the next. Bishop Doyle wrote a circular letter to his clergy in January 1828, recommending Sinclair's method of converting the potato into flour, but the elaborate procedure was far beyond the resources of his flock. The impractical suggested, as they were later to repeat during the famine, that the poor should extract and store the starch from the potato, all oblivious to the fact that 'potatoe starch alone would be a very starving diet even for an infant'.[65]

The English patriot now saw Ireland, no longer as the successful pioneer of potato culture, but as a dreadful pointer to the fate which awaited his country if it plunged into a potato economy. The bright and shining noon of the Irish potato, which Arthur Young had seen and praised, had already turned to evening when Wakefield made his tour; now that it was approaching midnight it is little wonder that William Cobbett so reviled it. He adopted his most famous phrase from a poem of Dr William Drennan's called 'To Ireland', first published in 1815, in which he spoke of the Irish:

> ... hungering for a *lazy root*
> Food for a soft contented slave,
> Not for the hardy and the brave.[66]

Clearly the uncompromising Belfast patriot of 1798 condemned the potato for its pacific properties. Cobbett, on the other hand, denounced it for economic reasons as the 'root of misery' and the 'root of extreme unction', although his considered opinion was more moderate and rational: 'as garden stuff and used in that way it is very good...it is the using of it as a substitute for bread and meat that I have deprecated'.[67]

The reality of the contrast in the prosperity of two periods only about sixty years apart is confirmed in many sources. The most comprehensive is Bicheno's comparison of life in Young's period with that revealed by evidence from the *Poor inquiry*. Binns found that conditions had deteriorated in County Kerry since Dr Smith wrote in 1756.

Of course, the realisation of the ultimate unsoundness of the potato economy was bound to come with time, but the speed of the decline was hastened, not only by the postwar depression of agriculture, but by a number of ancillary causes. A significant change, particularly for the west, was the rapid development during this period of an improved road system, which facilitated the carriage and export of grain and other agricultural products. For instance, in 1812 there were no means of taking cereals to market in the roadless area of north Mayo. A little was used locally for food; much was converted into portable poteen which could be 'taken out of the country on horses' backs, over moors and mountains, upon which even men find it difficult to walk'.[68] On the eve of the famine, Mr Brett, county surveyor, could report to the Mayo spring assizes that, in the past nine years, upwards of 200 miles of new roads and about 150 bridges had been constructed, and that the mileage of roads improved and maintained had increased ten- to fifteenfold in the same period. Some of the little roads, such as those that ran down to the coast in Clare and Galway, facilitated the small-holder in gathering seaweed and coral sand as manure, but in general, every improvement in transport facilitated the movement of the agricultural products so much in demand in Britain and forced the Irish tenant to fall back more and more on a poor potato diet.[69] The establishment of a regular steamship link between Ireland and England contributed further to this end, although it also meant that more and more of the wheat exports took the form of flour (which under the slower and uncertain transport of earlier years tended to arrive in England in poor condition) and thus led to a great increase in the number of flour mills in Ireland.[70]

Another of what must have seemed to the hard-pressed population a conspiracy of hostile factors was the postwar trend towards pasture. 'During the war, a great deal of good land was turned up, and since that, we are getting it to grass as quick as we can.' Thus the potato crop, vital to most of the population, was progressively forced deeper into the bogs and higher into the hills. 'In Cork, and some wild counties, they are getting up the mountains and tilling those which might be called the wild lands; that is almost entirely due to the dense population.' 'The nature of the times has forced the people to extend their farms up the ascent of the mountain, and to take in some of the land to meet the demands upon them; they have done more in that way in the last four or five years than in the ten before.'[71]

The short-term palliative which the people grasped in their despair proved to be no more than another step on the downward path. The inferior varieties, adopted because they gave greater bulk even on poor and scantily manured land, did not, as might be expected, keep well; an increased gap between the inadequate old crop and the late new crop made the summer months a period of annual and ever-increasing distress. The remedies of urgent immediate hunger – to eat the stock reserved for seed, to sample the new crop as soon as the tubers were formed – were quickly paid for at a dreadful price. In the west and south, regions of greatest want, recurrent failures of the new varieties gave warning that the potato economy was nearing the end of its tether.

So, at an accelerating tempo, the condition of the people spiralled down to an ultimate and unavoidable disaster. A sense of brooding catastrophe hangs over John Wiggins' compassionate and prophetic book written on the eve of the famine. 'The condition of Ireland becomes worse and worse.' It is 'a house built upon sand...and must inevitably fall the moment that the winds blow and the waves rage, or even with the first and slightest adverse gale'. 'Something must be done...*now*'.[72] It was already too late. As he wrote the tiny fungus which was to bring the whole rotten structure to the ground was already making its way into Europe. But even if potato blight had not come, the crisis could not have been long delayed.

* * *

We have proposed here a broad chronological pattern of the rise and decline of the potato in Ireland, into which fit not only the jigsaw pieces of evidence cited by Davidson and Salaman but also the additional data quoted here; only the isolated and discordant claim of the *Montgomery manuscripts* is rejected. It provides a background against which, for instance, both Young's enthusiasm for the potato and Cobbett's hatred of the root are seen to be consistent in their historical contexts. It underlines the necessity of relating each piece of evidence to its own time; it is a not uncommon error to treat Young's brilliant snapshot of Irish life in the late 1770s as if it were a representative panorama of the last hundred years or so before the famine.

It is, however, a broad pattern, typical mainly of the south and west of Ireland. Complete domination by the potato was never achieved in the extreme north-east, where the best varieties of earlier days (the Black and the Apple) continued to be widely grown, despite their poor yields, right up to the famine. In this region, other foods, particularly oats, played an important part; in the comfortable orchard areas of the Lagan valley, fruit was commonly eaten, sometimes in odd and, to modern ears, repulsive combination with the potato:

> The 'farmer's pudding' (which makes a good dinner for a family) is made with apples and potatoes mixed, about equal quantities of each, cut up into slices and tied into a large towel or bag, and let boil three or four hours, when a little milk mixed with sugar is used along with them by way of sauce.[73]

In no country other than Ireland did the potato economy run its full course. Even in the Scottish highlands, the use of the Lumper or similar potato varieties, other than as cattle food, appears to have been uncommon. The situation in the remainder of Scotland, parts of northern England and Belgium was similar to that of Ulster, i.e. a stage in the potato chronology about a hundred years behind that general in Ireland. This is the main reason why the ravages of potato blight were to have more serious consequences in Ireland than elsewhere.

It remains, in the immediately following sections, to show that the sequences of potato diseases and of varieties are consistent with, and supplement, the chronology which we have outlined.

The successive ailments of the potato in Ireland

A new crop, grown on a limited scale and in separated stands, tends to escape serious disease; but as it comes into widespread cultivation, it becomes progressively vulnerable. Denser populations in pure stands invite disease. Thus, soya bean cultivation in the USA expanded about tenfold in the mid-twentieth century; simultaneously ten plant diseases, four of them previously unknown, emerged from obscurity to become major and costly enemies of the crop.[74] It is, therefore, significant that there is no reference to disease in the potato crop in Ireland or indeed in Europe, prior to 1750.[75] Were the potato in very general use prior to that date, this uncharacteristic healthiness could be explained only on the hypothesis 'that in the earlier years of its general introduction, this crop was not as liable to disease as in later times'.[76] However, apart from specific disease, the potato is very subject to direct weather damage, and it was not until 1726 that the crop was reckoned of sufficient importance to have losses due to severe frost damage put on record.

Damage by abnormal weather conditions

The meteorological hazards liable to damage the potato are continued drought, excessive rainfall, and severe frost either early or late in the growing season; to these may be added the breaking of plants in high winds in exposed places and damage caused by sea spray carried inland by the wind.[77]

Drought has rarely been a major problem for Irish agriculture except on thin sandy soils, as in the Aran Islands; Boate records 'a common saying in Ireland that the very driest summers there never hurt the land'. In his comprehensive review of previous seasons, Wilde mentions drought as restricting potato yields in 1765, 1785, 1800-1, 1822, and 1825-6, but the result was, at worst, distress rather than famine.[78]

The potato, prior to the coming of blight, throve best in wettish seasons, but when excessive rain fell in a country where the crying need was for improved drainage, the potato crop suffered severely from waterlogging and subsequent rotting. It had been earlier noted by Maxwell that washing potatoes prior to storing them increased the danger of rot, whereas, if they could be harvested and stored in a dry condition, they remained sound.[79] Weather conditions in Ireland often made this impossible; indeed there were wet years like 1829 when it was reported that 'the potato is quite blasted. In the low grounds the water is up to the top of the potatoes.' Other years in which excessive rainfall damaged the potato crop included 1821 (when the floods 'literally swept away whole crops of potatoes'), 1830 and 1839; according to Wilde arterial drainage in many parts of the country had reduced the risk of damage by flooding in the years preceding the famine.

As regards low temperatures, we have already suggested that the frost damage in the bad winter of 1739-40 was related largely to the early practice of leaving the potato crop in the ground during the winter. A shortage of potatoes in Dublin in the severe winter of 1783-4 may be attributed in part to an interruption of supplies from country areas. An exceptionally sharp frost in the first week of November 1807 is reported to have destroyed nearly half of the potato crop, but this, in the absence of subsequent distress, is almost certainly an exaggeration.[80]

With a late planting date autumnal frosts must, in the early nineteenth century, have been a greater menace than those of late spring. One instance deserves mention, since Wilde, reporting it out of context, thought he had found a possible appearance of potato blight as early as 1816 in England. He writes[81] that:

the accounts of this (1816) epidemic in England state that early in September the potatoes were 'blackened and spoiled; they smell at a distance the same as after a frosty night late in October' – symptoms which indicate a similarity between the epidemic of that period and the one with which we have lately become so familiar.

We have traced the original quotation to the *Irish Farmers' Journal and Weekly Intelligencer* of 21 September 1816, in which the 'London letter' gives the following account of the state of the crops in Cumberland:

The weather has been remarkably unfavourable since my last. Sunday, the first of September, was extremely cold for the season of the year; a strong northwest wind blew in the day; at night it cleared up and there was a keen frost, which continued that and the following night. The whole face of the country was white like a winter morning; ice was hanging at the heads of corn in the field, and water was frozen in some places. The potatoes are blackened and spoiled, they smell at a distance the same as after a frosty night in the latter end of October. How far the corn may be injured, I am not able to know yet...

It was, in fact, a simple case of frost damage; the same journal reports that considerable injury was also done to potato crops in Ireland by frost in the early part of September, 1816.[82] The reverse of Wilde's error was common in Ireland in the autumn of 1845, when the effects of the first blight attack were frequently attributed to frost damage.

The curl of the potato (from c. *1764)*

The curl, a virus complaint, was recognised as a disease of the potato in England about 1764. The date suggests that the disease might have been introduced with American varieties brought home by British soldiers returning from the war with the French in North America, which officially ended in 1763, but was virtually terminated in 1760. A variety known in England as American Reds was introduced in this way,[83] about the same time, James Howard obtained from America a new sort which became famous as the Howard or Cluster, a potato which yielded heavily and was in demand for stock-feeding.

There is, however, an early comment by Maxwell which can be interpreted as evidence that the effects of virus infection were present before the disease was recognised as such:

In Galloway we find that potatoes for seed, as well as other seed, require changing, not only from one ground, but also from one country to another; so, when we have opportunity of purchasing any from England or Ireland, we chuse them, and find that the produce is greater than from our own potatoes.[84]

It may therefore be that the curl developed when the potato spread as a field crop in Britain, where the dry calm climate is more favourable to potato virus disease than the more humid and windy Irish environment.

Indeed the curl never caused spectacular loss or serious alarm in Ireland; its main consequence there was a gradual 'degeneration' or frittering away of the yield of potato varieties which had been long in use:

> The tendency of potatoes to degenerate is a frequent cause of the shortness of crops, when the culture of a favourite kind is followed up too long. It is observable that as they diminish in size, they generally improve in flavour.[85]

The last remark is interesting; it is a variant of the popular opinion that as a variety loses vigour it tends to become 'more dry and floury', which Davidson traces back no further than 1853.[86]

The advent of the curl set off a series of consequences. It gave a stimulus to the exchange of seed potatoes, and a great demand for those from bog and mountain land:

> Turf bogs and moory grounds seem to possess the quality of preserving potatoes from degenerating, as well as that of throwing out considerable crops; and in this county [Down], where those soils are frequently applied to their culture, the curl is little known, and frequent applications for change of seed are made from other parts where this advantage is not enjoyed. Of the cause of curled potatoes I have never yet heard a satisfactory account, but I think I can say that frequent changes from boggy and moory soils, to those of a different quality, are found the best preventative; as such it is considered in England.[87]

Within Ireland, this exchange of seed seems to have been on a local and unorganised basis, but Scotland soon built up a considerable trade in seed potatoes. A scheme for the establishment of an Irish disease-free potato seed industry, under the aegis of the Agricultural Society of Ireland, was proposed by Niven in 1835.[88]

The second major consequence of the curl was the encouragement it gave to the breeding of new varieties in the search for a potato resistant to the disease. The early writers mention only five to seven sorts; by 1797, Maunsell, in a quotation previously given, speaks of the 'great variety of potatoes we now have' and Dubourdieu claims that 'there are an infinite variety of potatoes, and every day new varieties are produced from seed'.[89] We shall discuss the 'Irish Apple' in detail later; Davidson mentions other varieties developed in England in the period 1750-1800, including some remarkable for early maturity and others, abundant but of poor quality, designed for stock-feeding. These developments enabled potatoes to be eaten throughout the year; table potatoes were now available that ripened early or that kept reasonably sound for upwards of twelve months.[90] Once started, the multiplication of varieties continued at an ever-increasing rate. Sinclair writes that:

> the number of kinds are so considerably increased from sowing the seed contained in the potato apple, and confounded by local appellations, that it is difficult to convey accurate information on this head.[91]

It is true that the same potato variety tended to have 'more names than eyes', but there is abundant evidence of the wider range and greater specialisation of the varieties developed in this period. Aitken says that the growing of new kinds, early and late, 'has added incalculably to the value of the potato, by extending its use throughout the whole year; not only at table, but as food for almost every description of cattle'. He considers that the main developments in this respect had taken place in the last twenty-five or thirty years, but elsewhere he dates the emergence of new varieties from *c.* 1780; it is clear from other evidence that it had already commenced by 1770 and possibly somewhat earlier.[92]

Both the trade in seed potatoes and the development of new varieties, which the progressive farmer was anxious to obtain and test, led to a considerable international exchange of potatoes, not only within Europe but even across the Atlantic, a trade which was bound to accelerate the spread of new diseases. We have seen that the curl was first noted in England; it is somewhat ironic that the varieties developed there to resist it should apparently have carried the disease to continental Europe. Appel cites contemporary evidence that the curl, which arrived in Germany about 1775, came with imported English white potatoes, which had become popular as food for pigs and cattle. A warning was issued in 1803 against planting the 'curled' British cattle varieties close to native German potatoes. Once introduced to the continent, virus disease caused really serious losses and much concern.[93]

One of the methods most strongly recommended for avoiding the curl was to take up the tubers before they were fully grown. This remedy, which, in practice, involved either late planting or early harvesting, was, apparently, an influential factor in altering cultural practices in England, if one may judge by the vigour with which it was denounced there after blight had made its appearance.[94] In Ireland, social and economic circumstances – and, in particular, the priority claims of increasing grain tillage in the second half of the eighteenth century – were probably more important causes of the trend towards later planting and earlier lifting of the potato crop. Thus, for example:

> Lord Doneraile...many years ago...had a farm at Shanakilly, and wishing to be early in sowing his wheat he obliged his labourers, to whom he set potatoe ground, to dig them out at Michaelmas (29 Sept.). Such a deviation from the old routine could not fail at first to alarm the tenants who thought they must be starved, but they became at length reconciled to the practice, seeing that their potatoes kept better than their neighbours', and were as fully grown.[95]

The taint or dry rot of the potato (from c. *1832)*

In the period 1832-6 an 'unmistakable epidemic attacked the potato in spring throughout Ireland'.[96] Crops affected with the taint, as it was called in England, partially rotted in storage; diseased seed potatoes tended to 'miss' (i.e. to rot in the ground without giving rise to a new plant), or to set up a weak and sickly growth.

It was the first potato disease to cause serious alarm in Ireland. In July 1834, the Royal Dublin Society offered gold and silver medals for the best essays 'upon the cause of the recent partial failure of the potato crop, and upon the most effective means of preventing a recurrence of the evil'. The disease was a problem in Scotland also at this time, and a similar premium was offered by the Highland and Agricultural Society; both sets of essays are reviewed by Aitken. Germany was another country affected by taint; there it did not reach its greatest intensity until 1841, when it provided the stimulus for the famous study of potato diseases by von Martius.[97]

Excellent descriptions of the disease are given in the cited works; the essay by Ninian Niven, curator of the Glasnevin Botanic Gardens, which was awarded second prize in the RDS competition, is particularly sound. Useful information is also provided by Townley and by Wilson. A comparison of the symptoms which they describe with those of the disease, caused by *Fusarium spp.*, now known as dry rot, leaves no doubt as to their identity. [98]

Aitken mentions that dry rot of the potato caused losses in Scotland as early as 1812; it is very possible, as Wilson suggests, that the attack in the 1830s was merely a virulent form of a complaint which had been known since the previous century; the reliable Berkeley says the causal fungus had been originally described by Tode towards the end of the eighteenth century. Certainly a succession of hot dry planting seasons contributed towards the damage done by the disease in the early 1830s.[99]

The immediate consequence of the dry rot epidemic was to give a fresh impetus to the development of new varieties. They multiplied apace. The French Society of Agriculture had a collection of 177 potato varieties in 1846 and the Horticultural Society of London had rather more.[100] The number of varieties grown in Ireland was estimated to be as high as 200; Niven mentions that he himself had developed more than fifty sorts from seed. It was not an enthusiasm confined to the professional; small farmers and maiden ladies took an active part.[101] No wonder that the *Irish Farmers' Journal* in 1845 considered the sorts of potatoes to be 'innumerable' and the situation confused by local names. In fact, the number of varieties in widespread use was not excessive; Smee considered that 'not more than 20 kinds are commonly sent to the London market'. The multiplicity of little-used kinds came into their own in 1845-6 in tests of resistance against potato blight.

Immediate success in developing a variety resistant to the taint was not forthcoming, and a demand arose for a 'renewal of the stock' by bringing a fresh supply of potatoes from South America. This is significant, for the demand continued right up to 1845, and may have provided the carrier which brought the blight fungus to Europe.[102] It would seem that the first positive action was taken in Ireland; Niven speaks of the experimental planting in Dublin of a new species of potato 'recently imported from

South America' which proved to be large and productive – some of the tubers weighing 4 or 5 lb.! This may explain Dyer's mysterious remark that 'the Irish government got over a fresh strain from South America' which proved to be susceptible to disease; no later importation of this kind to Ireland has been traced. A Scottish grower refers in 1845 to his use 'of a kind [Hannah's Prince Regent] imported from South America some ten years ago'.[103]

Meanwhile, the regular international exchanges were accelerated as growers tested foreign varieties for their resistance to dry rot. Johnston gives examples of recent potato importations from the USA to Scotland, and from France to the USA.[104]

Cultural practices were appreciably modified as a result of the dry rot epidemic. Formerly it had been the practice to cut the seed potato into 'as many pieces as it has eyes'; where this was done, dry rot caused the greatest havoc and the trend now was to plant the whole tuber.[105]

> At one period the smallest portion of a potato having an eye was deemed quite sufficient for seed; but since the failure of the crop has become of such frequent occurrence, the whole tuber has been preferred for planting, and the practice is extending.[106]

Simultaneously it became common to plant more thickly, so as to compensate for any tubers which failed to germinate and to obviate the necessity for late replanting in case of an extensive failure. 'More than three times the necessary quantity of seed is used, and the plea for such useless expenditure is that if one or two of the "sets" fail, a third may grow.'[107]

Losses by taint when tubers were sown in dry soil were aggravated by late planting, and the onset of the disease set off an agitation for earlier planting, in reverse of the earlier trend. But for many Irish potato growers the advice was impractical; 'they must plant their crop whenever they can, 'tis no pick and choice matter with them'.[108] It was not until the famine had transformed the social situation that the potato planting time in Ireland reverted to an early date.

Potato blight, 1845

The final consequence of the dry-rot epidemic was to create utter confusion between the two diseases when blight made its appearance in quick succession in 1845. This confusion, which has persisted to the present day, is the less excusable since the more authoritative contemporary writers were in no doubt of their separate nature.[109] Soon after blight appeared, Niven made the following accurate and convincing distinction between the two diseases:

> The origin of the 'dry rot disease' was in the tuber, not on the leaf, as in the case of the present epidemic; it likewise was chiefly developed in spring, at the time

of planting, and was evidenced either by blanks in the crop, or by the sickly, wire-like stems that sometimes appeared from the infected root. In the present case the development of the disease is towards the end of summer and during the autumn, and is generally most destructive when the previous growth had been most luxuriant. The 'dry rot' or 'root disease' prevented the growth upwards; the 'wet rot' or 'leaf disease' destroys the growth downwards. Alarming as were the failures of 1832, 1833, and 1834, they soon afterwards passed away or became extremely partial.[110]

The decrease in intensity of the taint, to which Niven refers, was a phenomenon largely confined to the maritime countries of north-west Europe. Even in the years of consecutive dry springs, dry rot had not struck uniformly; it was claimed, for instance, that it had never appeared in the Ballina area of County Mayo. With the return of normal rainy springs, the damage caused by the disease decreased, although some complaints continued to be voiced almost every year.[111]

With the curl and taint in restraint, the potato, in the five years preceding the famine, suffered only from certain localised and partial complaints, which were a nuisance rather than a menace. The identifiable minor diseases include scab and blackleg. But, in practical terms, the official *Farmer's Guide* was justified in its claim that potatoes had 'never been more healthy than at present'.[112]

It was the lull before the storm, for blight, which was first recorded in Ireland in late summer 1845, was to prove a far more comprehensive and destructive plant disease than any previously known.

The sequence of outstanding potato varieties in Ireland

Research into the history of potato varieties was largely pioneered by Davidson.[113] He discusses twelve famous varieties which appeared in the period prior to 1845. We shall illustrate this facet of the rise and fall of the potato in Ireland by considering, in rather more detail than Davidson gives, the four kinds which, in turn, dominated the Irish potato scene – the Black, the Apple, the Cup and the Lumper.

The Black

The Black potato, first mentioned by Rye in 1730, is the 'first really outstanding variety' which can now be traced; it continued in high regard for a hundred years. It was, apparently, just coming into general use in Rye's time, and its outstanding quality was that it kept longer than the varieties it supplanted:

It is the Black potatoe (not that the pulp is black, but that the skin is very dark) that is most valued by those who know it; the pulp affords a strong invigorating diet to the labourer; it keeps till potatoes come again...Since the people of this country found the peculiar goodness of this potatoe they will scarce cultivate any other.[114]

Under the name of the blue potato, one of its aliases, it figures amongst the seven varieties listed by Maxwell as being used in Scotland. Dubourdieu says that in Down, at the turn of the century, it 'still keeps its ground, as it is prolific and requires less manure than other kinds'. Indeed, it was in the extreme north-east of Ireland and in Scotland that the Black potato made its last stand. Sinclair speaks of it still being grown 'in some places'.[115] An essayist from Comber, Co. Down, in discussing the gradual degeneration of all varieties, comments that the Black Seedling, formerly one of the best potatoes, is now 'on the point of departing'. It did not, in fact, bow out for another ten years. The first report of blight in the extreme north of Ireland occurs in a letter dated 18 September 1845 from a farmer living near Ballycastle, Co. Antrim; he reported that the Black potatoes had suffered most. A report from Antrim confirms that 'there is a serious failure by rot in the potato called Black Seedling'.[116] The variety did not survive the first attack of potato blight.

The Apple

Apart from the Black, one other of the 'five sorts of potatoes' was praised by Rye; 'the round red is a good potatoe and increases much'. It is very possible that it was the ancestor of the next two outstanding varieties, both of which had a red pigmented skin. 'The Irish Apple has deep green foliage, with roundish tubers, much hollowed at the ends and reddish eyes.' The Apple was undoubtedly the aristocrat of potatoes; 'too much could not be said in praise of this wonderful potato'.[117] First reference to it occurs, according to Davidson, in 1770 in an enthusiastic report to the RDS by John Baker, who praises it for the uniform size of the tubers and its superb mealy quality. It had, he said, a 'prodigious dryness'.

The attribute which recommended the Apple most strongly to the people was its excellent keeping quality, a fact which suggests that either Rye exaggerated this aspect of the Black potato, or else that the earlier variety soon lost its excellence in this respect

> The Apple potato is the only kind, in general, that preserves its originality, because its shoots are not so forward as the others, and is fit for sowing when all other kinds are in the ground, and the poor man's ready to till; this should be called the poor man's potatoe, because Providence has, in a most kind and benign manner, withheld its shoots till he has time to begin his tillage.[118]

The Irish Apple was at the zenith of its career at the time of Arthur Young's tour; it was the variety above all others which established the reputation of the 'Irish potato'.

By the turn of the century, the variety had begun to fall off in yield. But it kept its other excellent qualities and Dubourdieu forecast that 'the Apple potato, by being the best for late use, though not very productive, is likely to keep its place'; he considered that, with care, it might be kept sound for over twelve months. At this time, the variety was still the food of the common people; 'since the cultivation of the Apple potato has become general, the poor continue to eat them until new potatoes come in'.[119]

But the Apple was soon to pass on its crown of 'the poor man's potato' to more abundant varieties. Less than ten years later, it was considered that

> the Apple potatoe, which, in quality, surpasses all others, has so greatly degenerated in produce in the last thirty years, that its culture can no longer be recommended on principles of economy.[120]

Smallholders were already abandoning it, but it continued to be grown by the more comfortable because of its excellence:

> The most generally valued, though not the greatest producer, is the Apple potatoe, which far exceeds all other kinds in the important article of keeping. The quality it seems to owe to the hardiness of its shoots, and the long continued growth of its stalk. Other kinds quickly attain their full size, after which the stalks immediately quail and wither. The Apple, which is seldom planted at an early season, retains its verdure until the arrival of frost, and in the south part of the county [Cork], is sometimes green in December.[121]

Despite occasional hopes of regeneration and repeated testimonials to its unique excellence, the Apple continued to lose ground. 'The Apple, the king of potatoes at one time, is fast hastening to decay.' It remained the favourite variety of the Irish well-to-do until blight swept it finally out of existence; after that there remained 'only the reminiscence of what a richly-flavoured mealy potato – a little loaf in fact – really was'.[122]

The Cup

When first mentioned by Dutton, the Cup potatoes were already in widespread use as human food in County Clare: 'there are more Cups planted than any other kind; they are reckoned not only more productive, but vastly more nutritive, being more difficult of digestion and, as the country people say, "they stay longer in the belly"'. The variety can scarcely have been introduced later than 1800, for ten years later it was in general use in County Cork also:

> the common farmers prefer a new kind of potatoe (sometimes called Cups and sometimes Minions) to the Apple. It is more productive, but very inferior in every other quality. The Apple potato, indeed, does not thrive on cold moory soils, such as compose a large portion of the western part of this district, where this preference of an inferior kind is therefore justified by necessity.

The *Annals of Horticulture* describes the Cup as a 'good flavoured Irish variety', with 'upright dark green foliage, and large uneven shaped tubers, of a dull reddish colour'.[123]

What quality of potato was the Irish Cup? Clearly, from the quotations given, there were varying opinions; in fact, the verdict depended largely on the basis of judgement. If one compared it, as Townsend did, with the Apple which preceded it, the Cup was undoubtedly 'a coarse kind of potato'; compared with the inferior varieties which followed on its heels, it could be described as 'of the firmest quality'. The Apple far outshone it in wholesomeness and keeping quality.[124]

The poorer keeping quality of the Cup represents the first reversal of the trend, set up by the Black and the Apple, towards a potato variety which was usable throughout the year, and is a factor with important social consequences; it is reflected in increasing food distress in the summer months in the thirty years before the famine. In Lecale, Co. Down, where 'the Apple potato is common among the better class of farmers' it was stated that 'Apple potatoes keep good for a longer time by two months than the Cups; Apple potatoes go out early in July'.[125] No doubt standards of fitness for eating of old potatoes were higher in this oats-eating region than elsewhere, but the fact that Cups did not keep as well as Apples is the significant point.

The factors which brought the Cup into general use were its hardiness and high productivity. It grew 'on all sorts of soil and under all conditions of treatment' and was 'well adapted for upland culture'. In the barony of Fews, Co. Armagh, Cups were grown 'for the consumption of the peasantry...principally, says Mr Bruce, because they are hardier and more plentiful, and don't require the ground to be as rich as Apples'. In the barony of Lecale, Co. Down, 'the potatoes most grown here for general use are Cups, because they yield a more abundant crop than Apple potatoes by at least one-fourth, according to the statement of Mr Nevill, but they decline in fitness for eating much sooner'. The qualities of sturdiness and high yield led to the spread of the Irish Cup to England, Scotland and Canada. Outside of Ireland, it was mainly in favour as cattle food, the Irish Apple and other choice varieties being recommended for table use.[126]

Even in Ireland, it is an exaggeration to claim, as Davidson and Salaman do, that Cups were a luxury potato and the food of the rich between 1810 and 1846. The potatoes of the well-to-do were the Apple and good early kidney varieties. As late as 1846, the Cup could still be called 'the poor man's potato', but this was strictly true at that time only for the more prosperous parts of the country. Nevertheless, when the poorhouse guardians of Cork advertised for potato tenders in 1845, they called for good Cup potatoes, with samples; the corresponding Killarney board also opted for Cups. No doubt this was partly due to the fact that many farmers who grew inferior kinds for their own use cultivated Cups for sale.[127]

Alternative names for the Cup were 'Fegan' in the north and 'Minion' in Cork, and elsewhere in the south and west. The latter form is variously given as 'Minion', 'Mignon', 'Mignonne', and even 'Million': 'they [vagrant beggars] are often useful in spreading really advantageous information. It was by them that the million potatoes (a very productive kind) were first brought into Roscommon.'[128]

The early references to the Cups suggest that they first came into use in the west and south; in Scotland, they (or a sub-variant) were sometimes referred to as the 'Connaught Cups'. A writer in 1835 says that Cups were fairly recently introduced in the Dublin area although they had long been cultivated elsewhere.[129]

Like its predecessors, the Cup potato eventually began to degenerate; in 1835, it was remarked that the Cups were not so hardy or productive as they formerly were. But this time there was a significant change in the tempo of succession; the new challenger, the Lumper, was already taking over long before the Cup went into decline. The dominant force requiring a still higher yielding variety was now economic rather than one arising from the regular agricultural cycle.[130]

The haulm of the Cup was, as we have seen, upright rather than sprawling. This created a microambient less favourable to the development of blight, and when the disease struck in 1845, the Cups in many places put up longer resistance than most popular varieties. 'The Cups held out a little longer than most other kinds, but have likewise given way.' The variety did not long outlive the famine; it had almost disappeared by 1852.[131]

The Lumper

The Lumper is first mentioned by Dutton in his work (1808) on County Clare: 'the kinds of potatoes usually planted are apples, blacks, cups, leather coats, grenadiers, lumpers, a few red-nose kidney by gentlemen...' It is ranked sixth in a list of seventeen named varieties; he does not single it out later for special mention as he does the Cup. It was grown in the west, but it had not yet come into prominence. Townsend, writing of Cork, does not mention the variety two years later; in fact, he contrasts the 'pleasant, mealy and nourishing' potatoes cultivated by the Irish, using their expert knowledge of how to breed, grow and cook the vegetable, with the 'watery and ill-flavoured' potatoes which had been developed in England. However, by the time Dutton came to write of County Galway he found that 'Lumpers are much used, as they are more productive with a little manure than any other kind, but they are a wretched kind for any human creature; even pigs, I am informed, will not eat them if they can get any other kind.'[132] Between the dates 1808 and 1824, no significant references to the Lumper have been traced. Joyce quotes 'a satire on those Irish farmers and small gentry who became rich and cut a great figure during the Napoleonic Wars, but who came to their level after "Boney was down" in 1815'. Two lines of the song are as follows:

> Our gentry who fed upon turtle and wine
> Must now on wet Lumpers and salt herrings dine.[133]

There is no evidence as to when or in what part of the country the song was composed. It seems doubtful that the Lumper emerged from the obscurity of the west of Ireland before the end of the Napoleonic Wars.

Rarely can a potato variety have been so unanimously condemned as was the Lumper. Here are a few representative denunciations from the hundreds, all of one voice, which can be found in the books, newspapers, agricultural journals and official reports of the period:

> A species of potato called the Lumper has been brought into general cultivation, on account of its great productiveness, and the facility with which it can be raised from an inferior soil and with a comparatively small portion of manure. The root, at its first introduction, was scarcely considered food enough for swine; it neither possesses the farinaceous qualities of the better varieties of the plant, nor is it as palatable as any other, being wet and tasteless, and, in point of substantial nutriment, little better, as an article of human food, than a Swedish turnip.[134]

> The Irish are reduced to the necessity of entirely subsisting on the Lumper potato, a kind that grows somewhat better in the poor man's impoverished land than the potatoes of good quality. The Lumper is not indeed human food at all. Mix them with any other kind of potatoes and lay them before a pig, and she will not eat one of them until all the good kind are devoured, even if her hunger be not at all abated.[135]

> As regards this part of the country [Limerick], these white Lumpers form the sole food of the poor labouring class and about five sixths of the entire produce...White potatoes are not suitable food for human beings, and it may be a mercy of God to destroy the seed.[136]

> It is of a soft watery quality, and is both unwholesome and unpalatable food; pigs do not thrive on it, though it gives milk to the cows, as it approaches the nature of a turnip.[137]

> I would wish a penalty imposed on anyone who would retain the Lumper kind; they are bad food for pigs, but in no country but this would they be deemed fit for human beings, much less for men engaged in hard labour, who use them through necessity.[138]

> The watery Lumper, on which he [the labourer] knows from sad experience it is impossible for a man to work.[139]

The iniquity of the Lumper runs like a theme through the whole of the *Poor inquiry* reports. Not only elsewhere in Appendix (A), but also in (D) (Supplement: answers to q.3), in (E) (Section on 'Food'), in (F), (Section on 'Nature and state of agriculture') and in Bicheno's summary in (H), part ii, pp 9-10. All the poor qualities of the variety are there reviewed and illustrated; the Lumpers were 'little better than turnips'; pigs fed upon them did not thrive well or fatten quickly, and even crows rejected them if a Cup was to be had.[140]

Alternative names for the Lumper were the Horse potato or the Common White potato. The name was possibly applied to more than one distinct variety, of which the common characteristic, apart from colour, was that they were basically 'cattle kinds...waxy and watery'. It will be noted that it was the first all-white potato to come into general use in Ireland; it was the precursor of the popular trend away from pigmented potatoes which set in after the famine.[141]

We have seen that, from about 1770, varieties of this kind were being evolved in England. This was natural, for there the potato was regarded primarily as an animal food; there was, apparently, a strong stimulus towards developing specialised varieties particularly suited to milch cows, i.e. something like a cross between a potato and a turnip. In Ireland, on the other hand, the feeding of pigs and other farm animals on the potato arose as a secondary use of a vegetable mainly regarded as human food; there was little demand, except amongst the bigger farmers, for a distinct cattle variety.

All the evidence suggests that the coarse stock-feeding potatoes were evolved in England and tried in Ireland by the larger cattle farmers. The earliest such variety was the Howard, also called Cluster or Turk, brought to England from America in 1765. Young reports that in 1776 a Mr Longfield, of Castlemartyr, Co. Cork, grew the English Cluster extensively for his cattle, but, significantly in this heyday of the Apple, 'nobody will eat them'. Thirty-five years later, two prolific white cattle potatoes, the Woodley and the Meldrum, were being raised in Cork; by then it was considered that the latter, at least, was 'also good for human food'. Later came the 'farfamed Mangold Wurzel potato' and the even more prolific Russian Heads, whose names alone make description superflous. A similar variety, the Rohan, was developed on the continent.[142]

Outside of Ireland, a distinct line was drawn between potatoes for men and animals. The Mangold Wurzel was very moist and of bad quality, despite being a large bearer; both it and the Rohan were 'very fit for cattle, but much too coarse for table'. They were not even particularly good for pigs; a large hog fed on good mealy potatoes fattened at a rate some 35–50% faster than on the same amount of Mangold Wurzel potatoes.[143] Where the Lumpers were cultivated under that name outside of Ireland it was specifically as a stockfeed. Rothwell speaks of the Lumper in the north of England as the worst of 'the watery sorts, or what we call cattle potatoes'; Johnston describes it in Scotland as 'a large coarse potato, generally used for cattle, horses, etc.'[144]

If the Lumper originated as an English white cattle potato, how was it that it first appeared in Ireland in the far west, so that, indeed, it was sometimes described as the Connaught Lumper? A clue is given by the name of the variety. Henry Mayhew's account of the poor of London, the masterpiece of that great social historian, was collected over many years and first published in 1851. Amongst the occupations he describes is that of the *Lumper*, a dock labourer employed in discharging cargoes of timber. 'In the summer a great many Irish labourers seek for work as lumpers. They come over from Ireland in the Cork boats.' They constituted upwards of a third of the entire work force during the summer months, which was the peak of the seasonal lumber import trade.[145] Cork was the natural port of exit for south Connaught migrants; Townsend speaks of an 'annual influx of western peasantry' there. Irish navvies working on the railways in Britain sometimes wore blue jackets known as lumpers' coats; Handley takes this to be a nickname derived from the potato variety, but it seems far more plausible that, like the later lumberjacket, it derived from the occupation.[146] It is suggested, then, that the Connaught lumpers, on returning home from seasonal work in England, brought with them some of the fashionable English white stock potatoes, and the variety was named after them in Ireland.

The Lumper went down the most heavily and fatally of all varieties in the first blight attacks of 1845-6.

* * *

The concept of using the sequence of potato varieties as a parameter to indicate the increasing level of distress in the first half of the nineteenth century is no academic conceit:

> I have, in the course of my life, witnessed the fact of the poor people having passed through three phases of this root – first the Apple which was rather nutritive – then the Minion, less so – and for many years past, the Horse potato or Lumper, which, upon chemical analysis, has but 2% of nutrition, giving repletion which allays the cravings of hunger and little else.[147]

Two quantitative estimates of the relative value of the three potato varieties in question may be given. The specific gravities, as estimated from 56 lb. of each sort in 1835, were:

Apple	1,116
Cup	1,096
Lumper	1,084

The figures are not above suspicion, especially as the varieties were grown on different kinds of soil, but they tend to show that, by modern standards, the Apple was a superb variety, the Cup average and the Lumper inferior. As regards market price, Apples were quoted in Dublin in June 1845 at 2s. 6d. to 3s. od. per cwt, Cups at 1s. 10d. to 2s. 2d. and Lumpers at 1s. 4d. to 1s. 6d.[148] The price differential was, of course, at its greatest at this time of year, because of the relative keeping qualities of the different sorts.

The status of the three varieties in the Dublin area at this time is so excellently described in the *Poor inquiry* that we reproduce it in full here:

> There are three descriptions of potatoes cultivated here – the Apples, the Cups, and the Lumpers. The first-named are of the best quality, but produce the least

in quantity; the Cups are not so good in quality as the Apples, but produce more; and the Lumpers are the worst of the three in quality, but yield the heaviest crop. For these reasons the Apples are generally sent to Dublin and other large towns for sale. The Cups are grown for the consumption of the smaller towns, and are eaten by the larger farmers, and the few of the small occupiers and labourers who are in better circumstances than the generality of their class; and the Lumpers are grown by large farmers for stall-feeding cattle, and by most of the small occupiers, and all the labourers (except a few in constant employment, and having but small families), for their own food. Though most of the small occupiers and labourers grow Apples and Cups, they do not use them themselves, with the few exceptions mentioned, except as holiday fare, and as a little indulgence on particular occasions. They can only afford to consume the Lumpers of coarsest quality themselves, on account of the much larger produce, and consequent cheapness, of that sort. The Apples yield 10 to 15 per cent less than the Cups, and the Cups 10 to 15 per cent less than the Lumpers, making a difference of 20 to 30 per cent between the produce of the best and the worst qualities. To illustrate the practice and the feeling of the country in this respect the following occurrence was related by one of the witnesses: A landlord, in passing the door of one of his tenants, a small occupier, who was in arrears with his rent, saw one of his daughters washing potatoes at the door, and, perceiving that they were of the Apple kind, asked her if they were intended for her dinner. Upon being answered that they were, he entered the house, and asked the tenant what he meant by eating Apple potatoes when they were fetching so good a price in Dublin, and while he did not pay him (the landlord) his rent?[149]

If one fact alone were to be chosen to epitomise the level to which many of the Irish had fallen by 1835, it might well be the status accorded to a reasonably dry potato 'as holiday fare, and as a little indulgence on particular occasions'.

Regional and seasonal aspects of the food problem in Ireland on the eve of the famine

We have seen that there were regional differences, linked in large part with the geographical distribution of poverty, in the rate at which the potato displaced other foods, and in the readiness with which inferior varieties were adopted. In the remainder of this chapter we shall consider the regional variation and annual cycle of food usage in the decade preceding the famine. Quantitative information on these is needed for a fuller understanding of the distress which occurred even in normal years and of the varying impact of the famine when the potato crop failed.

The distribution of the Lumper, c. *1835*

Davidson claimed that 'by the year 1838 the cultivation of Lumpers was universal in Ireland'. He presented the statement as if it were a direct citation from the *Drummond report,* and thereby deceived later writers.[150] In fact the *Drummond report* is far more restrained: 'in many counties of Leinster, and throughout the provinces of Munster and Connaught, the Lumper now constitutes the principal food of the labouring peasantry'.[151]

A more specific definition of the geographic spread of the variety by 1835 is given in fig. 1. The double-hatched area is that in which the Lumper was the normal staple food of small farmers and labourers. In the single-hatched area, both Cups and Lumpers were in use as human food by these classes, depending on relative poverty. For the unhatched area, no reference to the use of the Lumper as human food has been found.

Fig. 1 is based primarily on the very detailed evidence contained in the *Poor inquiry*; the relevant sections have already been listed under 'the Lumper'. An important error occurs in Bicheno's otherwise accurate summary; he cites the barony of Kilconnel, Co. Galway, as one into which the Lumper had not found its way. This claim is refuted in the evidence.[152]

That in the north-east the competition lay more between the Cup and the older varieties like the Apple is illustrated by evidence in the *Poor inquiry* from the baronies of Lecale, Co. Down, and Fews, Co. Armagh, which we cited earlier when discussing the Cup.

Representative evidence for the boundary lines shown in fig. 1, taken from three north Leinster counties, illustrates the reality of the regional differences:

> The peasantry of this county cultivate the kind of potatoes called Lumpers for their own consumption, on account of the abundance of its produce, although it is the coarsest kind known, and in many counties only cultivated for feeding pigs and cattle [Barony of Portnahinch, Co. Laois].
>
> The kind of potatoes usually cultivated for the consumption of the peasantry is that called Cups...Some of the poorest families, however, grow Lumpers for their own use [Barony of Upper Dundalk, Co. Louth].
>
> The kind of potatoes most cultivated here for the consumption of the peasantry is the Cup which is found to unite, in the greatest degree, quantity and quality of produce. The Lumpers are considered too coarse here for human food [Barony of Upper and Lower Kells, Co. Meath].[153]

In the south-east and extreme north-west the outer boundary line for the use of the Lumper is shown as a broken line in fig. 1 to indicate the lack of positive evidence either way in these areas. Some testimony before the Devon commission, in which food usage in Donegal is compared with that in Kerry and Galway, suggests strongly that the Lumper was never in use in County Donegal for human consumption.[154]

Two arrows appear in fig. 1 to indicate areas of apparent recent progress in the use of the Lumper. Thus, in the barony of Trughenackmy, Co. Kerry, 'for the last few years the white potato has been getting into considerable favour, because it will produce a greater quantity with less manure; it is considered inferior food, and will not feed cattle so fat as other potatoes'. There was similar evidence from the *Poor inquiry* in respect of Iveragh, Co. Kerry, and Conello, Co. Limerick, and also for the barony of Moyfenrath, Co. Meath.[155]

The latter direction of spread is later confirmed by a letter, dated October 1845, which speaks of the use in the Kells area of 'the vile Lumper that even the swine, three years ago, would turn up his snout at'. Otherwise, there is little evidence of any substantial extension of the domain of the Lumper in the ten years following 1835; thus, a report dated 19 September 1845 from Glaslough, Co. Monaghan, says: 'By far the greater part of the potatoes grown in this part of the country are Cups; indeed the poorer classes generally plant very little of any other description.'[156]

The distribution shown in fig. 1 is consistent with data previously considered which suggests that the Lumper was first grown in Clare and Galway, and later diffused to the south and east. Indeed the areas in Britain where the Lumper was known under that name were those most frequented by migrant workers from the west of Ireland.

Bicheno comments generally on the close interrelationship between the geographical distribution of the Lumper and of poverty. Fig. 4 shows, by separate shading, the sixteen counties of poorest housing (percentage represented by the two worst kinds) and of the highest percentage of illiteracy. The data comes from the census of 1841, as presented in percentage form by Grimshaw.[157] As measured by these two parameters, fig. 4 shows the area of greatest distress as comprising the western half of Ireland together with a broad belt running across the northern midlands to the east coast. Within its limits of accuracy, it agrees well with fig. 1.

The oatmeal zones

The areas in which oats continued to form a regular part of the diet of the people throughout the year are indicated in fig. 2. This is based primarily on the answers received by the poor law inquiry to q.3 (q.8 as issued) of its questionnaire: 'What is the ordinary diet...of labourers in your parish?' The proportion of those including oatmeal, gruel, stirabout or oatcakes in their answers is taken as a fair guide to usage. It averages 28%, and varies from a maximum of 63% in Antrim to zero in Kerry, Limerick and Waterford. In general, these figures are probably conservative in respect of the agricultural poor, in so far as the question was, strictly speaking, concerned with labourers only.

The double-hatched core of the oats-eating zone in the north-east had, no doubt, an historical in addition to an economic basis; Sydney Smith had commented, on the theology of the Scottish church, that he knew it had something to do with oatmeal, but beyond that he was in utter darkness. Wilde considered that the 'stirabout-eaters' of Ulster had 'inherited the peculiar appetites and culinary knowledge of their Scotch ancestors'. Dowdall defines the corresponding area as that north of a line from Dundalk to Finnea, Co. Westmeath, and thence to Ballyshannon, but excluding the counties of Cavan and Donegal.[158]

The secondary areas, in which oats continued to form some part of the normal popular diet throughout the year, are single-hatched in fig. 2. Altogether it is calculated that about 30% of the humbler classes had at least an oatmeal breakfast in place of the full potato diet which was the fate of their counterparts in the remainder of Ireland. The line xy on fig. 2, which is intended to indicate the boundary of the unshaded areas to the north-east of it which had recently seceded from the oats-eating zones, is necessarily tentative. A representative piece of evidence is that from the barony of Gowran, Co. Kilkenny:

> The cultivation of potatoes has increased considerably in consequence of the greater poverty of farmers and labourers, which obliges them to live more on potatoes, instead of the meal and other produce which they consumed formerly; also from the increase of population and because more pigs are kept and more cattle stallfed (in great part on potatoes) than formerly.[159]

Fig. 3 shows the density of oats cultivated by county in 1847, the first year for which official figures are available, expressed in terms of each thousand acres of crops and pasture. The figures vary from 313 in Down and 310 in Armagh to 75 in Clare and 66 in Kerry. Approximate isopleths are shown for the 200 and 120 levels. It is true that fig. 3 shows the gross extent of the oats crop, irrespective of whether it was to be sold elsewhere or used locally as food; but it is in good agreement with fig. 2, which, in turn, is a fair counterpart to the Lumper distribution in fig. 1.

The annual cycle of agricultural work

The true picture of the recurrent summer distress in Ireland, and its relationship to the food problem, can be understood only in terms of the chronology and fluctuations of the agricultural year in the 1840s.

The sequence of agricultural operations is shown in figure 5, which is based mainly on Doyle, the *Farmer's Guide* and the *Irish Farmers' Journal*.[160] The more common and important farm activities are shown in the upper half of the figure; the lower section is devoted to crops such as turnips (little grown in pre-famine Ireland), flax (largely confined to Ulster) and bere (a cruder and less important form of barley). The dates recommended for the winter housing of cattle are almost certainly idealistic.

Early potatoes, properly so called and referred to in the lower half of the diagram, had no significance from the point of view of the food of the people. Even in former days, they were confined to 'private gentlemen' who, indeed, 'vied to outdo a neighbour in early potatoes'. Townsend comments that the early Kidney 'is in no repute with the common farmer, by whom it is seldom planted, except near great towns for the purpose of supplying the early market'.[161] The *Munster Farmers' Magazine* confirms that no Kidneys are cultivated except by gentlemen. It goes on to stress the need for a good yielding dry early variety; more than twenty years later the

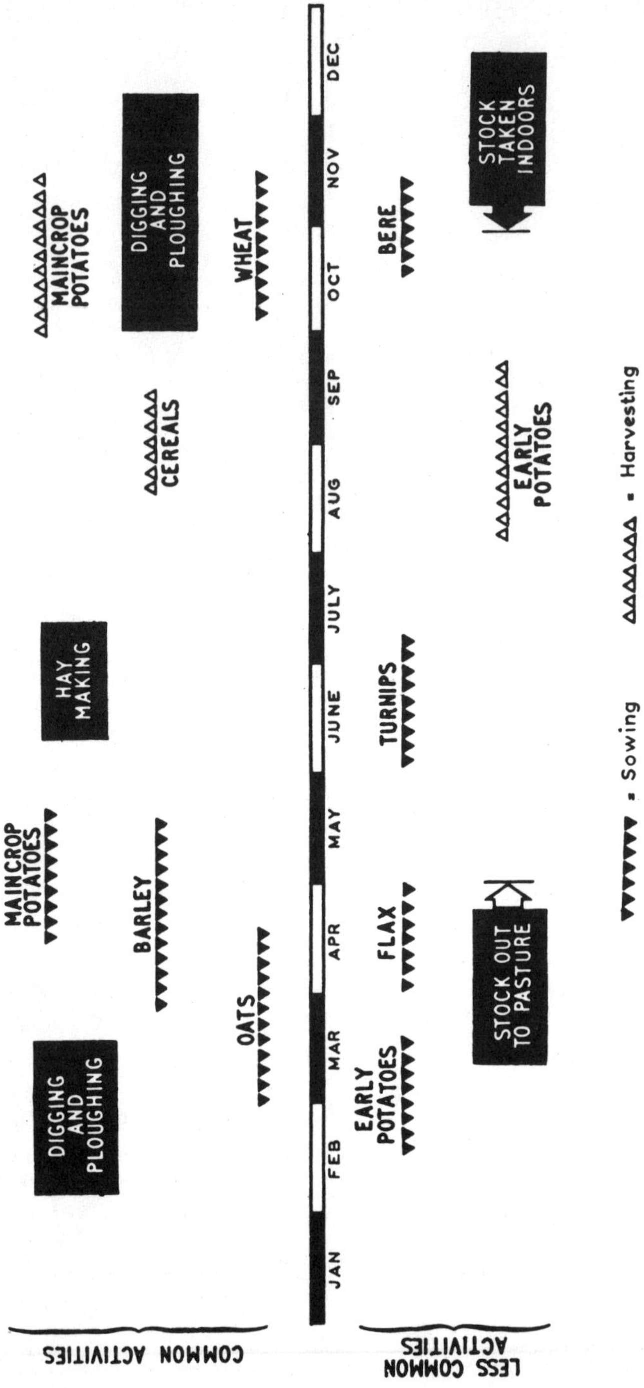

Fig. 5 Annual cycle of agricultural work, c. 1840

cry was still re-echoing: 'a general want is felt here for some good early potato'.[162]

The fact is that, unlike Arthur Guinness and despite the advice of Martin Doyle to the poor to grow 'a few stone of Kidney potatoes', small growers could not afford to cultivate the low-yielding early varieties, for exactly the same reason as they were forced to abandon the good-keeping Apple once it had passed its peak of productiveness.[163] It is significant that all the early potato varieties then grown in Ireland were developed in England; indeed, in some four hundred years of potato growing, no important early variety has ever been bred in Ireland.

It is symptomatic of the extent to which the potato had conquered the wealthy that there was a lucrative trade in Dublin city for a really early and expensive potato. Radcliff gives a fascinating account of this trade. The variety used was locally known as the Wicklow Banger, but was, in fact, imported from Cumberland. It was sown in September, in small bog islands in the marshy coastal strip between Kilcoole and Wicklow town, where the influence of the sea and shelter of the mountains (not to mention the laborious human devices which Radcliff mentions) largely protected the crop from frost. Prior to marketing, the potatoes were hand-picked, washed, graded and scraped free of blemish. (How far we have progressed!) Marketed in early May, the first few pounds to market could command a price as high as five shillings a pound, surely a fortune in those days:

> And the too happy carman, grinning with delight, is borne upon the shoulders of applauding basket-carriers, nor ever suffered to touch the ground until, amidst the general and vociferous acclamation of the bagpipe, nearly the whole of the money is nobly dissipated on... whiskey, to the infinite satisfaction and festivity of his attendants and himself, and much to the *credit*, if not to the profit of his master.[164]

The spade cultivation of potatoes on isolated bog islands surrounded by water was laborious and hazardous, and later the Wicklow trade tended to decline, although it appears to have continued to some degree up to the famine. Meanwhile the more readily worked farms of coastal north Dublin had begun to specialise in early potatoes, which were planted in autumn or winter at this time.[165]

The critical factor for the practical consideration of the food question is the maincrop potato or the 'people's crop'. The dates of planting and harvesting of this crop are of vital importance, and we shall consider in a little detail the justification for the mean dates shown in fig. 6.

Time of potato planting

We have seen that the historical trend, at least until 1830, had been towards later planting of potatoes. There does not appear to have been any substantial change in the average planting date between 1800 and the famine. Dubourdieu gives the date for the maincrop as 'the latter end of April or the beginning of May; in boggy ground, any time in the month of May or even the beginning of June'. The recommended period is given by the *Munster Farmers' Magazine* as from 20 April to 10 May.[166] This target was rarely achieved by the harassed cottier; potatoes were 'generally planted too late in the season, frequently with the poor not before the end of May'. The system 'pertinaciously adhered to' by those who had a choice 'was to plant their general crop (to use their own words) "between the two Mays" – meaning between the first of May, new-style, and the first of May, old-style'.[167] The gradual realisation that this was too late is reflected in the *Irish Farmer's and Gardener's Register*:

> an opinion very generally prevails amongst farmers that the best season to plant the general crop of potatoes is between the 'two Mays', viz, from the 1st to the 12th of this month; but when the ground can be got ready in time, which it always may if properly drained, April is certainly the proper season.[168]

For the famine years, the following quotations are representative:

> The beginning of May was formerly very generally regarded as the proper period to plant the potato crop, but for some time past an earlier seed time has been employed – now much of the crop, in some districts, is planted by April. Early planting is the best means to guard against recent failures.

> I plant as soon as possible after April 20th.

> Although the general planting of potatoes is now (4 May) nearly over, there will be, for various causes but more generally from the difficulties the poor man encounters in all his little operations, some little to be done.

> Potato planting should, if possible, be finished by the middle of May.

> The usual season of planting in Ireland is from the middle of April to the middle of May; sometimes, indeed, it extends even to the beginning of June.[169]

The persistence of late planting, in June or even July, is well attested. It was common amongst the poorer farmers and labourers, and was sometimes attributed by the righteous 'to that improvident spirit which no sufferings or experience can forewarn'. In fact, it arose variously from delays in obtaining seed, conacre land, and manure, and from the necessity to work for others during the peak spring period.[170]

The overall picture shows an average potato seeding time about a month later than became the practice after the famine. The exact dates depended in part on the character of the spring weather, but, in the mean, it extended from mid-April to mid-May, and straggled on, in some cases, into June.

Time of potato harvesting

The time of lifting the crop was correspondingly delayed. When the constabulary were reporting in the second half of September 1845 on the state of the potato crop, many commented that it would be impossible to give reliable information until the general digging took place. This they variously timed as beginning 'in October' (Louth), 'by the end of October' (Carlow), 'at the latter end of October' (Carlow), 'in November' (Mayo) and even 'about the middle of November or early in the month of December' (Down). Trevelyan differentiates between 'the early crop of potatoes, which is generally about one-sixth of the whole, and is dug in September and October' and 'the late, or what is commonly called the "people's crop" and is taken up in December and January'. The latter dates are certainly too late; it was a matter for comment when any substantial part of the crop was still in the ground at the end of November.[171]

However, since the growing time of the maincrop varieties was about six months, those planted by April were nearing maturity in September, while those not planted until the end of May were not ready for lifting, other than in frosty autumns, until November. In this sense, one could speak of an early and late maincrop and this was not uncommon. 'None but the early kinds of potatoes are got out before October'; 'what is called the early crop, now digging for use'.[172]

But for the bulk of the maincrop, and despite the pressure exerted by wheat farmers, it was considered that potatoes 'can scarcely have time to ripen if harvested so early as the beginning of October'. Newenham adds that 'every farmer must be aware of what essential benefit a week or ten days' growth is to the potato at the time of its ripening'.[173]

For the general maincrop, lifting took place in October-November, consistent with a planting time of April-May.

The annual cycles of employment and of distress

An important factor in the lives of a great number of Irish labourers and small farmers was the fluctuation during the year in the demand for agricultural labour. The typical cycle is shown in figure 6(a) which is based on the mean of three numerical tables given in the *Poor inquiry (D)*. The data refer to conditions in County Meath; that they are representative of the country as a whole may be seen from the answers to query 5 of the poor law inquiry questionnaire.[174]

The annual cycle of food stress was compounded of a number of factors – of diminishing potato supplies in the months of spring, of the deterioration due to poor keeping quality in the old potatoes immediately following, of the early summer slump in rural employment, and of the lateness of ripening of the main potato crop. The rise and fall in intensity of the food problem in an average year is represented schematically in figure 6(b). The amplitude and the intensity of the mid-summer wave of distress varied from year to year, but it was a regular feature of the Irish social scene for the thirty years preceding the famine. *'Tous les ans, à peu près à la même époque, on annonce en Irlande le commencement de la famine, ses progrès, ses ravages et son déclin.'*[175]

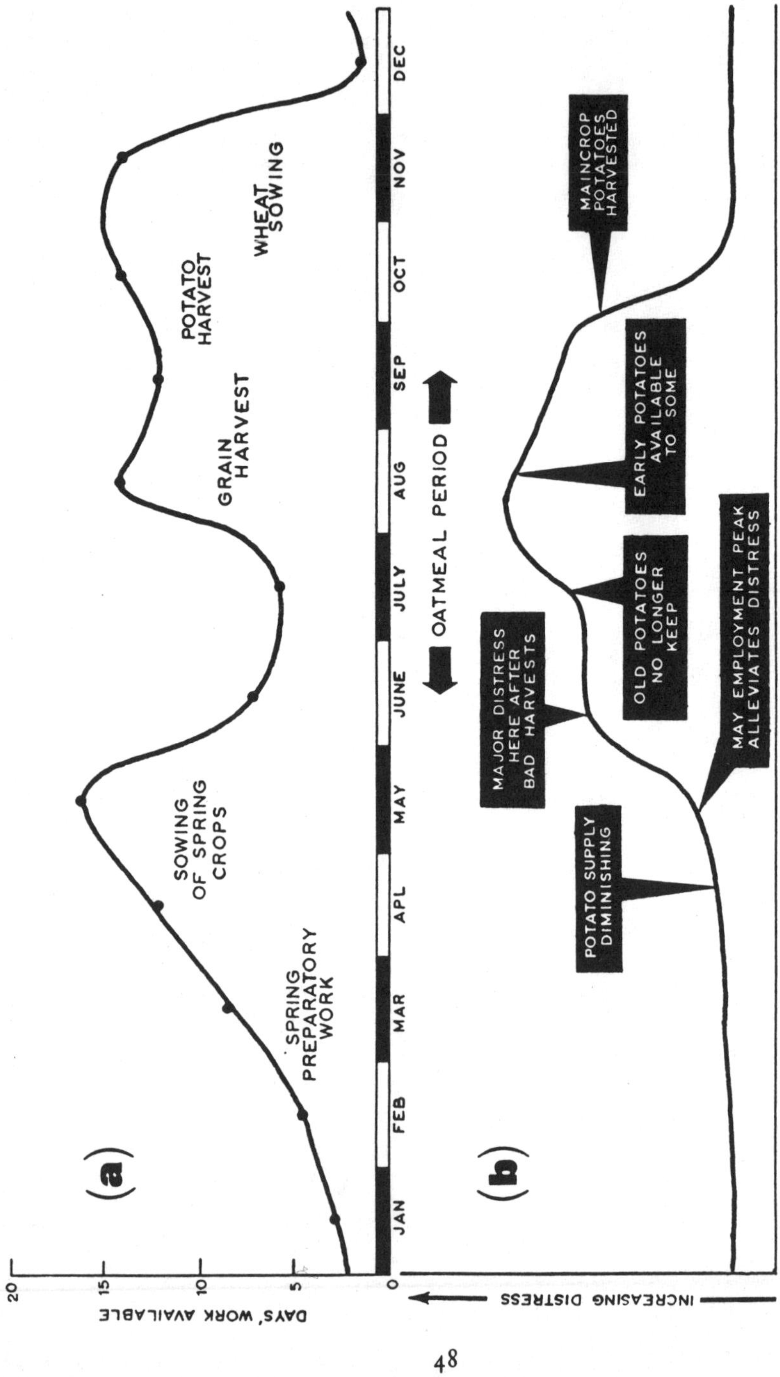

Fig. 6(a) Annual cycle of demand for agricultural labour and 6(b) mean annual cycle of food stress (diagrammatic).

The oatmeal period

The 'potato gap', or the interval between the old and new crops of potatoes, is so important a feature of pre-famine Irish life that it deserves a little closer examination:

The distress of the peasantry is in proportion to the extent of time that thus intervenes, and the universal opinion that it is the most frightful evil in Ireland is but too strongly confirmed by the wretchedness that it annually renews or increases in the shape of regular periodic visitation which only varies from great privation to absolute famine, according to the season, the price of food, employment and other local circumstances of the district.[176]

Trevelyan presents the simple concept of an average interval of two months of the oatmeal diet in an otherwise exclusive potato regime:

The potato does not, in fact, last even a single year. The old crop becomes unfit for use in July, and the new crop, as raised by the inferior husbandry of the poor, does not come into consumption until September. Hence, July and August are called the 'meal months' from the necessity the people are under of living upon meal at that period.[177]

Chart too denominates July and August as 'meal months'.[178] The poor law inquiry heard the most comprehensive evidence on this question; it illustrates that the summer shortage of potatoes in the immediate pre-famine years was, in fact, occasioned by a complex of causes.[179] We may distinguish four major factors:

(1) *the difficulty of many of the population in growing an adequate supply of potatoes*

'The labourer never has any of his conacre potatoes remaining at the period at which they become unfit for use, the greater number have used them all at the beginning of April, and scarcely one has a potato remaining at the 1st of May.' Clarke confirms that this was a problem in all except years of abundant yield.[180]

Those in employment, or whose credit was good, supplemented their own crop by the purchase of potatoes in these months in normal years. In the years following a poor potato harvest, shortage and high prices made buying impossible. After the partial failure of 1845, the Athy board of guardians decided to store farina 'for the months of April, May and June, which are generally the period that the poor are the worst off for potatoes'.[181]

(2) *premature digging of the potato crop*

Dr Doyle speaks of how the poor man recalls with regret, 'the waste, the havoc committed in his little garden by digging the produce of it in August or September; but with this recollection and regret upon his mind he will and must dig it up again the next year, and every year of his life'. 'Many a journey does the housewife take with basket in hand and spade on shoulder "to try the potatoes", as it is called; and many a time does she return unsuccessful from the field, with disappointed looks, to boil the unwelcome stirabout for supper.'[182] 'The want of employment in June and July is to the last degree injurious to the labourer because, when his stock of potatoes is run out, he is obliged to dig the new ones, though at that time scarcely larger than marbles.' 'Sometimes they go to the best-looking stalks on the ridge, and root out the young potatoes with their fingers, then turn back the mould that they may injure the growth as little as possible.' 'I have seen them, in the beginning of summer, digging the wild potato stalks to get at, not the young, but the old potato that the stalk was growing from.'[183]

In a year (1835) which 'was, perhaps, the most favourable in every way that can be remembered', the commissioners saw for themselves families living entirely on their new potatoes in the first and second weeks of August, when the tubers 'did not exceed the size of a walnut'. Often they were eaten, in the fine phrase of a witness, 'when only hunger could see them on the stalks'. During the period of food shortage in County Sligo in 1822, the local committee decided that any person who dug potatoes before 20 August would be removed from the relief list.[184]

(3) *the unfitness for use of the old potato crop*

'The potato is generally unfit for use after the middle of June or the 1st of July.' 'By the month of July all potatoes have become bad, except Apple potatoes which, unfortunately, are not the produce of the poor man's garden; Lumpers and Cups begin to deteriorate in June, and they are the ordinary food of the people.' But the poor who were lucky enough to have some of their store left were not amongst 'those who can afford to have an opinion as to the quality of their potatoes'.[185] 'Is there any kind of food used by human beings in any country under heaven more insipid, less nutritious, more unwholesome' than the old potato in summer, asks Dr Doyle; and adds that 'every person knows how nauseous, how disgusting almost, are potatoes in July and August'.[186]

(4) *the lateness in maturing of the current people's potato crop*

'Of the new crops, the Cups (middle quality) are fit to eat by the 1st of September. Lumpers...are not fit for human food till the middle of September or beginning of October; until then they are generally too soft for a man to work upon.'[187] Even this date is probably optimistic, certainly for the late sown maincrop, but it was common to anticipate the general harvest by digging out current needs from day to day; where this sampling did not begin until September, the overall loss of yield was not substantial.

* * *

Various combinations of these four factors gave a normal summer oatmeal period which varied, according to circumstances, from nil to three months or longer. For those who grew Apple potatoes and who had early varieties for the months July-September, it could be claimed truly that 'in reality, no time intervenes between the old and the new crops'; in a sense, this was true also of the very poor who ate the old crop after it was unfit and tried the new before it was ripe. Over the community as a whole, one may consider the average oatmeal period as covering what has been called 'the bitter six weeks'; for the remaining 10½ months the potato reigned virtually supreme.[188]

Relationship between potato yield and distress

Two final points may be made regarding the productivity of the potato crop and its influence on the level of distress. Where the yield of the potato crop was below normal, it was extremely rare, prior to 1846, for the produce to be insufficient to meet immediate winter needs. Thus the season of distress began early in the year following the failure of the potato crop. Several instances of confusion between the year of distress and the year of crop failure will be found in the analysis of previous famines given by Trevelyan.[189]

The repercussions of a failure in the potato crop were not confined to the year immediately following. For the following crop, seed potatoes were scarce and dear, credit was tight and deposits for conacre land hard to come by, and there was a natural tendency to use the new crop prematurely, with consequent scarcity two years after the original failure. Thus the acreage under potatoes in 1846 was down by over 20% on that of the previous year, while conacre was reduced by nearly 40%; a marginal note on the crop returns from Kilkenny states that 'the landlord...will not let conacre without security for payment'.[190] The repercussions from a poor potato crop bore hardest on, and persisted longest for, the class least able to bear them.

Similarly, the effects of a good potato crop were not confined to the season in which it was eaten. Seed potatoes were cheap and easy to reserve, the pigs prospered and multiplied, rents were paid, credit was good and conacre land rather more readily available. After the good harvests of 1842-4, the potato planting of 1845 was extensive, increasing by nearly 6% between 1844 and 1845, with the acreage under conacre potatoes up by 10%.[191]

CHAPTER 2

'The visitation of God': the role of the potato in Ireland on the eve of the famine*

Michael Brennan, aged about 14 years, apprentice to James Reilly, a sweep, was sent up a chimney by his master at Mr Egan's brush factory, Thomas Street, on Monday to clean the flue, but not returning in due time, or making answer when called to, another lad was sent up after him, and found Brennan stuck fast in the mason work, and unable to speak or move. He was brought down with some difficulty and found to be without any appearance of life. The body was conveyed to Barrington's hospital, where James Bennett, Esqr., coroner, held an inquest, and the verdict was – 'Died by the visitation of God.' (Report in the *Limerick Chronicle of* 3 September 1845, at the time when the early signs of potato blight were appearing in Ireland)

The breakdown of potato usage in Ireland and the availability of other food crops provide a reasonable yardstick with which we may assess the role of the potato in Irish life just before the famine.[1] So dominant was its position as a food that its influence dictated the level of rents, depressed the value of labour, and indeed touched on almost every aspect of rural life.

The potato as a human foodstuff

In terms of population, it has been calculated that 3.3 million people lived exclusively on the potato, that for 4.7 million it was the predominant item of diet, and that less than 0.7 million, on 25% or less of a potato diet, could be said to be independent of the foodstuff.[2]

We may, using the data in the publications quoted, calculate the contribution made up by potatoes and cereal crops to the diet of the population as a whole; it emerges, in broad figures, that potatoes made up 60% of the nation's food supply, oats 16%, wheat 9% and other foods 15%. The figure for 'other foods' is uncertain, unless we can assume that overeating by the rich exactly compensated the hunger of the poor; the calculation is based on an adequate diet for the population as a whole.

A third method of presenting the importance of the potato as an article of food is in terms of the average amount consumed each year per head of

* From 'The potato, blight, weather and the Irish famine' (Ph.D. thesis, NUI, 1967), chap. 2.

the population. This information is given in the following table together with comparable data for the mid-twentieth century.[3]

AVERAGE INDIVIDUAL CONSUMPTION OF POTATOES IN IRELAND

(a) *Pre-famine* (all Ireland)	
In the agricultural community	*c.* 2,300 lb. per annum
In the non-agricultural community	*c.* 1,000 lb. per annum
In Ireland generally	*c.* 1,900 lb. per annum
(b) *1950* (Republic)	
In Dublin city	267 lb. per annum
In large towns	346 lb. per annum
In small towns	364 lb. per annum
In farm labourers' families	435 lb. per annum
In farming families	529 lb. per annum
In congested districts	683 lb. per annum
In Ireland (Republic) generally	440 lb. per annum

Thus, in agricultural areas, the per capita consumption of potatoes as human food before the famine was at a level of about a ton a year, or over six pounds a day. (It may have been on a similar basis of calculation that Wakefield found that 'the average consumption of each member of a potatoe-eating family, according to my notes, is 5½ pounds').[4] Over the country as a whole, it was over five pounds a day, which was more than four times the level a century later and nearly three times the value returned for the congested districts.

How adequate nutritionally was a monodiet of potatoes? The Scotsman, Bain, was in no doubt:

> Whatever may be the misfortunes of Ireland, the potato is not implicated. It, on the contrary, has *more* than done its duty, in giving them bones and sinew cheap...There is no other crop equal to the potato in the power of sustaining life and health.[5]

Connell presents an analysis of the content, in terms of calories, protein, minerals and vitamins, of ten pounds of potatoes and one pint of whole milk, and concludes that this amount of food per day represented a nourishing if monotonous diet for an adult man.[6] The difficulty of basing firm conclusions on this kind of approach to the calculation of food needs and to determining the adequacy of diets is discussed by McArthur.[7] An added uncertainty is introduced by equating, as Connell does, the chemical composition of modern potato varieties with that of the sorts in use in pre-famine Ireland. It may be significant that, of the witnesses with Irish experience whom Connell quotes, Young, at the time of good potato varieties, was enthusiastic about the healthiness of a potato diet; Wakefield, in the transition era, was doubtful, and Doyle, in the age of the Lumper, was hostile.[8] An Irish witness giving unrestrained approval to the potato as an exclusive human diet is difficult to find after 1820.

Even if adequate for those in good health, a bulky and coarse food like the potato was scarcely good for the ailing. 'The food on which the Irish chiefly subsist may be well suited to the support of life, whilst the vigour of youth animates the frame; but in declining age, and when the vital spark is on the point of expiring, surely some further help is needed, some comfort to assuage the pangs of disease and smooth the bed of illness.'[9] Twenty years after the famine, Thompson wrote that the 'higher standard and greater variety of diet had diminished greatly a distressing class of cases which formerly prevailed extensively in the early summer months, commencing with flatulence and dyspepsia, and ending in dysentry and fever, thus incapacitating the labourer from work at a time of year when his labour was most valuable to him'.[10] The major factor in this seasonal illness was, doubtless, the short supply and poor quality of the old potatoes in early summer.

Apart from the nutritional and health aspects, there were serious disadvantages to a potato monodiet. Familiarity has dulled our astonishment at the fact that the potato should have attained the position as a food which it held in Ireland in the 1840s; in fact, it is historically unique that a single foodstuff, other than a storable grain, should dominate the diet of a people living in a temperate climate. Dr Knox asks, 'Is it not a lamentable consideration that a whole race of men should, like the beast of the field, be reduced to one description of food; to live on one root, however wholesome, however good...a root, too, which cannot be preserved as food for a single year.'[11] Dr Knox did not, however, 'consider the potato to be the real national malady' or the reason why there were 'three or four million people living within the pale of a seeming civilisation, but in a condition inferior to that of the savage'. The basic cause he saw to be 'feudality – the *land* does not belong to the people'. It was an unorthodox opinion for a Briton of his time.

Twenty years before the famine, an anonymous writer in the *Edinburgh Review* pinpointed the basic weakness of the situation:

When wheat and beef constitute the principal part of the food of the labourer, and porter and beer the principal part of his drink, he can, in a period of scarcity, *bear to retrench*. Such a man has room to fall – he can resort to cheaper articles – to barley, oats, rice and potatoes. But when he is habitually and constantly fed on the very lowest species of food, he has plainly nothing to resort to when deprived of it. The labourers, who are placed in such circumstances, are absolutely cut off from every resource. They are already so low, they can fall no lower. They are placed on the verge of existence. Their wages, being regulated by the price of potatoes, will not buy them wheat or barley or oats; and whenever, therefore, the supply of potatoes fails, it is next to impossible they can escape falling a sacrifice to famine.[12]

On the basis of an erroneous acreage figure for 1846, Salaman deduces that the supremacy of the potato was scarcely shaken for thirty years after the famine.[13] In fact, as the following table shows, the production of potatoes fell abruptly after the famine and, even allowing for a reduction in population, never subsequently reached a level at all comparable to that of the 1840s.

AVERAGE POTATO PRODUCTION IN IRELAND

Period	*Potato crop* (thousands of tons)
Early 1840s	*c.* 15,000
1847-56	4,423
1857-66	3,407
1867-76	3,361
1877-86	2,642
1887-96	2,740
1897-1906	2,647
1907-16	3,088
1917-26	2,976
1927-36	3,470
1937-46	4,116
1947-56	3,844

Dun, having discussed the rising cost of boarding servant girls on Lord Waterford's estate, harks back nostalgically to more frugal times:

The tea, bread, small portion of bacon, and other etceteras consumed by master and servants, inexpensive and reasonable although they appear, I am told by careful housekeepers, add 20s. per week to the expenditure on a farm of one hundred acres, as compared with the moderate commissariat expenses of thirty years ago, when potatoes, stirabout and buttermilk constituted the dietary both in parlour and kitchen.[14]

The trend of human potato consumption in the century following the famine is discussed in some detail by Bourke, who concludes that the evidence

tends to indicate that, ignoring regional variations, the use of the potato as human food dropped abruptly at the time of the famine to about one-third of its previous per caput value, then fell more slowly to a minimum value about 1900, and may have risen somewhat in later years.[15]

It is symptomatic of rising prosperity that the use in Ireland of potatoes, in common with bread and household flour, has again dropped in recent years.

The potato as a food for animals

In 1951 the consumption of potatoes by farm animals was stated to be 44% of the total production; the amount used as stockfeed was almost double that used for human food.

In 1845, on the other hand, the dominant use of the potato was as food for humans. The 33% devoted to stockfeed represented no real safety valve in case of shortage, for the main animal consumer was the pig, which could not readily be dispensed with without doing serious damage to the already borderline economics of the poor. It is remarkable, in fact, how many pigs survived the famine; the total (in thousands) was 622 in 1847, gradually rising to 1,085 in 1851, as compared with the 1841 figure of 1,413. In other words, the percentage drop in pigs in the intercensus period which straddles the famine was little greater than in the human population.

The potato and the value of labour

The claim in the *Edinburgh Review* that the wages of agricultural labourers were depressed in proportion to the cheapness of the food which they ate is only part of the truth. The vast majority of the Irish labourers, unlike their counterparts in England, were paid, not in money, but in land or in food.[16] The abuses which the truck system in potatoes and oats gave rise to are vividly described by Ryan in his prize essay; his evidence is all the more convincing since, as Church of Ireland vicar of the parish of Rathconnell, Co. Westmeath, he was a disinterested witness.

In England, he claims, it was illegal to pay a labourer in kind, or even for a farmer to sell food to his employees. In Ireland, on the other hand, it was usual, for example, to pay labourers on road construction in the form of provisions, the value of which was assessed at a high retail price, 'with a little addition arising from the lack of competition'. The overseer, to whom the road construction or repair had been assigned, worked through a deputy, a procedure which introduced further opportunities for graft. The overseer recovered his inflated expenditure at the next grand jury assizes; the landlord (often himself the overseer) benefited by the improved roads which facilitated the transport of grain and livestock to market; the exploited labourer was grateful for the handful of potatoes which kept hunger at bay for another day.

> Such is the anomalous situation of the Irish peasantry, that they consider themselves greatly favoured by being thus employed and paid. The kind consideration of the overseer is frequently a theme of praise; and I sincerely believe that many of them [the overseers] think they are very disinterestedly discharging an important duty, without ever calculating the profits.[17]

This is a recurrent feature of pre-famine life which is very striking. The victim, trapped in a system under which his condition constantly deteriorated, accepted thankfully anything which gave him that day his daily potato, whether it was land rented at an impossible price or the temporary use of 'chance lots of ground' to grow conacre potatoes at high cost.[18]

In England, the allotment system was feared by some farmers lest it make the labourers too independent; in Ireland, under the form of cottier tenancy, it created a pool of ill-paid, ill-treated, but grateful labour:

> I never yet knew an Irishman rendered so independent of his employer as to become a saucy and bad servant from his possessing his bit of land; it is attended with a contrary effect, for his dread of losing it is such that he is made much more subservient, and much more to be depended on, than the casual day labourer. He becomes, indeed, an interested person, and I have known him even submit to a blow from his employer, rather than leave his service and lose his land.[19]

On the other hand, the exploiter saw himself as a good Samaritan helping his less fortunate brother; the evidence of the usurer, Patrick Rooney, is a remarkable example.[20] In Ireland, a 'good' landlord was one who took no more than his full pound of flesh.

The potato and the rent of land

'Land is, to the Irish peasant, a necessity of life, the alternative being starvation.'[21] The rapid rise in population in the early nineteenth century intensified the scramble for potato ground and led to frantic overbidding for land by the man 'to whom it is an object to obtain subsistence for the passing day, though at the remote inconvenience of contracting a debt that he can never discharge'. One lived for the moment; tomorrow was another day; by overbidding one was 'sure of time'.[22] Again, it is a theme which recurs repeatedly in the evidence. In taking conacre land, the advantage is 'above all, that he gains time by the mode of payment'.[23]

The landlord's main defence of the level of rents was the law of supply and demand. 'Where there is a greater competition, we must expect to let at a higher rent.' When the landlord was told that his rents were too high, his natural reply was that 'everything is worth what it will bring'.[24]

Justification more morally warming than the cold dictates of economics was put forward by a clergyman:

> Was the generosity of a landlord to make a considerable deduction from a tenant's rent, in order to enable him to live with more comfort, it is by no means improbable that the abatement, instead of bettering his condition, might make it worse. By diminishing the necessity of laborious exertion, it might encourage an idle and dissolute habit, and make him eventually less solvent than he was before.[25]

It is an argument not without its faint echoes in recent times in Ireland.

It is important to note that it is a gross oversimplification to contrast a small group of grasping landlords, English and Protestant, with a great mass of exploited tenantry, Irish and Catholic. The prevalence of division and sub-tenancy created an extremely complex system of land tenure:

There was a man who appeared before us, and it happened to come out in the course of his examination that he paid thirty days' work for four perches of ground, and he built a house upon the ground himself. The person he held from held eight acres and a half, and he paid £3 8s. 5d. an acre, the outside value of the land being about £2 an acre. He held it from a middleman, that middleman held from another, and he held again from the head landlord; and I should say that such cases are not rare.[26]

It was thus true that 'in Ireland, the same man is constantly changing character, being in one sense a landlord, and in the other a tenant'. The only true landlords were the handful of land owners, whose first lettings were normally at close to the real value of the land; the only true tenants, at the other end of the escalator of successive rent increases, were those with small patches of land, normally held as cottiers or in conacre. The tragedy of the system was that 'the class in the community which has the least means has the highest rent to pay'. It enabled the bigger man, when his rents were criticised, to say that the worst abuses were at the lowest level, when the poor dealt directly with the poorest: 'It is when they come to traffic amongst each other that they come to deal in that conacre system; it is that that is destructive to the poor.'[27] Evading responsibility himself, he could thus attack 'the frieze-coated farmer who, without capital, skill or industry, stints the land of labour, the labourer of hire and the landlord of rent', and sympathise with the lot of the agricultural labourer,

the poor, abused, wretched, demoralised victim of a system which compels him, in exchange for a scanty supply of the meanest food, to surrender himself a bond slave to the most unpitying and unscrupulous of masters, the peasant farmer of the south of Ireland.[28]

In so far as the small farmer exploited the cottier or conacre tenant, his action may be understood, if not condoned, in the light of his own land problems.[29] Before he took possession of the land at high rent from a middleman, a great part of his small capital was sunk in a 'fine', as a deposit for security.

If the landlord employs an agent, he is also to be handsomely compensated, for doing no more than his duty by his employer if he acts honestly, and for defrauding him if he does not; another expense is the law agent's charge for leases, generally double his fair claim. The wife of the landlord or agent must also be complimented; and often the good word of some man, who is supposed to have influence with the latter, is secured by a handsome present. To these expenses I am aware there are exceptions, but they are few, and the state of the country is influenced by the practice in the greater number of instances where it prevails.[30]

But the letting of land in conacre was not a practice confined to the small or medium farmers. 'Proprietors of large estates may be seen thus proportioning out their land, and constantly suing the improvident conacre tenant at the quarter sessions, thus adding, by legal expense, twelve per cent to the original rent.' The temptation was considerable;

'a man with 100 acres of land at 30/- an acre pays a large proportion of the rent if he can conacre 12 or 15 acres of that land at £12 an acre'. Land on Lord Ponsonby's estate in County Cork, rented at 16s. a statute acre, was sub-let as potato ground to labourers, who were required to manure it themselves, at £6 and over per acre.[31]

In an excellent analysis of the conacre potato system given before the Royal Agricultural Improvement Society, W. Herbert Saunders instances a man who rents 'the use of an acre of ground' for £4 or £5 from a middleman who pays his landlord £1 or £1 10s.:

> Upon it he expends his dunghill, gathered by the whole previous year's labour of *all* his family, his seed potatoes, and the labour again of *all* his family...to sow, earth, and dig them. To pay the £4 or £5 for the usufruct of the acre of ground, which he afterwards leaves highly manured and valuable, he *trucks* his labour at the rate of 6d. per day...The labour of the potato-fed population of Ireland goes for little more than a tenth of its value.[32]

Conacre was, in fact, fundamental to the agricultural system in many parts of Ireland; together with other systems of leasing potato land, it enabled many farmers without capital to pay their rents and to employ cheap labour:

> The conacre system was hitherto the universal plan of conducting the labour of farms in this part of the country [County Cork]. According to the quality of land, it was charged to the labourer at from £6 to £8 to £10 an acre per annum, the most worthless heath being let, when limed, at £6 per annum. The rent was paid by the labourer's work; the system was, to let out as much land as paid the whole labour bill of the farm. In every way the necessities of the labourer were taken advantage of. The highest rent was charged, and that was paid by the lowest rate of wages. This system of course fell to pieces when the potato failed; and the farmer, having no capital to pay his labourers in cash, failed also.[33]

The conacre system was obviously wide open to abuse, and with no effective legal restraint upon 'avariciousness and rapacity' in the face of enormous demand, every advantage was taken of the helpless labourers:

> When a gentleman or his agent determines on letting a tract of land for con-acre, the first object to be considered is the appointment of a trustworthy person to explain the terms, take in the names of the applicants, receive the 'earnest', have the crop watched, and finally receive the rents, for which a remuneration of 2½ per cent, and sometimes upwards, is allowed by the proprietor to said collector. It very rarely happens that any respectable land agent would lower himself to do such business; consequently the lot falls to the under agent (if such there be), or to some friend or nominee of his, who is appointed to perform the business. Notice is duly given, and on the appointed day vast crowds assemble to deposit the 'earnest', without which none need expect to be enrolled. The 'earnest' given, the next business to be done is to divide the land, in the performance of which it is very natural to suppose there will be favour observed; as in large tracts there must be a difference in the soil, there may be angles where cattle were fed, sheep dressed often, or where the drainings of dung-yards run occasionally, all these little advantages in point of locality are immediately pounced upon by

the worthy functionary 'appointed to do justice', and those favoured spots are either planted for his own use – perhaps gratis by some of the creatures who must make such a sacrifice to retain his mighty favour – or given by him to some herd, ploughman, or other that may contribute in some measure to aid him in his purpose. The *learned surveyor*, of course, does his own part – divides the land into acres, and acres into divisions and subdivisions of half acres and roods; and when the number of applicants exceed the number of subdivisions, as almost always happens in populous districts, the surveyor's chain is cut short to retain the number of '*earnests*', and each subdivision frequently is found to contain little more than from 30 to 35 perches, as it happens; for the surveying of each of those subdivisions is charged 6d., for 'earnest' on the same from 1s. to 1s. 9d. or perhaps 2s.; so that when the whole is made up it frequently exceeds 10s. per acre. This is wrung from the poor at the hardest season of the year, never to be allowed a farthing for it at the time of paying the rent; and such is the severity of those petty tyrants, that no poor man, however honest, need expect a perch of land without handing down his 'earnest', although his integrity were known to be unimpeachable. I have known poor men to be obliged to give their subdivisions to others after having prepared them to receive the seed, in consequence of not having the full price of it at the market, and support their poor families at the same time, and be obliged to go to England to work and let their wives and children go beg about the world till their return.

All this time the proprietor may be ignorant of how matters go on, and so may his agent, perhaps; and it is only when the rents become due he can form even the most distant idea that matters are not all right; and then, too, he will be made to think all the fault rests with the poor cultivator, who may be represented to him as an idle, lazy fellow, who did not cultivate his land right, and that if he did he would have more than the value of his rent, seed, and labour.

The last mentioned is of little value where little employment is to be had, but the rest, I think it will be admitted, is pretty high at from six to ten pounds an acre in many places, without any manure, or the least assistance towards cultivation.

The days of rent becoming due are the 1st of November and Christmas – if they are paid at November, no additional charge is made to former rent, 'earnest', &c.; but should they remain unpaid till Christmas or Candlemas, the rent is increased from 1-10th to 1-6th of the whole amount in proportion to the time given. The question that then presents itself is, how the rents are to be made up: some may have a few barrels of oats, but it is then selling at five and six shillings a barrel; others may have no means except their labour. But who is to employ them? Some may be fortunate enough to have from 5s. to 10s. to spare after planting the potatoes, and they repair to England to earn the rent, but are not returned perhaps in time to dig the potatoes, they remain undug till the frost comes and destroys them, in which case the landlord as well as cultivator may become the sufferer.[34]

For all the abuses with which conacre was attended – and they are attested again and again in the evidence from the *Poor inquiry* – the system was an unavoidable corollary of the later stages of the potato economy and of the land tenure of the early nineteenth century. 'The country would starve were it not for conacre.' It was not the farmers who rented out potato ground, at however high a rate, who provoked the anger of the labourers;

it was those who declined to do so that had their pastures ploughed up by the land-hungry mob.[35]

The potato and land reclamation

McAdam lauded the potato as 'one of the great instruments by which our bogs are reclaimed'.[36] Those who were unable to obtain potato ground otherwise were forced up into the mountains or out into the bogs in the grimmest struggle of all for survival.

There is a third class of improvers who used to be the most numerous of the three, but who are now rapidly decreasing, viz., those known by the name of 'squatters', who were, for some reason or another, allowed to settle on the land, sometimes paying a slight acknowledgment, sometimes nothing at all. These squatters' first care was to erect a mud-hovel, without a window or chimney, and covered with sods resting on a few rough pieces of bog-pine, a residence in every respect inferior to a fox-earth or a rabbit-burrow, these last always having a rise at the end, which ensures the occupants a dry bed, a luxury by no means always to be found in a squatter's cabin.

On one occasion, two friends of the writer taking shelter in one of these cabins, when benighted, had great difficulty in extracting their horse from the one apartment in which it shared with them the owner's hospitality, in consequence of its being *bogged in the middle of the floor*.

Having built his house and buried a few bushels of seed potatoes, the squatter had nothing to live upon until potato harvest, and accordingly he closed his house and set off on a tour in England to raise a little money by haymaking, harvesting or hop picking, whilst his wife and children wandered around Ireland picking up a precarious existence by asking the 'loan' of a few potatoes from the more thriving farmers. If an accurate and circumstantial account of the wanderings of some of these poor souls could be published, probably it would surprise every one, even the 'faculty' themselves, to learn how much privation and starvation the human frame could endure and still return to tell the tale.

Under favourable circumstances, the steadiest and most industrious of the squatters gradually reclaimed a sufficient portion of land to create a diminutive farm, but the potato disease made a squatter's life impossible, and there are comparatively few of them now left.[37]

Thompson adds that all land improvement of this kind was based on an excessive expenditure of time and labour, under the goad of hunger; it would not pay as an agricultural operation in normal conditions. It was the last resort of men who had no capital except time, effort and a spade.

Cheap labour under the potato economy was also the foundation of the official bog reclamation scheme undertaken by the Board of Works at Kingwilliamstown, near the source of the River Blackwater on the Cork-Kerry border, and at a height of 850 feet above M.S.L.

The land was worked by conacre labour. That is, the people assembled in Spring and agreed to pay £6 an acre for the use of wild heath land to grow potatoes. They got lime for it, put in the seed and tilled the land at their own cost, giving their labour on the farm till it paid this exorbitant rent. A second crop of potatoes was taken, dung being applied to the land and the rent proportionately increased. The land was then ready for turnips and oats, after which it was sown out with grass seeds and laid to pasture. The moor was thus converted into grass at no other expense than that of seed, inasmuch as the labour of the people in cultivating their potato crops reclaimed it from its natural state, and the rent they paid for the use of the ground repaid their labour in the subsequent process of improvement. As long as the potato remained sound, the experiment prospered; but now that money wages must be paid, it does not succeed.

The success of the system was thus totally based on the potato; and the scheme seems rather to have been intended to show how many people could be kept alive by the cultivation of waste lands, than to exhibit an example of *an improvement in the condition of the people* resulting from the reclamation of the land. Better far that this tract should be left to the undisturbed possession of the curlew and the solitary raven, than that it should be made the means of perpetuating a system which only thrives through the misery of the people.[38]

This indignation is all the more striking as coming from one who had earlier regarded Lord Lucan's clearances with equanimity; but Caird, who was a careful observer, had learned much from his travels in the interim.

Nimmo gives a detailed account of reclamation for potato growing in the western bogs; after a few seasons, the reclaimed bogland tended to revert to its original condition; the patch appeared perhaps a little greener than its surroundings but was often scarcely distinguishable. Cultivation rose, in the exposed mountains of Mayo, to a height of 500 feet above M.S.L., and descended into the edges of the bogs until stopped by the wetness. Hall says that in some cases hills rising to one thousand feet above the surrounding country were cultivated nearly to their summits.[39] Evidence of cultivation to even above this level may still be traced on the sheltered slopes of the Wicklow mountains.

The potato and the manuring of the land

'No crop grown by the farmer is more dependent on a due application of manure for its success than the potato,' and in Ireland the grower was almost totally dependent on the potato. A small addition to the yield could avoid weeks of misery in the early months of the following summer; as a consequence, 'manures were collected and applied with a degree of industry and perseverance that appears almost incredible now'.[40] It was, literally, a matter of life or death. This aspect of the influence of the potato, which is fundamental to an understanding of the agricultural situation before and after the famine, has been virtually ignored by most commentators apart from Barrington.

In the previous century, Young had observed that 'nineteen-twentieths of all the dung in the kingdom is employed' on the potato. Maunsell confirms the preoccupation of the 'lowest class of the people' with manure for the potato crop; 'should they be so fortunate as to have sufficiency of manure for the gardens, they sleep in ease'.[41] A premium-winning Cork smallholder waxed poetic: 'manure put pinions on me to fly above the world, thank God!' The importance of manure tended, if anything, to increase as the population grew, and with it, the pressure on land. 'The only way in which the people in Cork can live is by the quantity of manure they draw...They can afford to pay more where there is a greater facility for manure.'[42] There was something frantic in the search for fertilising materials on the eve of the famine:

> The extraordinary activity which prevails in this country from the beginning of April to about the first of June must strike everyone acquainted with its rural population. The efforts then made to collect manure; the risks run in the plunder of the roads, of bogs, of ditches; the scrapings and gatherings; the careful admixture of the dungheap; and the ultimate stretching out of the compost, all show that when it comes to the point of sowing for the ensuing year's provision, our people are all alive to the importance of having manure for the purpose.[43]

Every available material was turned to use as a manure. It is true that the number of cattle was comparatively small, but the number of people was over eight million; the subject of human manure was considered indelicate but there are sufficient tactful references to confirm that the use of 'night soil' was widespread.[44] The more fastidious tried in vain to eradicate the eyesore of the essential manure heap beside the cabin door:

> The bishop's wife, my mother, and three or four other ladies were zealous of good works in those days...[They] made excursions into the fetid alleys of the Irish town, endeavouring to induce the inhabitants to remove the dungheaps accumulated round their wretched dwellings...[They were] probably too high in their bearing, too patronising in their ways, without meaning it, to stir the hearts of a people wary of strangers, and of a singularly sensitive and suspicious nature, and little real success attended their efforts.[45]

It was, no doubt, to be deplored that 'the dwelling of the peasant' should be no more than 'an inhabited dungheap'; but the more clear-eyed compassion of the Quakers saw that it was necessity which ousted hygiene: 'a doorway half blocked up by the dungheap is a sure sign of comparative wealth'.[46]

One feature of the growing demand for manures in the second quarter of the nineteenth century was the rise of the seaweed trade. Its potash content made it an excellent manure for potatoes and it was brought deep into the country sometimes as far as thirty Irish miles or more from the coast. For example, many hundreds of thousands of tons of seaweed were harvested annually at Youghal, whence it was carried up the river and across the mountains as far as the Clogheen district in County Tipperary. The seaweed was used extensively in the Curry area of south Sligo, to which it was carried over thirty miles from the sea. The demand for seaweed led to violent disputes and to complicated legal battles as to the ownership of the weed growing on the foreshore or in deep waters, and of the storm-loosed wrack floating on the sea or cast upon the shore.[47]

The most remarkable development arising from the demand for 'sea manure' was the construction of man-made sea farms for the encouragement of seaweed growth. In the previous century, Young had remarked on the industry of the people who had placed stones in Strangford Lough to encourage seaweed growth; this arose from a local scarcity of kelp, used as a bleach in the linen industry. Now the practice became widespread all around the coast as a source of manure. Of the many seaweed farms which were set up at this time, the most spectacular and best preserved example survives in Mill Bay, in Carlingford Lough; other specimens may be seen in Achill Sound and Lough Swilly. The extent to which this harvesting of the sea had developed by the eve of the famine is illustrated by an account of the situation on the east side of Galway Bay. The foreshore had been divided into 'acres', let in lots of from one to fourteen or more, which were in as keen demand as dry land. Shores which had already been prepared by laying down rows of rocks for seaweed anchorage were rented at £7 per 'acre'; those which had not yet been so 'reclaimed' at 30s. 'The nobleman who owns the land gains thus a considerable portion of his annual income.'[48]

The proprietors, while welcoming the lucrative sideline which the seaweed trade represented, were more dubious of its advantages (from their own point of view) as a manure. Excellent for the potato crop to which it was first applied, its effect was more 'transient' than that of dung and it did not so highly benefit later grain crops.[49]

Here we find the key to the general high level of crop yields before and immediately after the famine; the enormous effort devoted to manuring the potato crop at the time when it was vital to the life of the people carried over its beneficial effects to the oats, barley and wheat crops subsequently grown on the same land. Indeed it was considered that a grain crop following a well-manured potato crop yielded better than if the manure were put on with the grain. The manuring requirements of virtually every other crop grown in pre-famine Ireland were provided for in the care given to the potato; when the potato lost its dominating position after the famine, yields generally went into a sharp decline as soon as the momentum of accumulated manuring effort had run down.[50]

Those who rented out land, particularly in conacre, were very conscious of this profitable by-product; in fact part of the detestation of the Lumper potato by the well-to-do arose from the very property that commended it to the poor, i.e. its ability to bulk on a limited supply of manure. 'The little manure required in the growth of them deprives the farmer of about half the produce of wheat and oats in the succeeding crops.'

One of the early features of the famine which caused dismay to the landlords was 'the gradually increasing apathy and discouragement which, I regret to hear, are creeping over the poorer classes as to the necessity of providing their usual stock of manure for the ensuing season'. The landlord of Carbery, who wrote these lines, was moved belatedly to offer premiums to those of his tenants who continued to collect manure. 'However small the heap collected by each poor individual, I am convinced the aggregate loss of it would be seriously felt.' And, then, the astonishing *cri de coeur:* 'A total severance of interests between the farmer and the labourer is fraught with future mischief; it is giving up a link in the social chain!'[51] The labourer was, alas, too busy dying to respond to this despairing appeal for one last effort to shore up the collapsing social structure which had ground him into the earth.

The potato and agricultural efficiency

The yields of agricultural crops in Ireland in the 1840s were remarkably high. It is true that they are considerably below those now being obtained, but allowance must be made both for the greater area cultivated in the earlier days and the peculiar problems then posed by social conditions. Less than 2 million acres are now under crops in the whole of Ireland as compared with 6.4 million acres in 1845. If the present cultivated area were expanded more than threefold, to take in much land of lower fertility, it is problematic whether the mean production would be superior to that obtained in pre-famine years.

How can this relatively high productivity be reconciled with the picture of Irish agriculture as 'deplorable' and 'defective', so uniformly presented at the time, especially by English and Scottish agricultural writers?

It was primarily a matter of what was meant by 'efficient farming'. In the mechanical sense, of obtaining the maximum result from the minimum effort, Irish agriculture was clearly defective. The same applied to the economic concept of obtaining for the cultivator the greatest monetary return from the least expenditure. The pre-famine commentators frequently remark that many of the characteristic agricultural operations – from bog reclamation to pig rearing – would not pay as economic projects divorced from the peculiar social conditions of the time. But from the point of view of simple subsistence farming, with the primary object of obtaining the greatest possible amount of food per acre without regard to the amount of time, trouble and labour expended, pre-famine Irish agriculture was – and indeed was forced to be – as efficient as the circumstances of the time permitted.

> I have never seen any field cultivation in England, except perhaps hops, where more diligence is discovered [than in growing potatoes in Ireland]. Every ounce of manure is carefully husbanded, and every weed is destroyed. The drainage is made complete; and the hoe, or rather the apology for that instrument, is constantly going.[52]

The criticism of the agricultural 'improvers' must be interpreted in the light of their preconceptions as to what farming should be like, and their blindness to the fact that local practices, based on long painful experience, had been moulded to meet the difficulties of Irish conditions, both social and climatic.

The 'improvers' saw the turnip as the key to agricultural progress. They did not appreciate that, in the Irish conditions of the day, the potato carried out all the functions that had made the introduction of the turnip an important break-through in English agriculture. It represented a root crop to replace fallow as a preparation for cereals; it provided winter food for livestock; indeed, as a sturdy pioneer for breaking new ground and clearing land, it was far more suited to Irish conditions than the less vigorous turnip which needed a well prepared seed bed.

For the 'improvers', the replacement of the spade by the labour-saving plough represented agricultural progress. But the plough was ill suited to the bogs and the hills; and, in any case, the spade, laborious though it was, gave a far greater produce than the plough. 'No gardener would think of planting potatoes, carrots or cabbages in ploughed land if he could get it dug, for the difference of produce far more than compensates for the difference of expense.'[53]

The 'improvers' favoured the neat drills made by the plough, and despised the broad raised ridges on which most of the Irish grew their potatoes and oats. In one form of cultivation, the ground on to which the earth from the trench was piled was left unbroken; it may have been from the French '*laisser*' – as in *laisser faire* – that the term 'lazy bed' was derived. Whatever its origin, the name provided an added weapon to those who ridiculed the ridges. The irony of the situation was that the lazy beds represented, in fact, a 'laborious system of culture'.[54]

The controversy on the merits of drills and ridges was one of long standing. Maxwell recommended that new ground and wet land should be cultivated with the spade 'after the Irish manner'; the beds should not be more than about two yards wide. In Limerick, 'the Palatine mode of sowing in drills' was not adopted by their Irish neighbours, although their ridges were 'attended with greater expense and labour'. Sinclair considered that the lazy bed method was well adapted for damp soils and wet climates, and for breaking new coarse land; otherwise drilling was faster and cheaper, and might be more economical even if giving a lesser crop.[55]

In fact the ridge method of cultivation, laborious as it was, provided an essential element of drainage in the waterlogged soils of Ireland; indeed it was used elsewhere where climatic conditions were similar, as in parts of Scotland, the Isle of Man, Lancashire and Cheshire. It had, in fact, many advantages in the conditions of the time.[56] Since the ridge was moved in the subsequent year to where the trench was previously located, it guaranteed uniform usage of all the available ground; it also provided a measure of surface cold air drainage from the ridge to the trench which reduced the risk of frost damage, which is particularly frequent in bog land.

Nor was the lazy bed merely a traditional practice blindly followed without regard to special circumstances. On the exposed shores of the

Mullet, Co. Mayo, 'the ridges are made in a direction from north to south; quite low on the eastern, and raised about two feet on the western side' to protect the growing crop from wind damage in westerly storms.

This was no isolated example of agricultural alertness. One cannot read the agricultural journals of this time without being impressed by the keen discussion of matters which were later to be revived as 'modern' topics; such as the most efficient placement of presprouting potato seed for earliness and abundance. It can scarcely be entire coincidence that the type of wind-permeable walls used in the west of Ireland should make, as recent research has shown, the best kind of shelterbelt; certainly in Inishbofin, fences were deliberately erected to serve as windbreaks.[57] And experience in England has shown that the indiscriminate removal of boundary fences to make larger fields has sometimes led to reduced yields due to wind damage.

As regards lazy beds, the wheel has also come full cycle. In the 1960s, official experiments took place in England on a 'revolutionary system of potato growing' using beds 56″ wide, containing three rows of potatoes and separated from the next bed by a wheel track![58]

The potato as an instrument of disaster

In retrospect, it is only too clear that an unrestricted potato economy contained the seed of its own ultimate destruction; there were limits to the extent to which an expanding population, unsupported by industry and outstripping rural employment, might eke out even a bare existence by the subdivision of land, the cultivation of barren hillsides and of bog, and the use of the worst varieties of the cheapest food. For at least thirty, and perhaps up to fifty years before the famine, the Irish economy was moving closer to inevitable disaster, and indeed, as we have seen, each desperate new resort served only to sink the people deeper into the morass of hunger and helplessness.

Did no one at the time hear the rumblings of coming disaster? They were loud enough after the partial crop failures of 1816 and 1821, and during the dry rot scare of 1832-4. Dr Doyle saw the danger clearly, more than twenty years before the famine, in his letters on the state of Ireland: 'should a dearth of provision occur, famine and pestilence will set in together, and rid us probably of a million'.[59] According to Wilde:

> The late Bishop Brinkley, one of the most profound thinkers we have ever had in Ireland, who predicted the loss of the potato many years ago, and calculated mathematically the extent of ruin which was likely to follow, declared to his relative, the late Dr Graves, that he was unable to sleep for an entire night, owing to the effect that it had upon him.[60]

No details of his calculations which gave rise to Bishop Brinkley's insomnia have been traced, despite the help of many kind collaborators.

No doubt his reasoning followed broadly the lines of the analysis given above. If so, he had good reason for disquiet. In case of a general failure, what efforts could save the 1.6 million people in the families of landless men outside the oatmeal zone? An unprecedented relief operation would be needed to help another 3.1 million people, slightly better placed, who were still wholly or largely dependent on the potato. That the fall in population between 1841 and 1851 so closely approximates to the calculation of the number of the almost inevitably doomed throws additional doubt on the tradition of the ineffectiveness of public and private relief during the famine years. The fact that it fell far short of meeting the full needs of an overwhelming disaster should not blind us to the unprecedented extent of what was actually done.

One may more reasonably criticise the inertia which allowed the disastrous situation to develop to a point that it became out of hand. Why was nothing done during the years 1800-45 to divert the country from its headlong course towards the abyss?

For one reason or another, the majority of the people, in Ireland as in England, denied or ignored the menace of the situation. Many had a vested interest in the continuance of the potato economy, upon which the whole structure of Irish life rested. In the philosophic climate of the times, the prosperous tended to regard the problem more as a matter of moral outlook than of economics. God rewarded the industrious and right-thinking man with wealth and security; the poor were the architects of their own misery. Distress was dismissed as the inevitable result of the lazy Irish deliberately choosing a lazy root and growing it in lazy beds:

> No other crop produces such an abundance of food on the same extent of ground, requires so little skill and labour either to rear it or prepare it for food, and leaves so large a portion of the labourer's time unoccupied. Now, these are great temptations, and it requires forethought and energy to overcome them. When they go to England or America, they *earn* their subsistence. It no longer depends on the potato, the crop which fosters, from the earliest childhood, habits of indolence, improvidence and waste.[61]

If one accepted, against all the evidence, that the general adoption of the potato as the staff of life had been a free and voluntary choice of an indolent people, all else could be satisfactorily explained. The undue use of the potato had, it was argued, led amongst the poor to

> an indifference as to the higher comforts and conveniences of life, and a remarkable deficiency in these respects, when contrasted with their more polished neighbours...Hence the working days are few, and the days of loitering, of sight-seeing and amusements many.[62]

Interpreted in terms of social, religious and national prejudice, the argument took on a harsher note:

> That the Irish peasantry are poor, no man need doubt; but in what country of the world is the labourer rich? Opulence never was made, and never will be made, by

the mere labour of the hands...Yet, if in addition to the natural disadvantages of that state in which man must earn his bread by the sweat of his brow, he shall disqualify himself by a taste for rioting and whiskey, spend a large portion of his year on Popish holidays, and spend another portion in travelling across the country to monster meetings, faction fights, and the usual crimes and absurdities of itinerant or local treason, who shall wonder if Pat continues poor?[63]

The kindlier took refuge in the comforting illusion so beloved of the prosperous, that the poor man, free of care, had chosen the better lot.

The poorer Irish appear to me the most easily contented, and the most philosophically and truly happy of any peasantry I have ever seen; faithful, generous, warm-hearted, fearless and reckless, they smile in peace over a handful of bad potatoes, and devoutly thank the Providence who provides it.[64]

The more thoughtful observers saw that it was superficial to blame the potato as 'the curse of Ireland'; the fault was inherent in the social system which would have produced a similar wretchedness even without the potato, although the number of victims would have been fewer. The few who looked beyond

the prevalent idea that the manners of the lower order of people were radically and incorrigibly depraved, and that [their poverty] did not arise from any exterior causes, by gradual removal of which their condition might be ameliorated and their manners improved,[65]

soon saw that the poor were the helpless victims of a cruel social organisation. Ryan was one of the first to make a thorough and sympathetic analysis of the situation; his conclusion that the Irish agrarian system was in need of overhaul gained wider acceptance during the 1830s.[66] As the anxiety of men of foresight grew, the government set up a series of parliamentary inquiries to report on the state of Ireland, and to suggest remedies. Each in turn lifted the lid of the cauldron, looked helplessly into the mess of injustice, prejudice, starvation and despair, and quietly put the lid on again. Within the accepted ideas of the rights of property and the duties of government, they found only the weakest palliatives to suggest.

We should take stock before we condemn out of hand the many sincere men who baulked at the problem of rectifying a situation which may well have already progressed beyond the point of no return, and who found themselves helpless before the entrenched forces of property and position. It is a humbling exercise to study the situation described in the *Poor inquiry*, and to attempt to devise an adequate solution which did not involve a complete overthrow of the social system. Again, even today, there are many parts of the world – Central America, in the Middle East and in Asia – where the rights of property and the protection of investments take priority over the welfare of distressed humanity. Accepted ideas have altered since 1845 but in their new form they still dominate the minds of men; those who feel the world is in danger from an atomic holocaust are helpless in the face of the inertia of the many who hope for the best. The problems change; human emotions and reactions remain the same.

If, in this analysis, we have neglected to consider some of the factors which have traditionally been blamed for much of the misery in pre-famine Ireland, it is because we feel that their role has been much exaggerated. Whether a head landlord lived in Ireland or abroad made little difference to the mass of the people whose immediate landlord was the small or medium landholder. The 'absentee landlords' were a convenient whipping horse for many who bore a more immediate responsibility for local distress. 'Not much of the misfortune of Ireland is to be attributed to their absence. Their return, without a change in the system of letting land, can avail little. The condition of the peasantry is equally wretched in the estates of resident and absentee landlords.'[67]

Nor can we feel that the union with Britain had seriously aggravated the agricultural situation, or that repeal at a date even well in advance of the famine would have avoided or minimised that disaster. An Irish government of the landed and the propertied – as it would inevitably have been at that time – would have regarded any meddling with the social system with the same doctrinaire horror as a London government, and would indeed have had a more direct vested interest in maintaining the status quo. An undoubted evil of the union was to place in unfamiliar hands the control of 'a country of which Englishmen in general know something less than of Kamchatka or South Australia'.[68] They had no direct experience of the potato economy or of the extent to which it had come to dominate Irish life. There is an air of honest bewilderment in many English comments at the time of the famine; 'the question of how the Irish alone, of all the populations of Europe, arrived at the condition of abject wretchedness in which we find them, remains unanswered'.[69] As so often, the Quakers saw clearly to the heart of the matter:

> Truly the sins of the fathers, in a political as well as a moral sense, are visited upon the children to the third and fourth generation! England is now reaping the sad effects of bad government; and with all the honest desire of those in power to remedy the evils, they know not where to begin, or what change to make.[70]

As we see it, then, the potato economy, under the pressure of unwise laws and unrestrained extortion, got gradually out of control; the factors which accelerated its career to disaster in the nineteenth century were less the local developments which have been traditionally blamed than external factors such as the end of the Napoleonic Wars, the improvement in international transport with the coming of steam and the increased demand for Irish agricultural produce in industrial Britain. It is not unreasonable, in fact, to claim that the doom of Ireland was finally sealed at the battle of Waterloo. No doubt, the defeat of Napoleon meant the overthrow of an ambitious and ruthless military machine, but it also meant victory for the forces of privilege, position and property. The rise of democracy was retarded, and the warped remnants of feudalism lived on, in most of Europe, to fight a rearguard action against the rights of the 'little man' for more than a century.

In this interpretation the potato, although freed from the charge of responsibility for the misery of the people, becomes the essential foundation upon which the whole evil social system was based. Again the Quakers saw this clearly. Jacob Harvey wrote in April 1848,

> I do not know whether to rejoice or not at the improved prospect of the potato crop; if they should prove as prolific as formerly, what is to prevent the labourers and small farmers from falling back upon them as their only food. This is the great danger to my mind and I confess I am anxious as to the result.[71]

On the other hand, the landlords, large and small, looked to the return of the potato economy 'as their chief hope of better times':

> The easiest remedy for this disastrous state of things would be the revival of the potato and its renewed cultivation. To this, many landlords cling with desperate hope. Things will mend, they say, if we can 'get over' a year or two. With the revival of the potato, conacre labour will return, farms will be cultivated, rates reduced and the whole machinery be again set in motion.[72]

When the potato appeared to be doomed, there were a few tentative efforts to find a substitute; turnips, swedes, Jerusalem artichokes and even dahlia bulbs were suggested. No doubt, many of these ideas were intended only as famine relief foods; but this was clearly not the case in the consideration of 'new farinaceous roots' used by the Indians in North America. Two in particular – the mus-quasete and the saa-gaa-ban – were recommended for adoption and development in the same way as the potato had been. The more responsible Irish commentators insisted that there was 'no sound policy or philosophy in perpetuating cheap and capricious food under any form' (except as adjuncts to better food, as in England or Scotland). 'Would any man think himself the benefactor of Ireland if he could grow chestnuts and pignuts as food for the population?'[73] It is a moot point whether the question was as rhetorical as the writer thought.

In fact, the machinery of the old social order was never again to run smoothly, and many felt that even the dreadful visitation of the famine was not too high a price to pay for its passing. Emergency surgery had removed the cancerous growth which was 'the system by which they [the labourers] and the industry of the country is enthralled' and gave new hope; 'I yet confidently look to the ultimate results as placing society on a sounder basis, and largely contributing to the happiness of both rich and poor.'[74]

If the potato was no more than the passive instrument of misery and famine, who then wielded the weapon? An answer based narrowly on Irish history does not explain parallel developments in Scotland.[75] An answer based solely on political or sectarian divisions ignores the fact that many of the sub-landlords, and most of the bailiffs, drivers, gombeen men and usurers who battened on the potato system were Irish and Catholic. James Connolly puts forward a broader theory; 'no man who accepts capitalist society and the laws thereof can logically find fault with the statesmen of England in that awful period'. A later study finds that Connolly's sketch gives a picture of the period which is essentially correct, even if strained a little to fit a doctrinaire frame. [76]

We feel, more simply, that the basic responsibility for Ireland's plight rested on human greed; on the selfishness, not just of the few, but of the many in situations of some power and authority. Experience, under all social systems and in every time (including our own), illustrates the lengths to which greed and self-interest will go if not tightly contained either by regulation or by public opinion. The real responsibility of the British lay in the laws and practices which left a great part of the people wide open to exploitation; the poor were below the law and the propertied above it. The origins of the unbalanced social system lay far back in Irish history; the streams were bitter because the springs had been poisoned. In the final stages the government would, no doubt, have tried to set things right in Ireland if it could have seen a way to do so, but, having earlier released from its bottle the terrifying djinn of human cupidity, it could not get it back under cork again.

We differ from Connolly in our feeling that, given the circumstances, the ideological system was not a material factor. There is a sardonic Polish riddle, based on dual experience, which neatly summarises the matter:

Q. What is the difference between capitalism and communism?

A. Under capitalism, man exploits his fellow man;
under communism, the reverse is true.

The final years of the potato system

It is a remarkable thing how often a dying man, in the final stages of a long illness, will suddenly appear to rally and hold out spurious hope of recovery. It was so with the course of the potato economy, which had been ailing since early in the nineteenth century, and had seemed on several occasions to be on the point of death. Now, in the last few years before the famine and as the result of several excellent harvests, it took on a remarkable appearance of health. Hope sprang up afresh; the tide of emigration was temporarily stayed. Ireland had never been 'so contented, so tranquil or so likely to become prosperous'.[77]

The harvest of 1845 looked equally promising until the blight came:

Crops of all kinds exhibit a most cheering luxuriance. Wheat looks quite healthy and abundant. Oats has improved rapidly and looks right well, and never was there such a prospect of potatoes or such a breadth of them planted; they appear most healthy and vigorous. The seasonable rain of last night and this morning should inspire us with gratitude to a gracious Providence.[78]

What, in fact, did life promise for an average Irish countryman in a 'good year', such as 1845 had every appearance of proving? We may usefully round off this chapter with a synthesis of the cumulative effect on one family of the individual factors we have been considering, as provided 'by an intelligent and observing peasant'. He lived in a relatively prosperous area (County Cavan), had a garden and children at work, and could find temporary employment, so that his state, if no Utopia, was far better than that of many of his contemporaries.

From March till May, one year with another, he usually earns from £1 10s. to £2; of this £1 goes to pay the rent of his cabin, and for as much as can be spared of the remainder he buys wool, tow and flax which, in the course of the summer his wife manufactures into frieze, drugget, and coarse linen to clothe the family; but every year does not afford this. A good part of May and June is taken up with setting and landing his potatoes and cutting his turf; this turf the wife and children rear during the succeeding months. By the latter end of May his stock of potatoes is out, and he then gets more, or some oatmeal, on credit at high interest; he then repairs to the counties of Meath and Dublin, or perhaps to England, to haymaking and harvesting and returns in the month of September...in time to avoid a civil-bill process by paying up the price of the oatmeal he was credited for; from this, until the potatoes are dug, he may earn from £1 to £1 10s., and his pig, now a year old, sells for about £3, making, in all, about £4 10s. or £5. But now his half-yearly rent is again become due, above £1, his conacre rent more than £2; his frieze and linen are ready, and the tailor and weaver must be paid. He wants a pair of brogues for the winter; the wife an apron, shawl and cap, but, as to shoes, it is a small chance for her; he wants himself a fine shirt for Sunday. The earnings of his elder children at service are too small to clothe them; and the wife (let things go as they will) must get 5s. to buy flax, that, with spinning it through the winter, and selling an odd hank and a few eggs, she may struggle from week to week to get salt, soap, blue, starch, an odd herring, and, with great saving and care, a few pounds of meat at Christmas. Besides this, he has to replace the pig, or how is he to pay for his conacre next year?[79]

CHAPTER 3

The agricultural statistics of the 1841 census of Ireland: a critical review*

Ireland is fortunate to have a series of annual statistical returns of agricultural produce which stretches back to 1847. Had the surveys begun some ten years earlier they would have been invaluable as a measure of the changes brought about by the famine. As it is, the quantitative pre-famine picture must be built up from diverse statistical material contained in the 1841 census returns, the report of the Devon commission, the *Poor inquiry* and elsewhere, after the data have been subjected to critical assessment and all possible quality control. The purpose here is to draw attention to just such a synthesis of pre-famine statistics, the overall design of which may have been masked by its publication piecemeal in different journals over a period of nearly twenty years.

The first step was to clear rubble from the site by removing, as far as possible, ambiguities of unit and definition. This involved, for example, a recasting of early statistics of area and yield which had been largely expressed in terms of Irish or Cunningham acres, of returns of farm size which ignored waste land and of cattle surveys which excluded young calves from the definition. The next procedure was to test each set of data for internal consistency; to ensure, for example, that there were no major unexplained differences of the total area of all farms in consecutive returns, that the consumption of major crops used as human or animal food (potatoes, oats, wheat) was in good agreement with acreages and normal yields after allowance had been made for exports, seed and other use, that the extent of pasturage was consistent with cattle numbers, and that the total area under crops and hay when added to pasture agreed with the available land area. Finally the figures had to be shown to fit well with post-famine statistics when allowance was made for changed circumstances.

The main subsections of this research have been published, each as a self-contained paper complete with the argument to sustain it. Ideally, however, the different sectors should not be judged in isolation, but considered as part of an interlocking system in which the fact that each component fits snugly with the others can be advanced as evidence of the

* From *Economic History Review*, 2nd ser., xviii (1965), pp 376-91.

essential accuracy of the overall picture. The whole can claim to be more than just the sum of its parts.

The principal subject of each paper is obvious from its title but in some cases the discussion ranges fairly widely. Thus the article on crop yields before the famine also reviews the trends of acreage and yields of the potato, oats and wheat crops in Ireland over the period 1847-1966. Elsewhere some quite significant secondary statistics are derived which have no obvious relationship to the main topic under discussion. A case in point is the number of agricultural labourers who did not hold land apart from seasonal conacre, probably the most vulnerable group in pre-famine Ireland. They had been enumerated at 567,441 or 7.3% of the total population in the census of 1831. The poor law inquiry commissioners estimated that the number had risen to 585,000 by 1834. Curiously the great 1841 census did not enquire into the number of landless labourers, but its tally of the number of farmers and agricultural workers exceeded the poor law figures of persons holding land in however small a quantity by 650,921. The total of men without land and dependent on potatoes grown in conacre had thus risen to 8.0% of the total population, a reflection of the evergrowing competition for land. Together with their dependants the landless agricultural group totalled over two and a quarter million persons on the eve of the famine. It can be calculated that their food requirements of potatoes at normal yield would call for some 470,000 acres of conacre land. In fact the extent of conacre potatoes in 1845, at 350,000 acres, reached only 75% of this target so that in a year of average yields, the harvest would have fed the group only until April/May of the following year. This deduction is in good agreement with evidence given before the poor law inquiry: 'The labourer never has any of his conacre potatoes remaining at the period when they become unfit for use; the greater number have used them all at the beginning of April and scarcely one has a potato remaining at the 1st of May.' Broad consistencies of this kind tend to confirm the essential reliability of the analysis.

* * *

The first of the regular annual surveys of agricultural produce in Ireland was made in 1847.[1] It deals with such matters as size of agricultural holdings, extent and yield of different crops, and number of livestock, but does not provide figures for the extent of grassland. The first published census of pasture and of fallow was made in 1851.[2] All these statistics refer to the agricultural situation as disrupted by famine conditions after 1845.

Accordingly abnormal interest attaches to such agricultural data as are included in the 1841 census of Ireland.[3] The prestige which rightly attaches to this monumental work as a demographic survey has tended to mask deficiencies in some of the supplementary data which, at the time of collection, were officially regarded as secondary to the 'more essential object' – 'the enumeration of the people'.[4] It should be remembered that the agricultural survey carried out in connection with the 1841 census could not foresee that, before the next census, the situation would be so drastically altered that the agricultural returns, a sideline of their work, would have unique importance. In contrast, the annual surveys which began in 1847 were carefully designed to give as accurate a picture as possible of the agricultural situation, and profited from the experience gained in 1841. Furthermore, the fact that they were carried out annually from 1847 permits a comparison of successive reports which establishes that, apart from slight evidence of teething troubles in the earlier returns,[5] the post-famine agricultural statistics are free from major error.[6]

Part 1. Number of agricultural holdings of different sizes

Introduction

The statistics for size of agricultural holdings given in the census of Ireland, 1841, have been discussed in detail in an earlier paper.[7] Here it will suffice to summarise the argument on the basis of a tabular comparison of the official figures for 1841, 1847, and 1851:[8]

Table 1

Size of holding	*Number of agricultural holdings in Ireland* (1841–51)		
	1841	1847	1851
Above 1 acre and not exceeding 5 acres	310,375	139,041	88,083
Above 5 acres and not exceeding 15 acres	252,778	269,534	191,854
Above 15 acres and not exceeding 30 acres	79,338	164,337	141,311
Above 30 acres	48,623	157,097	149,090
TOTAL	691,114	730,009	570,338

Inconsistencies in the data

Table 1 is a familiar one, quoted many times in the past hundred years, to illustrate the effect of the famine on agricultural holdings. However, even a simple visual examination of the figures, making due allowance for the fact that patches of ground of up to one acre are not included, brings certain puzzling features to light:

(1) The fall, from mid-1841 to mid-1847, of over 170,000 in the numbers of the smallest category of farms, representing the elimination of more than half the families in this group in a relatively short period of full famine conditions contrasts strangely with the fall of less than 51,000 in the same group in the four years, mid-1847 to mid-1851, during which distress continued at a very high level. There are similar sharp discontinuities in trend in the sequences for the other farm sizes.

(2) There was a general similarity of life amongst all smallholders at the time. Comparing the 1847 and 1841 figures, it is difficult to reconcile the rise in all categories above 5 acres, and in particular the doubling of the numbers in the 15-30 acre category, with the fall of more than half in the number of the smallest farms.

(3) At a time when the smallest farms were disappearing rapidly, it is paradoxical to find an increase in the total number of holdings between 1841 and 1847.

None of these arguments, in itself, conclusively undermines the 1841 figures. In each case, at least a partial explanation can be devised. Thus, some of the contrast discussed in (1) and (2) above might reflect the undoubted 'phase lag' in the impact of distress between the very smallest and the larger landholders. As regards point (3), the rise in the total number of holdings in 1847 was noted as an inconsistency at the time, and was attributed to the fact (a significant admission) that some holdings were recorded in 1841 in Irish acres, with the result that some smaller farms fell below the category limit of 1 acre in 1841, but not in 1847 when great care was taken that all the returns were expressed in statute acres.[9]

However, there is a further argument, based on a simple arithmetical check of the total area of farming land represented by all the holdings, which discredits the 1841 figures. If one assumes an average farm area for each of the four categories in table 1 as 3, 10, 22½ and 85 acres respectively,[10] then the total area represented by the 1841 figures is less than 9½ million acres while the corresponding totals for 1847 and 1851 are close to double this (approximately 20 and 18 million acres respectively).[11]

The source of the incompatibility of the 1841 census figures of farm size with later data is twofold:[12]

(1) An ambiguity in the term 'acre'

The enumerators of the 1841 census were asked to give farm data in 'acres', without further specification or explanation. (This error was not repeated in or after 1847.) The vast majority of the returns were naturally expressed in Irish or plantation acres, the unit in common use in the country (and the one, incidentally, which put the extent of the farmer's land at the lowest numerical value).

(2) An ambiguity in the concept of 'farm size'
In the forms used for the 1841 census, the 'size of holding' was not, in fact, requested as such, but rather the number of 'acres' in the farm under three separate headings, 'arable', 'pasture', and 'waste'.[13] The size of holding was then computed by adding 'arable' and 'pasture' and ignoring waste land.[14] From 1847 onwards a radically different procedure was followed; the classification was based on the full farm size, including waste land and the area occupied by farm buildings, yards, etc.[15]

Each of these procedures tended to reduce the recorded farm size. The first factor diminished the apparent size of a holding in the approximate proportion of 1 to 1.5.[16] The amount of waste land was found in 1853, the first year for which it was published, to be 23% of the total area of farmland.[17] The second factor thus diminished the recorded farm size in the approximate proportion of 1 to 1.3. Together the two factors led to a reduction of about one-half in the apparent farm size.

The 1841 census figures of farm sizes could thus be brought much closer to the true picture, by simply doubling the classifications, thus:

Table 2

1841 CENSUS RETURNS OF AGRICULTURAL HOLDINGS, CRUDELY AMENDED

Size of holding	*No. of holdings*
Above 2 and not exceeding 10 acres	310,436
Above 10 and not exceeding 30 acres	252,799
Above 30 and not exceeding 60 acres	79,338
Above 60 acres	48,623

This correction still involves a measure of distortion since the proportion of waste land, for which a uniform average adjustment had been applied, is, in fact, much greater in the larger farms than in the smaller ones.

Alternative data on farm sizes before the famine
Luckily there is available an independent summary of pre-famine farm sizes which was prepared in 1845 by the land commission office from returns provided by the poor law commissioners.[18] This was considered by the Devon commission in conjunction with the corresponding 1841 census returns. It was adjudged that the former returns, 'having been taken with a view to taxation, and being subject to periodical revision for this purpose, are probably nearest to the truth'.[19] The poor law returns are expressed in terms of 'the number of persons holding land' whose holdings are of a specified size, which is not quite the same thing as the

number of holdings of the same size; also, not unnaturally, they found a number of holdings (less than 4% of the total) which they were unable to classify, mainly due to joint tenancy. The summarised figures, however, give a rational picture and stand up well to arithmetical checks.[20]

Table 3

NUMBER OF PERSONS HOLDING LAND, 1845[21]

Size of holding	*Number*
Less than 1 acre	135,314
Above 1 acre and not exceeding 5 acres	181,950
Above 5 acres and not exceeding 10 acres	187,909
Above 10 acres and not exceeding 20 acres	187,582
Above 20 acres and not exceeding 50 acres	141,819
Above 50 acres	70,441
Unclassified	30,433
TOTAL	935,448

The categories of size between 5 and 50 acres differ, unfortunately, from those used in the census and in the agricultural returns, thus making a direct comparison difficult. It is possible to reclassify the data approximately by the mathematical device of accumulating to the given breaks (5, 10, 20, 50 acres) and fitting a suitable curve. A new break at 15 acres can thus be introduced with some confidence, but the large amplitude of the 20 to 50-acre group makes the introduction of a new break at 30 acres a more uncertain process.[22] That section of the reclassified data which can be put forward with reasonable confidence is given in table 4, together with the comparable data for 1847 and 1851.[23]

Table 4

AGRICULTURAL HOLDINGS IN IRELAND (1845-51)

Size of holding	*1845*	*1847*	*1851*
Above 1 acre and not exceeding 5 acres	181,950	139,041	88,083
Above 5 acres and not exceeding 15 acres	311,133	269,534	191,854
Above 15 acres	276,618	321,434	290,401
TOTAL	769,701	730,009	570,338

If table 4 is compared with table 1, it will be found to show a change over the famine years both less sensational and more credible. The fact is that by far the greater part of the apparent change in land tenure which has, on the basis of table 1, been attributed to the immediate effect of the famine arises, in reality, from the peculiarities of the 1841 census figures.

Part 2. Livestock numbers

The inaccuracy of size of holdings in the census of 1841 naturally invalidates also the returns of the number of farm animals *held on holdings of different sizes*, and these returns may not correctly be compared with the corresponding statistics for 1847 and later years.

However, the national and regional totals of livestock given in the census of 1841 are considered to be reasonably accurate.[24] The alarm created at the enumeration of farm animals, which is reported to have occurred 'in remote districts', led, no doubt, to some underestimation of the number of poultry, but in the case of pigs and other larger animals, there was little possibility of concealment, nor indeed much purpose, since the landlord normally enumerated them as security against rent.

The totals of different types of farm animals in Ireland in June 1841 are given in table 5.[25]

Table 5

LIVESTOCK IN IRELAND, 1841

Cattle	1,863,116
Sheep	2,106,189
Pigs	1,412,813
Horses and mules	576,115
Asses	92,365
Poultry	8,458,517

Although the essential accuracy of these figures is not in question, the enumeration of cattle in 1841 was made on a different basis from that used in later years, and the number of pigs in 1841 was almost certainly below the normal pre-famine level. These points are considered further in the following paragraphs.

Number of cattle

In the 1841 census of cattle, the enumerators were instructed not to include 'calves of the current year'.[26] In 1847 and subsequent years all cattle were enumerated. The 1841 returns cannot, therefore, be directly compared with the later figures.

In 1847 the proportion of cattle under one year to the total population of cattle was just over 20%,[27] and averaged about the same proportion in subsequent years. About 80% of the annual number of calves are born in the first five months of the year.[28]

Accordingly, the 1841 enumeration of cattle, made early in the month of June, represents a proportion of the total cattle population which is, approximately, either 80%, if the phrase 'calves of the current year' was interpreted to mean cattle less than one year old, or 84%, if the phrase was interpreted to mean cattle born after 1 January 1841. The corrected total population of cattle in 1841 thus lies between 2,220,000 and 2,330,000.

Number of pigs

A poor potato harvest in any one year, in the Ireland of the nineteenth century, led to a scarcity of food for man and pig in the following spring and summer, with a rise in emigration and a drop in the number of pigs.[29]

Following a good harvest generally in 1837, there were local failures in the potato crop in 1838 and 1839 and the crop was below normal in 1840. After an indifferent harvest in 1841, there were excellent crops of potatoes and other crops in 1842 and 1843.[30] These changes in the food situation, with the indicated lag of one year, are fairly closely reflected in the statistics of emigration for the period 1838-44.[31]

The scarcity of potatoes in the spring of 1841 must have induced many smallholders to part with their pigs before the date of the census (7 June 1841), and thus tended to make the 1841 pig enumeration lower than normal. Indeed, it is officially commented that 'pigs are on the whole less numerous than might have been expected',[32] and Dr T. W. Freeman has remarked that the 1841 returns show an absence of pigs on many of the smaller holdings, in spite of the common belief that 'the pig is the companion of the humblest peasant'.[33]

To what extent the 1841 population of pigs fell below the average pre-famine level it is impossible to say with any assurance.

Part 3. Land use and classification

Introduction

Table 6 summarises the official data on land use in Ireland as given in the census of 1841, the agricultural returns of 1847, and the census of 1851.[34]

The terminology of classification requires some clarification. The rather ambiguous word 'arable' here represents the total of land immediately available for agricultural use, excluding waste, bog and woods. It is the sum of the acreage under crops, in pasture and in fallow.[35] It is synonymous with the term 'cultivated' used in the wider sense of 'having had labour or attention bestowed upon it' and not in the narrower sense of 'dug or ploughed'.[36]

Table 6

LAND USE IN IRELAND (in statute acres)

	1841 census	1847 agricultural returns	1851 census
Crops (including hay)	–	5,238,575	5,858,951
Grass or pasture	–	–	8,748,577
Fallow and uncropped arable	–	–	195,053
Total cultivated or arable	13,464,300	–	14,802,581
Uncultivated (bog and waste)	6,295,735	–	5,023,984
Woods and plantations (including orchards)	374,482	–	304,906
Water	630,825	–	631,210
Towns	42,929	–	45,590
GRAND TOTAL	20,808,271	–	20,808,271

The terms 'arable' and 'cultivated' were used interchangeably, thus, 'The quantity of arable land in Ireland in 1841 was 13,464,300 acres; the amount according to these [1851] returns is now 14,802,581 acres, showing that the extent of cultivated land has been increased by 1,338,281 acres during the past ten years.'[37] The word 'hay' has been substituted for 'meadow and clover', as used in the earlier returns.

The sub-category 'fallow and uncropped arable' consisted of dug or ploughed land, which was either allowed to lie fallow as part of a deliberate agricultural rotation, or which had been abandoned because of distress and had not yet reverted to pasture or waste. Deliberate fallowing, normally as a preparation for the sowing of winter wheat, was an obsolescent practice,[38] and the total of 195,053 acres under 'fallow and uncropped arable' in 1851 probably largely represented recently abandoned land which had formerly been under crops. The category showed a continuous decline in the following years, under the heading 'fallow and uncropped arable' in 1851 and 1852, and simply as 'fallow' from 1853 onward.[39]

The area under 'water' depends on whether, as in table 6, 'the larger rivers, lakes and tideways' are included. If these are excluded, the area under 'water' (and, of course, the corresponding total area of the country) is reduced by about half-a-million acres.[40]

The term 'uncultivated land' is here used to cover bog and waste land. This is the normal meaning in the official returns of the times, but it is also occasionally used in a wider sense, e.g. to mean the total area under bog, waste, towns and water (exclusive of the larger rivers, lakes and tideways).[41]

Basis of the data

There was a radical difference between the methods of obtaining the land use data given in the census of 1841 and those published for 1847 and later years, which raises serious doubts as to whether the figures may properly be compared. The commissioners of the census of 1851 were clearly uneasy on this point, for having commented that the increase in cultivated land 'speaks favourably for the industry of the people, notwithstanding the great diminution of the population between the two periods', they added at once: 'We should here state that in 1841, the areas of the arable and uncultivated land, of the towns and the water, were computed from the maps of the ordnance survey; in 1851 they are taken from the agricultural survey of that year.'[42]

Three immediate deductions may be made from the fact that the figures for land use given in the census for 1841 were based on the ordnance survey maps:

(1) There is no ambiguity as regards units; the areas are expressed in statute acres.

(2) The data do not, in fact, refer to the year 1841, but to various dates over the period 1829-42 during which the relevant part of the first ordnance survey of Ireland was carried out in different parts of the country.[43] In this, they differ radically from the returns of 1847 and later years, which refer to the situation on a specific date.

The census of 1841 does not, in fact, explicitly present the figures of land use as data for the year 1841. This error seems to have been first made officially in the census of 1851,[44] and has been frequently repeated since.

(3) The figures should be interpreted with caution, since the task of correctly segregating, enumerating and totalling different categories of land use on over 1,900 six-inch maps is a formidable one, even were the maps perfectly adapted to this purpose. In fact, as is shown in the next section, there were substantial extra sources of error in endeavouring to distinguish between 'cultivated' and 'uncultivated' areas on the maps.

The first ordnance survey of Ireland

When the ordnance survey of Ireland was projected, its primary purpose was to provide a more just basis of taxation by an accurate determination of townland areas.[45]

The earlier maps, which referred to the northern counties, contained comparatively less detail, and, in particular, did not show field or farm boundaries, except where they coincided with the townland or other administrative boundaries.[46] Later, as a result of representations from Sir Richard Griffith, who was responsible for valuation, these deficient maps were revised, but the first resurvey (Donegal) was not commenced until 1845. The counties involved were Antrim, Armagh,

Cavan, Donegal, Down, Fermanagh, Leitrim, Londonderry, Louth, Monaghan and Tyrone.[47]

These facts help to clarify the description given in the census of 1841 as to how the figure for cultivated land was arrived at: 'The extent of arable land is now for the first time given on accurate grounds, being based on the Ordnance Survey. For the 12 Northern Counties it has been computed by Mr Griffith, the Chief Commissioner of Valuation, and for the remaining counties it has been admeasured directly upon the maps.'[48]

The '12 Northern Counties' here referred to are obviously those listed above, with the addition of Carrickfergus, which appears as a separate 'county' on the table which immediately follows the statement.[49]

It is not clear whether Griffith worked directly from the maps, as is suggested in the census of 1851,[50] or whether he used additional material provided by the ordnance survey such as the famous 'names books'. In the notes column of the latter, there often appear comments on the proportions of cultivated and uncultivated land, but these are expressed in such broad fractions (half, one-third, etc.) as to be of little practical value.

No direction was given in the original instructions to surveyors requiring them to distinguish between cultivated and uncultivated land,[51] because the authorities 'had not contemplated the demarcation of the boundaries of bog and uncultivated land with reference to their utility in the valuation'.[52] In 1831 they yielded to the pressure of 'the Valuators', despite obvious reluctance in view of

> the increase of labour and the expenditure of time and money incident to the Survey of the uncultivated land...But, in order to abridge the time required for seeking out the boundaries of cultivation where it is progressive and uncertain, in all such cases the nearest fence bounding cultivated land will be surveyed as the boundary, though cultivation may have partially extended beyond it. And all patches of about five acres or less will be considered as too trivial for notice, whether they be of uncultivated land in the midst of cultivation, or of cultivated land inclosed in masses of bog or uncultivated land, except where such patches are so situated as to be surveyed without any loss of time. It being a general rule that everything which contributes to the perfection of the Map should be inserted when it can be done without delay and expense. Upon this principle, though the boundaries of various qualities of uncultivated land are not absolutely essential, it will always be desirable where it can be done by the Officer in his local examinations or in any other way in the course of the works (without delaying its progress) to indicate rocky land, turbary or morasses by distinctive marks though these particular qualities should not be bounded on the plans by lines which (not being positively accurate) might mislead the Valuators.

None of this is calculated to instil confidence in the accuracy of the figures for land use computed from the maps, nor does an examination of the maps themselves suggest that greater detail 'without delay and expense' was often found to be possible.

Even in the case of direct examination by experienced observers, the line between poor pasture and waste land is difficult to draw, particularly in hilly areas. Thus the commissioners of the census of 1851 comment:

It is very difficult to ascertain the exact surface under uncultivated or unprofitable land in a country, especially where there are large tracts of mountains which, though unenclosed, are used for grazing, but which, to the ordinary observer, appear as unclaimed land of little value. These figures for 1851-4, however, being the results of actual observation and inquiries by the constabulary enumerators, who year by year traverse the country to obtain information, may be considered as a near approach to accuracy.[53]

From this it is clear that, of the several sources of error in distinguishing cultivated land on the maps which arise from Colby's instruction on the surveying of land use, the most serious is that which directed that cultivated land which was not fenced should be ignored. In comparing the county figures based on the ordnance survey maps with the census returns of 1851, we should expect the error arising from this cause to be most marked in counties where there is much mountain grazing.

Comparison of reported cultivated land, by counties

The increase in cultivated land by 1851, compared with the value given in the 1841 census, represents a nation-wide average of just under 10% (table 6).

A comparison of the figures, county by county, shows an extremely wide scatter. Six counties (Dublin, Louth, Meath, Westmeath, Kilkenny and Roscommon) show an apparent *fall* in the extent of cultivated land. At the other extreme, ten counties show a percentage rise higher than the national average, *viz.* Donegal (76), Kerry (49), Mayo (30), Clare (20), Wicklow (19), Tyrone (19), Galway (17), Fermanagh (16), Antrim (16) and Londonderry (11). By no means all of these are areas in which extensive reclamation might have been expected.

The extremes of apparent expansion of cultivated land were reached in County Donegal and County Kerry. In Donegal, which was surveyed in 1834-6, the figure for cultivated land increased from 393,191 to 693,301 acres, i.e. the addition of three new acres to every four which existed sixteen years earlier. The corresponding figures for County Kerry, which was surveyed in 1841-2, were 414,614 and 616,458 acres. Expansion of cultivation at this sensational rate is surely incredible, especially when contrasted with reports of little or no increase (or even a fall) in counties such as Roscommon, Longford, Westmeath, King's County, Tipperary, Kilkenny, etc. The inevitable conclusion is that the 1841 census figures for cultivated land, and the complementary figures for bog and waste, are completely unreliable and must be discarded.

Towards an alternative estimate

The rejection of the 1841 figures for cultivated and uncultivated land leaves very little quantitative evidence on land use in Ireland before the famine, and much of the analysis which follows is necessarily more subjective than other sections of this paper.

Let us first consider the direct effect of the famine on each of the three sub-categories of cultivated land (see table 6). The immediate result was a fall in the extent of land under crops from 1845 to 1846, and a much sharper drop between 1846 and 1847.[54] After 1848 there was a partial temporary recovery in the area under crops. Dowdall,[55] in a comprehensive contemporary study of the Irish agricultural economy which has been oddly neglected, estimated that the extent of crops (including hay) and fallow in 1845 was 7,948,000 acres. This is 2½ million acres above the corresponding figure for 1847 and nearly 2 million acres above that for 1851.

What happened to this vast area of uncropped broken land in the interval before the first complete agricultural survey in 1851? In the category 'fallow and uncropped arable', there remained in 1851 only 195,053 acres, representing in the main recently abandoned land. Over 600,000 acres had been taken up in the recovery of tillage after 1847 (table 6). Land recently 'reclaimed' from bog or mountain, which had not yet been consolidated, certainly reverted rapidly to its original condition. But the bulk of the 'lost' land, to the extent of not less than 1½ million acres, had, with the traditional rapidity with which grass springs up even on unseeded Irish ground when left to its own devices,[56] been transformed into pasture land.[57]

The factors which we have considered thus far led to a redistribution of land between the three sub-categories of cultivated land, without change in the total, apart from the reversion of some land to waste. Any major difference in 1841 from the 1851 census return of 14.8 million acres of cultivated land can have arisen only either from genuine reclamation of waste land, or from a spill-over, under pressure of numbers, of an expanding population of cattle or sheep into marginal waste land, leading to the latter being classified as pasture.[58]

We may dismiss the latter as an effective factor in the period 1841-51, since the amount of tillage land which reverted to pasture was more than enough to carry the increase of livestock in the decade. The extent of reclamation over the same period is a more controversial question. Apart from calculations based on the discredited 1841 census figures, two other sets of numerical returns must be considered:

(1) Some of the northern counties, where the original ordnance survey maps had lacked detail, and also parts of County Kerry, were resurveyed before 1851. It was thought at the time that a comparison of the original and revised maps would provide a measure of the amount of reclamation

of waste land in the interval between the two surveys. Dr Connell summarised the results obtained, on the basis of both published and manuscript sources.[59]

No more reliance can be placed upon these figures than on those, similarly derived, which were presented in the 1841 census report. The extent of uncultivated land at the time of the original survey was not, in fact, measured afresh on the maps, but was taken from the manuscript calculations, by parishes, which had been prepared for the purpose of the 1841 census.[60] The only new data consisted of measurements of the extent of land which, from the later series of maps, appeared to have been recently reclaimed. No doubt part of the changes shown on the maps between the original ordnance survey and its first revision represents authentic reclamation, but, given the instructions to the surveyors, another part can represent nothing more than the extension of the boundary fences of expanding grazing farms. For what it is worth, it may be noted that in County Donegal, the 'area of land reclaimed' between the original survey (which ended in 1836) and the revision (which commenced in 1845) is given as 32,434 acres, i.e. little more than a tenth part of the comparable figure of 300,110 acres, derived from the successive census values and quoted earlier in this paper.

(2) Dr Collison Black, in an analysis of land improvement resulting from state action, quotes a figure of nearly 180,000 acres which, under the direction of the commissioners of public works, had been drained in the years immediately preceding 1850 as a result of the land improvement act and the arterial drainage act.[61]

It is very doubtful whether this evidence is at all relevant to the problem of extent of land reclamation. Drainage and reclamation were considered to be quite separate problems,[62] and an examination of the detailed accounts of the different drainage projects[63] confirms that they were largely concerned with the betterment of land already in use for tillage or pasture. Crop yields were reported as having improved or even doubled as a result of drainage; scanty pasture was now abundant; wet and shallow land, formerly suitable only for potatoes, had become fit to grow turnips and other green crops.

The commissioners repeated a warning that drainage in itself, without further work, would not repay the expenditure involved 'except perhaps on pasture lands of superior quality', and a landlord noted with appreciation that 'land improvement' is a 'very comprehensive expression'.[64] The report refers to a limited amount of drainage of bog land, but, even in these cases, drainage represented only the first stage in the laborious sequence required for reclamation. It is clear that the bulk of drainage was applied, as it continued to be later in the century,[65] to the further improvement of land which already ranked as 'cultivated'.

Using the terminology of Dr Connell, we turn from the statistical to the literary evidence of reclamation. For the decade before the famine, this comprises mainly statements made before the Devon commission, which have been reviewed rather fully by Dr Connell.[66] He concludes that, while the evidence scarcely confirms the very rapid rate of reclamation indicated by the statistics, it does indicate that 'a fair amount was taking place in most parts of the country'.[67] The problem is to convert 'a fair amount' into a numerical estimate of the increase in cultivated land between 1841 and 1851, taking into account the small extent of most of the instances of reclamation reviewed by the Devon commission, the probability of the reversion to waste during the famine years of at least some of the ground gained, and the unlikelihood of substantial reclamation by private initiative during the period 1845-51.

Reviewing all the available evidence, it is judged that a figure of 100,000 acres is, if anything, an overestimate of the net gain in cultivated land in the decade 1845-51. An estimate of this order will not be readily accepted by those who, working from the 1841 census figures, have found it possible to give some measure of credence to a figure of 1.3 million acres.[68] There are, however, two numerical straws which tend to confirm that the wind of change in land use blew far less strongly than the official figures would suggest:

(1) When Dowdall had completed his estimates of the 1845 acreage under crops, he went on to consider the probable extent of pasture. Accepting the 1841 census figure of 13,464,300 acres of cultivated land, he found that he could remain inside this boundary only by assuming that one-fifth of all the cattle and one-third of all the sheep were fed on bog and mountain.[69] The acreage of pasture thus illogically excluded amounted to 1,253,000 acres, which would have brought the total calculated area of cultivated land just before the famine to 14,717,000 acres.

(2) The unacceptable figures for land use given in the 1841 census represent, in fact, the second thoughts of Richard Griffith.[70] Before he was beguiled by the unhappy idea of seeking greater accuracy from the ordnance survey maps, he had put before the poor law inquiry the following calculation for 1831:[71]

Cultivated land...	14,603,000 acres
Uncultivated land...	5,340,736 acres

From the form of these figures, it appears that the extent of uncultivated land is the basic statistic, the other being derived as a remainder in round numbers from an assumed combined area. This remainder, in the light of the better information on total area (excluding woods, water and towns) available from the 1841 and 1851 census data, may be amended to 14.4 or 14.5 million acres.

The best available estimates of the sequence of change in cultivated land, which are considered, if anything, to exaggerate the rate of expansion, are thus;

1831 ... 14.4 million acres
1841 ... 14.7
1851 ... 14.8

The indicated average rates of increase of agricultural land (30,000 acres per annum in the first decade, and 10,000 acres per annum in the famine decade) are not inconsiderable, but the broad picture is in closer agreement with Professor G. O'Brien's conservative ideas on the extent of reclamation[72] than with the conclusions of other commentators.

CHAPTER 4

The use of the potato crop in pre-famine Ireland*

Introduction

The first definite newspaper reports that potato blight had made its way into Ireland were published on 6 September 1845.[1] In London, Professor John Lindley at once realised the grim implications of the news,[2] but in Ireland itself there was little immediate reaction. This domestic complacency was in some measure due to confidence about the food situation; the extent of land under potatoes had increased by 6% over the previous year's sowing to reach a figure of 2.5 million statute acres,[3] and both potato and grain crops showed promise of above average yields. Thus on the very same 6 September 1845 an editorial in the *Leinster Express* began as follows:

> Our correspondents on all sides transmit to us the pleasing intelligence that the harvest will be abundant and of good quality, and the deepest gratitude pervades the hearts of the farmers for the bountiful dispensations of a gracious Providence.

The farmers were 'in the height of good spirits', the peasantry 'grateful and contented', the country 'happy and prosperous'. The editor foresaw, not the imminent famine, but 'the dawning of a bright and glorious era in the history of Ireland'. Indeed, the only ones not overjoyed were 'some knowing old farm labourers' who had, earlier, expressed 'their regret at having gone to the expense of sowing potatoes this season, they promise to be so cheap and plenty'.[4]

Had the yield been even an average one of 6 tons per acre,[5] it would seem from these and similar comments that the production of 15 million tons of potatoes would for once have met the various calls upon the crop. In the present paper, we shall attempt to draw up a balance of how this enormous crop would have been used.

There are difficulties in reaching an accurate picture of the consumption of the potato crop even in more recent times.[6] It may, therefore, seem a hopeless task to attempt to do so for the Ireland of the 1840s. However, the dominant role played by the potato as food for people and pigs, and

* From *Journal of the Statistical and Social Inquiry Society of Ireland*, xxi, pt. 6 (1967-8), pp 72-96.

the abundant information on amounts consumed in those days, makes the problem rather less difficult than in days of a more heterogeneous diet. In fact, in a pioneer effort which shows a remarkably modern approach, Dowdall[7] drew up in 1846 just such a balance sheet as a means of determining the acreage under different crops in the early 1840s. We shall follow his general line, with some changes in detail and presentation. This is far from being a mere arithmetical exercise or just a further check on the accuracy of the acreage and yield figures; it presents, in fact, a quantitative picture of the structure of the pre-famine population and of the relative dependence on the potato of the different classes of society and of farm animals. It provides the basic data necessary to understand the repercussions of the potato losses in the years 1845 and 1846.

Sukhatme[8] gives the following formulation of the structure of a food balance sheet:

$$P = G+F+(E-I)+M+W+S+(J_2-J_1)$$

where

P = production of the food during the year
G = human consumption
F = animal consumption
E = exports
I = imports
M = use in manufactures other than food
W = waste
S = used as seed
J_1 = stock in hand at beginning of year
J_2 = stock in hand at end of year

Questions of the adjustment for carried-over stock (J_2-J_1) do not arise in the case of the potato. P is known as 15 million tons. We shall consider each of the other items in turn.

Human consumption of the potato

To assess human food requirements, we need:[9]

(1) information about the food requirements of individuals according to age, sex and occupation (physiological data);

(2) information on the numbers to be fed, together with their ages, sex and occupations (demographic data).

The census of 1841 gives the second category of data; the first is provided in numerous official reports of the time, particularly those dealing with the poor law. We consider first the basic yardstick, the daily food requirements of a healthy adult male living exclusively on potatoes.

Consumption of an adult male

Connell[10] reviews much of the evidence regarding pre-famine human consumption of the potato and concludes:

Perhaps if we take 10 pounds a day as the average potato-consumption of the adult man from the 1780s to the famine we shall approach the real position as closely as our information permits: it is evident, however, that any such figure acquires its convenience at the cost of neglecting both any tendency there was for consumption per head to increase, and the undoubtedly wide regional differences.

Dowdall in his contemporary analysis sets the consumption of a potato-fed adult male in the 1840s at 14 lb. a day. In so far as there is any disagreement between the two conclusions, the weight of authoritative evidence favours the higher figure for the years immediately preceding the famine. Trevelyan[11] says that a hundredweight of potatoes will not last a man more than eight days; he is echoing evidence repeatedly given before the poor law inquiry,[12] where eight days is the period most frequently cited, but with occasional variants from five to ten days. In Tipperary[13] it was said that while a hundredweight of good potatoes would support a man for eight days, the same quantity of 'the inferior sorts' would last only six days. In County Down, it was considered that a labouring man would 'be hard set to do on' a stone of potatoes a day, and 'would want something with it to work upon'.[14]

Perhaps the most convincing testimony, not quoted by Connell, is contained in two consecutive reports by Hall and Hawley given in the sixth annual report of the poor law commissioners.[15] The authors were engaged on the necessary but difficult task of fixing a poor law dietary scale less abundant and of inferior quality than that of the majority of the labouring class. 'Evils that cannot be contemplated without dread are sure to follow' unless things were so arranged 'that the seeking of shelter of the workhouse should be the test of destitution, and that none but those absolutely in want should ever be induced to claim its shelter'.[16] As one step in this direction it was suggested, in line with the procedure followed generally in gaols and institutions, 'that two meals a day will be sufficient for the paupers in the workhouse, namely, a breakfast and a dinner but no supper'.[17]

To determine what the labouring poor actually ate, Hawley[18] did a careful survey in thirteen areas in Counties Limerick, Tipperary and Clare. The results show considerable uniformity. Just under 14 lb. of potatoes were eaten in three equal meals; in one area (Ennistymon) Cups, a superior variety, were specified. Supper was, according to Hawley, not always taken, especially where there was a shortage of potatoes or fuel.

Both Hall[19] and Hawley[20] give useful information on the theory and practice of dieting in Irish prisons and institutions. The act for consolidating and amending the laws relating to prisons in Ireland (7

Geo. IV, cap. 74) laid down alternative diets, per prisoner per day, as follows:

Bread diet – 2 lb. bread, 1 quart of pure milk

Potato diet – 9 lb. potatoes, 1 pint of new milk, 1 pint buttermilk

Mixed diet – 8 oz. meal for stirabout, 4 lb. potatoes, 1 pint of new milk and 1 pint of buttermilk.

In general, the Irish prisons adhered rigidly to this schedule. Most provided the mixed diet, but Wicklow Gaol and Parsonstown Bridewell, no doubt catering to a mainly rural clientele, served potatoes exclusively. Among the twenty-two 'public establishments' listed, the Limerick Mendicity Society offered least – 5.5 lb. of potatoes and 2 pints of skim milk per day. Despite this frugality, it was crowded, because discipline was low and the paupers managed 'to obtain extra supplies of food from their friends out of the house'. Limerick County Gaol supplemented the approved mixed diet by an extra three-quarters of a pound of potatoes. Although Hawley conceded that this was still inferior to the dietary of the peasantry, he notes with displeasure that it 'has been found to offer sufficient inducements to abandoned characters to commit crimes, in order to enjoy its advantages during the winter months, notwithstanding the terrors of the treadmill'.

The most marked disapproval is reserved for the County of Limerick Lunatic Asylum, which is excluded from the summary of public establishments 'because of its evident disparity'. It served three meals per day. Breakfast always consisted of 7 oz. oatmeal (called cutlins) in stirabout and a pint of new milk, and supper of 8 oz. bread and half a pint of new milk. Dinner was variable but far from frugal; on Wednesdays it consisted of 'half a stone of boiled potatoes to each and 1 pint of new milk'. Hawley does not say whether abandoned characters were induced to simulate madness, but it would seem to have been worth an effort.

There was an interesting exchange at the Maryborough sitting of the poor law inquiry[21] which supplements Hawley's evidence. The governor of the gaol remarked that the prisoners engaged in hard labour got nine pounds of potatoes and a quart of milk a day, and were in better health than when at home. This claim was vigorously contested by a number of those present who said that men in gaol got into bad health from the low diet. The governor then admitted that those prisoners who could supplement their diet ate a stone of potatoes a day.

The contemporary evidence can be multiplied at will. Wilde[22] estimates that 'nearly a stone of the root was taken into the stomach of the Irish labourer per diem'. Dr J. F. Hodges of Belfast put the figure at fifteen pounds.[23] 'No less than 15 lb.,' said Spooner,[24] adding that 'an Englishman would, I take it, find considerable difficulty in stowing away this enormous quantity of vegetable food, and how an Irishman is able to manage it is beyond my ability to explain'. Bain,[25] who had lived in County Cork, recalls that 'in wholly feeding with potatoes 90 or 100 people at harvest time, the custom was to lay down a weight, i.e. 21 lb., of potatoes to each of four men, to breakfast, dinner and supper'. This gives a figure of nearly 16 lb. to each man, but the circumstances were exceptional and Bain puts the normal daily requirements at 'only 14 lb.'.

The evidence is overwhelmingly in favour of a figure of 14 lb., when potatoes were in good supply. It is equally clear that as potato supplies diminished in spring, the tendency was to reduce to two meals rather than three. For the purpose of our annual food balance, we accordingly scale down the allowance to 12 lb. a day for an adult male, as defined in the census of 1841, i.e. one of over 15 years.

Consumption of women, children and the aged

Hawley,[26] in his investigations into the diet of the working classes in Limerick, Tipperary and Clare, found that adult women on a potato diet used 80% of the amount consumed by adult men. He comments:

> The quantity of food consumed by ablebodied women is invariably less than that consumed by ablebodied men, but in quality is precisely similar. Males up to sixty years of age fully consume as much as young men in the prime of life, and those above sixty very little less. There is more difficulty in obtaining any correct data as to the relative consumption of food by children of all ages; but, from the best information I can obtain, I am led to suppose that those upwards of ten years of age require fully as much as full-grown women to sustain them, at a period when muscular expansion and rapid digestion require equivalent support.

The problem of determining the consumption of the young arose from their irregular eating habits. McAdam mentions that in every cottage little children were allowed to roast potatoes in turf ashes for their own use as often as they pleased. 'As you ride by a cabin you frequently see a group of children run to the door, each holding in his hand a roasted potato.'

Dowdall got around the problem by basing the food requirement of young children on the dietary of the House of Industry in Dublin.[27] In his analysis the food consumption of an adult woman is taken to be 80% of that of a man; the same figure is adopted for children between 11 and 15 years and a value of 35% for children under eleven years.

Considering the altered circumstances, these figures are not radically different from those used by modern authorities,[28] and we shall adopt them without change.

The statistical family

The census of 1841[29] gives data which enable us to divide the population into adult males and females (over 15 years), into older children (11 to 15 years) and younger children (under 11 years).

Following the procedure suggested by Dowdall, we associate with each adult male the appropriate proportion of adult females (1.080), older children (0.417) and younger children (0.993), to make a statistical 'family' of 3.49 persons. This is, of course, an entirely artificial concept, but it provides a valid and effective method of dividing the population into reasonably homogeneous dietary groups on the basis of the occupations of the adult males.

Table 1

COMPOSITION OF THE POPULATION OF IRELAND, 1841

Adult males	2,341,895
Adult females	2,529,660
Older children	977,020
Younger children	2,326,549
TOTAL	8,175,124

The next step is to weigh each section of the statistical family in accordance with the food needs of sex and age, as discussed in the previous section. If an adult man in a particular occupational group eats, on an average, M lb. of potatoes a day, the daily consumption of the associated group of men, women and children (3.49 persons) may be calculated as 2.55 M lb., equivalent over a period of 10½ months,[30] to 0.364 M tons. For instance, in the section of the population which was entirely fed on potatoes and for which M = 12, the corresponding annual consumption of the statistical family is 4.368 tons.

Potato consumption according to occupation

The next important question is to define more precisely the social group which lived entirely on potatoes.

There is ample evidence of the complete identity in poverty and diet of small farms (of up to about 20 or even 30 statute acres) with labourers and cottiers.

Martin Doyle[31] was primarily addressing the small-holders of the relatively prosperous County Wexford when he wrote:

> After paying the necessary demands against you, there remains little or nothing for the support of your families. In winter, milk, so necessary to human life, is seldom within your reach; and meat is a luxury which never falls to your share, except at Christmas and Easter. I have often seen a very large family picking delicately

at one salt herring for dinner, the only addition to their potatoes, and even this relish not afforded every day, while the father of the family rented from 10 to 20 [Irish] acres of land.

A witness before the Devon commission[32] spoke of the farmers 'from thirty acres downwards' as being united with the labourers in opposition to the eviction of tenantry. The Society of Friends[33] considered that:

the landed gentry and the clergy formed the first rank of society; and there were very few between them and the lowest class, which was composed of the labouring peasantry and the small landholders. The latter were scarcely removed above the labourer, either in circumstances or education.

Green[34] found that, in the Lagan valley area, 'the division between thirty acre holdings and those below thirty marked a powerful social barrier'. There was, of course, another at a higher level; a witness before the Devon commission considered that 'when you come to a farm of 100 acres, you get a creature between a hawk and a hound, and it is difficult to know how to deal with him. He is not a gentleman, and not a farmer.'[35]

The limits of farm sizes which we may assign to the different categories of landholders is circumscribed by the sizes in which the reliable statistical evidence is grouped. We shall combine smallholders of under 20 statute acres with cottiers and labourers to form the group on an exclusive potato diet, and divide the remaining farmers into those holding below and above 50 statute acres.

Even outside the lowest group, considerable amounts of potato were eaten. Of the bigger farms, Salaman[36] says:

If necessity made the potato the food of the masses, the habit it created was certainly not confined to them. The middle-class, though free to choose a more varied diet, became confirmed potato addicts and consumed what we today would consider preposterous quantities. A vignette from one of Griffin's novels (*The half sir*, p. 123) gives one an intimate glimpse into a comfortable Munster farmhouse in the first quarter of the nineteenth century: 'Minny O' Lone was quietly seated by the breakfast table making a rapid progress through the reeking mountain of steak-coated potatoes and virgin-white milk that covered the board.'

The more prosperous Irish landowners, on tour in Europe, surprised the continentals by their addiction to potatoes. When the Polish Countess Myscelska called on Lady Mountcashell in Paris, she found her:

eating plain boil'd Potatoes for her luncheon in the middle of the day. She then heard for the first time that *that* was the principal food of the Irish, and immediately resolv'd on giving Lady Mount Cashell a breakfast in compliment to her country. We went there and literally found nothing but Potatoes dress'd in fifty different fashions.[37]

In the case of the different artisans and tradesmen, Dowdall illustrates that his estimates of their degree of dependence on the potato are reasonable in the light of their earnings and way of life. In assigning values to M for each social group as shown in table 4, we follow the proportions suggested by Dowdall, who had contemporary experience; in some mixed groups which are marked as 'unclassified' we use an average value of M = 6.

It would be pointless to discuss in detail the values assigned to M in table 4 for the various groups other than that made up of cottiers, labourers and smallholders, for they alone account for 75% of the total human consumption of potatoes. If we assigned a mean value of M = 6 to all outside this group, the value derived for total potato consumption would be only 3% higher than under the system we have adopted; if we assigned a figure as low as M = 4, the total would be reduced by only 4%. In other words, the rather arbitrary figures of potato consumption assigned to all except the lowest class may be altered to personal taste without creating any radical change in the deduced total human consumption.

Regional differences in potato consumption: the oatmeal zone

In any calculation of potato consumption allowance must be made for the areas in which oats formed a regular part of the diet of the people throughout the year. The core of the oatmeal zone was centred in Ulster, home of the 'stirabout-eaters' whom Wilde[38] considered had 'inherited the peculiar appetites and culinary knowledge of their Scotch ancestors'. Dowdall defines the main area as that north of a line from Dundalk to Finnea, Co. Westmeath, and thence to Ballyshannon, but excluding the counties of Cavan and Donegal. On the basis of a survey made by the poor law inquiry, Bourke[39] calculates that about 30% of the poorer classes had at least an oatmeal breakfast in place of the full potato diet which was the lot of their counterparts in most of Ireland.

Occupational groups and total human potato consumption

The census of 1841[40] gives a detailed breakdown of the occupations of 2,213,457 of the adult males of 15 years and upwards. In table 2, these have been grouped into seven major categories, and an 'unclassified' group of 128,438 added to agree with the total of adult males in table 1.

The large and heterogeneous agricultural section (group 1 of table 2) needs to be broken down into subsections according to size of agricultural holding. For this purpose the more reliable statistics[41] are the poor law returns. Table 3 summarises these returns as given in the *Devon report*.[42]

Table 2

SUMMARY OF ADULT MALE OCCUPATIONS IN IRELAND, 1841

1.	Farmers (452,940), agricultural servants and labourers (1,105,258), ploughmen, gardeners and herds	1,586,369
2.	Graziers, land agents, land stewards, gamekeepers and dairykeepers	7,318
3.	Workers in clothing, including weavers (104,987), boot and shoemakers (45,656) and tailors (34,944)	212,582
4.	Workers in the furniture, building, metal and associated trades, including carpenters (38,672), blacksmiths (24,875), stonemasons (16,450), coopers (9,278), etc.	158,349
5.	Miscellaneous workmen, consisting of non-agricultural domestic servants (59,692), labourers and porters (29,064), fishermen (8,918), carmen (8,279), sailors (4,218), boatmen, coach and car drivers	115,287
6.	Professional classes, including those concerned with health, charity, justice, education and religion; and merchant classes, including bankers, merchants, shopkeepers, vintners and tavern keepers, etc.	128,127
7.	Paupers (self-styled)	5,425
8.	Unclassified	128,438
	TOTAL	2,341,895

Table 3

NUMBER OF PERSONS HOLDING LAND IN IRELAND, c. 1845

Size of holding	*Number*
From less than 1 acre to 10 acres	505,173
Above 10 and not exceeding 20 acres	187,582
Above 20 and not exceeding 50 acres	141,819
Above 50 acres	70,441
Unclassified	30,433
Total number of persons holding land	935,448

If this total is subtracted from 1,586,369, the number of farmers and labourers, the residue of 650,921 represents the number of agricultural labourers who did not hold land except in conacre.

It is worth while to digress for a moment to consider the implications of this important statistic. The landless labourers, according to the census of 1831, totalled at that time 567,441 or 7.3% of the total population (not counting their dependants). In 1834 it was calculated that they probably numbered about 585,000. The figure of 650,921 derived above represents 8.0% of the population in 1841. The rise in proportion to the general population is a reflection of the growing competition for land.

TABLE 4

POTATO CONSUMPTION BY DIFFERENT GROUPS IN IRELAND, 1841

		No. of Adult Males	No. Including Dependants (thousands)	Basic Daily Potato Food (M. in lbs.)	Annual (10½ month) Use of Potatoes (thousand tons)
AGRICULTURAL	1. Cottiers, smallholders and landless labourers outside the oatmeal zone	940,573	3,283	12	4,108
	2. Cottiers, smallholders and landless labourers within the oatmeal zone	403,103	1,407	8	1,174
	3. Small farmers, holding between 20 and 50 acres ...	141,819	495	6	310
	4. Unclassified farmers mainly in joint tenancy	30,433	106	6	66
	5. Large farmers, of 50 acres and above	70,441	246	3	77
	6. Graziers, landagents, etc.	7,318	26	3	8
	SUB-TOTAL ...	1,593,687	5,563	—	5,743
NON-AGRICULTURAL	7. Clothing workers ...	212,582	742	6	464
	8. Furniture, building and other trades	158,349	553	4	231
	9. Miscellaneous workmen ...	115,287	402	4	168
	10. Professional men and merchants	128,127	447	1	47
	11. Paupers	5,425	19	6	12
	12. Unclassified	128,438	448	6	281
	SUB-TOTAL ...	748,208	2 611	—	1,203
	GRAND TOTAL ...	2,341,895	8,174	—	6,946

If one adds their dependants, the landless labourers represented a total of nearly 2,272,000 people, or more than one-quarter of the whole population. They were the most vulnerable and insecure section of the people, living their desperate lives under a constantly poised sword of Damocles. In 1845, the amount of potato land set in conacre was about 350,000 acres[43] representing an average produce of 2,100,000 tons, or roughly 75% of the food requirements of the landless group. On this basis, their potato supplies from conacre would be exhausted early in May; the *Poor inquiry*[44] confirms that 'the labourer never has any of his conacre potatoes remaining at the period at which they become unfit for use, the greater number have used them all at the beginning of April, and scarcely one has a potato remaining at the 1st of May'.

Returning to the main argument, the derived figure of landless men is added to the numbers of smallholders and cottiers holding up to 20 acres to give a total of 1,343,676. Thirty per cent of these, or 403,103 people, lived within the oatmeal zone and are assigned, in the mean, a two-thirds potato diet, leaving 940,573 as the hard core of the potato-eating population. This completes the basis for table 4.

In round figures, the total annual usage of the potato as human food in Ireland just before the famine may be taken as 7 million tons.

Consumption of the potato by farm animals

A Mr Lambert wrote:

> I calculate that five out of the eight millions composing the population had their food or living by the potato, the remaining three million being partly fed on them, and the immense supply of pigs altogether, beside the aid afforded to supply cows, horses and poultry.[45]

It is necessary, therefore, to consider the annual potato consumption by pigs and other animals. An enumeration of livestock was carried out in 1841.[46] The returns of cattle and pigs are considered to be on the low side; there is no means of adjusting the latter, but a corrected figure of 2,250,000 has been calculated for the former.[47] With this adjustment, the pre-famine totals of livestock are as shown in table 5.

Table 5

TOTALS OF LIVESTOCK IN IRELAND, 1841

Cattle	2,250,000
Sheep	2,106,189
Pigs	1,412,813
Horses and mules	576,115
Asses	92,365
Poultry	8,458,517

Consumption by pigs

While cattle and horses spent most of the year on grass, pigs were fed on the potato, and almost exclusively on the potato, for as long as the food lasted. They therefore represented the major item in this part of the balance sheet. It is unfortunate that the care and feeding of the pig in Ireland, being largely the poor man's chores, are not discussed in any detail in the agricultural books and journals of the period; nor is modern feeding practice any guide, since the pig of today has been altered so much by breeding and by new introductions as to be virtually a different animal.

Dowdall considers the average daily requirement of food for each pig, 'at a very moderate estimate' to be a stone of potatoes. He quotes no supporting evidence. The most specific witness before the poor law inquiry[48] said that:

> he had only one pig this year, which was as much as he could venture to keep, as potatoes were likely to be dear; if distress should not come on him, he would like to keep it for a twelvemonth; it cost him 18s., and it would eat a stone of potatoes a day, and more when grown large; that would be 1½d. or 2d. a day if he had to buy, but they were the small potatoes of his conacre; if not obliged to meet the wants of his family, he would sell the pigs about Christmas for, perhaps, £1 8s. or £1 10s. It would not be worth keeping pigs if one had to buy the food for them.

Another witness[49] said that the small man could not feed his pigs well; raised by gentlemen, they fetched twice the price.

This is confirmed by some results of experiments of the fattening of livestock on potatoes submitted by Blacker.[50] A pig weighing 120 lb. and costing 30s. was fed for six months on two stone of potatoes a day; at the end of this period the animal weighed 320 lb. This is consistent with Blacker's claim that each bushel of 4 stone of potatoes will put on 2 lb. of meat on a pig. The conversion rate of roughly 1 to 6 or 7 barley units is, of course, poor by modern standards.

In another example, Blacker says:

> My steward bought a pig in November 1835 for 7s. 6d., and sold him 1st December 1836, which pig weighed nineteen score seven pounds payable and amounted to £6 6. 0.

From the period of rearing, final weight (387 lb.) and conversion rate, it can be calculated that the daily consumption in this case also was about two stone of potatoes a day.

But the vast majority of pigs were raised by the small man, if only for the reason that it was uneconomic to feed the inefficient breed on potatoes other than the 'peelings and waste of those used by the family'.[51] The pig was unlikely to fare better than the head of the family. There are numerous references to under-nourished and even starving pigs which suggest that, in many cases, the food supply actually available was inadequate. Allowing for fluctuations around the year, we have adopted a mean daily rate of 12 lb. of potatoes per pig over 10½ months.

Consumption by cattle

Dowdall submits that:

> It requires one stone of straw and 36 lbs of potatoes to maintain a carefully housed cow during twenty-four hours. An Irish cow is generally so much exposed to the influence of the atmosphere and her necessity for abundant fodder thereby so much increased that less than 21 lbs of potatoes daily, for the time she is house-fed, would scarcely support life. That period cannot be estimated at less than three months; for although there be a greater number of cattle which, in all weathers except snow, are made to depend on the almost naked fallow or closely nipped pasture, still the livestock of farmers holding about 30 acres are for much more than three months stall-fed on potatoes.

The higher rates of feeding and the longer periods under shelter, as practised by the bigger farmers, are confirmed by Blacker's evidence.[52] In two cases the cattle were stall-fed for five months; in another for four. The rate of feeding was, in most cases, 4 stone of potatoes a day; in one case, as high as 6 stone. 'A ton of potatoes would nearly last a beast 40 days.' More would be needed 'if the beast consumes more than 4 stone, which they often do'. Of course, these feeding rates were designed to fatten the cattle for market. They gained weight at about 1½ lb. a day, at rates equivalent to about 1 lb. of meat to 32-40 lb. potatoes.

Similarly a Louth farmer of over a hundred acres, who claimed normally to use 30 stone of potatoes a day for 'people, pigs and horses' found that cattle fed on 4 stone of potatoes fattened more rapidly than on 12 stone of turnips. The potato, says Goodiff,[53] 'is a better food for cattle than turnips, producing sweeter milk and finer beef'.

The problem is to strike a mean between the practice of the big cattle men and the small struggling farmers. We accept Dowdall's compromise of 1½ stone of potatoes a day for each beast over a period of three months.

Consumption by horses

In the case of horses, for whom oats was commonly available as an alternative food, the situation is more complex.

Martin Doyle[54] considered that a sufficiently fed horse required, over the seven-month period from October to April, inclusive, a daily diet of one stone of boiled potatoes, plus seven pounds of hay, seven pounds of oaten straw and eight pounds of oats. A County Galway farmer[55] found no diet so good for the winter feeding of cart horses 'as upland hay, oats and bruised beans, assisted with 21 lb. of steamed potatoes each night, seasoned with bay salt'.

The problem is not, however, so much the quantity of food desirable for a horse, but rather the amount he actually received. Dowdall asserts that:

> the horses of the gentry were generally well fed on oats, those of the cottier tenantry half-starved on wastes and fallows; the horses of the farmers were, to a very large extent, during the winter and spring months, supported on potatoes.

Evidence before the poor law inquiry[56] illustrates the extremes of practice. In the better areas, horses 'are turned out to graze from May to November and have then no other food, but from November to May the larger farmers give theirs one stone of oats and one of boiled or steamed potatoes per day, and the smaller farmers two stones of potatoes without oats'. Again in the barony of Gowran, Co. Kilkenny, horses were allowed, from November until May or June, 'besides hay, from one to two stones of steamed or boiled potatoes, and from a ½ stone to a stone of oats per day, according to their work'. At the other extreme, some horses were given hay only during the winter months, and saw oats (generally the 'tale' or unsaleable grain) only during the spring working season.

Taking a conservative mean of these and other accounts, we may consider the horse as living on pasture alone for six months, existing, apart from hay or straw, on a stone of potatoes a day during the three inactive months of winter, and feeding reasonably well on a stone of oats a day during the three busy months of spring.

Consumption by other animals

Dowdall makes allowance for potatoes eaten by poultry. No doubt they fed in large part on potato refuse,[57] but it seems difficult to make any rational estimate of how much, if at all, they added to the total consumption. Probably they frequently helped themselves to the fringes of the pig's ration.

There is some evidence[58] of winter feeding of sheep on 4 to 7 lb. of potatoes a day per animal. It seems to have been an experimental procedure tried by some enterprising farmers, and was probably not widespread.

Total annual potato consumption by farm animals

Confining our attention to pigs, cattle and horses, the total annual consumption of the potato as animal feed is as shown in table 6.

In round figures, the total annual usage of the potato as animal food in Ireland emerges as 5 million tons.

Table 6

POTATO CONSUMPTION BY LIVESTOCK, 1841

	Number	*Rate and period*	*Total consumption* (thousands of tons)
Pigs	1,412,813	1 stone a day for 320 days	2,826
Cattle	2,250,000	1½ stone a day for 91 days	1,920
Horses	576,115	1 stone a day for 91 days	328
TOTAL			5,074

Exports and imports of the potato

Imports of potatoes are rather easier to assess than exports. In normal years, potato imports were mainly confined to seed potatoes for the more prosperous growers who wished to change seed or to grow the early varieties more common in Britain. In north Dublin, which served the city potato markets:

> great care is taken in the selection of seed; all the growers change their seed occasionally, getting it from distant parts of the country, and often from England and Scotland. They find the greatest benefit from this practice and go to considerable expense to pursue it. The vicinity of shipping-ports saves the small holders from the necessity of paying any exorbitant price for this change of seed.[59]

In County Meath:

> The gentlemen and large farmers buy seed from other parts of the kingdom, the smaller farmers and labourers content themselves with changing from light [to] heavy land, and vice versa.[60]

Niven[61] refers to such imports and suggests means of organising an Irish seed potato trade to avoid 'so many thousands of pounds being sent annually out of the country'.

It was, clearly, a fairly limited trade, which Niven's comment suggests did not total more than some thousands of tons, and is consequently of little importance to our balance sheet. It has, however, considerable significance from the point of view of plant epidemiology, for it provided a means by which tuber-borne disease would quickly find its way from Britain to Ireland.

As regards trade in the reverse direction, an immediate problem is the ambiguous way in which the word 'export' was used at the time. Thus when Townsend[62] speaks in 1810 of 'a large export of potatoes' from County Cork he is speaking primarily of an internal Irish trade; he goes on to give a most interesting account of the coastal potato trade as plied between Cork and Dublin. This domestic exchange between the areas of dense and sparse potato cultivation had been long in existence. Pococke,[63] writing in 1752, mentioned that Dungarvan was famous for an export of potatoes to many parts of Ireland. The *Drummond report*[64] of 1837-8 gives the main potato shipping ports, in order, as Strangford, Ardglass-Killough, Donaghadee, Belfast, Waterford and Baltimore (Co. Cork). Dublin and Balbriggan are named as potato importing centres. The annual amounts quoted, which include true exports as well as the coastal trade, are not impressive; Strangford shipped just under 10,000 tons. The figure given for Belfast (2,924 tons) is of the same order as the 3,500 tons given by Lewis[65] for the same port in 1845. A problem with the trade statistics given in the *Drummond report* and elsewhere, apart from their speculative nature, is that potatoes are not separately listed in all returns.

It does seem, however, that by the 1840s Ulster had emerged as a strong competitor in a potato trade which had formerly been the monopoly of Munster. Carlingford now shipped cargoes of potatoes to Dublin,[66] while Cork was forced to seek alternative markets in Limerick city.[67] Perhaps the northerners had a keener sense of marketing; Dubourdieu[68] gives an illustration of a mechanical potato washer which had been invented by Mr Crawford of Crawfordsburn, Co. Down.

That there was a persistent foreign market for Irish potatoes is clear from occasional unambiguous references. Rye[69] wrote as early as 1730 of exports from Ireland 'to our garrisons of Gibraltar and Portmahon, and to some other parts'. A list of Irish imports into Bristol in the period 1839-42 includes potatoes.[70] Cargoes of Irish potatoes were reaching the London market in 1844.[71]

The trouble in assessing the amounts involved is that the subject came up for active discussion only in seasons of food scarcity in Ireland; if, as seems possible, proposals to prohibit the export of potatoes in such seasons were designed as a diversionary tactic to draw attention from grain exports, then the extent of the potato trade may have been deliberately exaggerated. The matter had arisen, for instance, in the hungry spring of 1817.[72] The lord lieutenant of the time pressed Peel to authorise the stopping of potato exports from Ireland. Peel insisted on 'precise information' before taking action; the figures eventually obtained indicated that in the months January to March 1817, potato exports from Ireland totalled 391 tons and imports 967 tons. Peel was not unnaturally indignant:

> I cannot tell you how embarrassed I am...After having had a meeting of the Government...and seriously discussed the policy of immediately prohibiting the export of potatoes from Ireland, I must now inform those that attended that

meeting that the imports into Ireland exceeded the exports from it in the last two months in the proportion of three to one.

Did this experience temper Peel's attitude when the question of prohibiting potato exports came up again in 1845? And yet, the 1817 figures were quite unrepresentative of a complete year's exchange. Exports, even in a normal year, would largely take place soon after harvesting; in a season of internal food shortage like 1816-7, they inevitably fell off rapidly in the new year. Furthermore, the period of the test was that in which imports of seed potatoes of early varieties was likely to be concentrated.

Some references in 1845 may refer to the normal export trade. A policeman comments on 'the demand for Irish potatoes in the Liverpool and Glasgow markets. The export of potatoes to these markets by the steamers from the port of Londonderry has commenced.'[73] New potatoes were being sent twice a week by steam packets from Cork to Plymouth;[74] there was a similar trade with Devonport.[75]

A new development in autumn 1845, however, was a demand for Irish potatoes from the Low Countries where blight had struck early and destructively.[76] 'It is said that orders to the extent of 5 to 6,000 tons have been received in this country from affected continental areas.'[77] There was as yet no general alarm for the Irish crop; the *Dublin Evening Post*[78] was confident that 'a full average crop of sound potatoes will be available for home consumption even if we should export some to England and the Netherlands'. And so a considerable trade began, from Cork, Dublin, Belfast, and other ports to Holland and other parts of the continent.[79] By the second week of October, it was clear that the Irish crop was seriously damaged, and some concern began to be expressed about the potato exports. 'We have great fears that our country will shortly be drained of this crop also, if, in every port in Ireland, shipments are made in the same ratio as from Drogheda last week.'[80] But the trade continued unabated even as alarm about blight in Ireland mounted;[81] the argument aired now in the *Cork Constitution* was that it was advantageous to permit the export of potatoes which, if kept, might contract disease.[82] But local bodies[83] and the Dublin corporation brought pressure on the lord lieutenant, who in turn pressed Peel for instructions regarding the 'great cry' for the prohibition of the export of foodstuffs.[84] Peel echoed the earlier comment of the *Cork Constitution* in his answer:

> If potatoes have a tendency to decay, and other countries are notwithstanding ready to take them, and if a profit can be made by the export of them, and if with that profit other articles of subsistence can be bought, we are not adding to our available means by the prohibition of export.[85]

No doubt, both were pleased to read shortly that in both Holland and Belgium cargoes of potatoes from Ireland arrived in a rotten condition. In Antwerp, potatoes from Londonderry were seized by the police and thrown in the river.[86]

We are left with the problem of estimating the amount of potatoes exported in a normal year. No doubt it fluctuated with the abundance or otherwise of local supplies and with the extent of British demand. Two numerical guesses are available. In an editorial which, in other respects, is not particularly sound, the *Gardeners' Chronicle*[87] speaks of Ireland as 'an exporting country, sending her potatoes elsewhere in large quantities' and by inference, estimates these exports as high as 800,000 tons. Dowdall made no allowance for potato exports in his original calculations, and may have been called to task for the omission, for in a later postscript[88] he admits that allowance should be made for 'the land in Ulster devoted to the production of potatoes for exportation...Several captains employed in the transit trade between Ulster and Scotland variously estimated the exportation of the potatoes at from 100,000 tons annually.'

This does not allow for exports from Munster, probably on a lower scale. With considerable lack of confidence, we take a figure to cover potato exports of 250,000 tons a year; it may well be an over-estimate. We ignore the small potato drain caused by emigrants from Ireland to North America who were required to provision themselves on the long sea voyage; in any case, it was offset by the saving of food of seasonal migrants to Britain.

Use of the potato in manufactures

The main industrial applications of the potato are in the manufacture of farina, starch and alcohol.

The supervisor of rates for County Clare reported[89] in 1845 that flour made from farina had been ground in Ennis Gaol for the past eighteen years and sold in the London market. Potatoes bought at 3d. per stone produced a profit of 75% in this way.

The principal application of potato starch was in the cotton industry.[90] This may explain the location of a starch factory in County Laois, which formerly possessed several cotton mills; now, the starch was mainly sent to Dublin.[91] There was also, in Kilmonogue, Co. Cork, 'a manufactory of starch from potatoes alone'.[92] These are the only references which have been found to the commercial extraction of farina or starch from the potato in Ireland. Clearly the 'industry' was negligible.

The potato was used extensively, in France, Germany and northern Europe generally, for the manufacture of spirits.[93] It was even alleged to have made a contribution to 'the best brandy that comes from France', and to have been used 'to give added strength and richness' to the poorer French wines.[94] Aitken[95] says the extraction of spirits from potatoes had been tried in Scotland 'with different degrees of success'. McAdam[96] describes the use of potatoes in distilleries in France and in Guernsey; he makes no reference to any similar use in Ireland. Smee,[97] writing in 1846, discusses the industry in France, and says that potatoes are not used by any distiller in the UK at present because:

(i) of the high capital cost of new utensils and machinery;

(ii) the spirit from potatoes is inferior to that from corn, and

(iii) the operation of the revenue laws discriminates unfairly against spirit made from any material other than corn.

Some years ago a French enterprise had erected a potato distillery 'near Vauxhall turnpike', but it became insolvent because of the operation of the excise laws.

The revenue laws were no restraint to the use of potatoes for the making of poteen, but the greater bulk of the raw material and the lower prestige of the end product seem to have been effective deterrents. It is still the opinion in the west of Ireland today that spirit distilled from potatoes is markedly inferior to that distilled from grain. Connell,[98] despite spreading his net wide, found no evidence of other than recent use of potatoes in making illicit spirit. Wilde,[99] in a passing comment, says the potato was 'occasionally' made into poteen; an ambiguous reference in Rutty[100] suggests that a 'liquor like ale' was produced from the potato, it 'being malted and managed as Barley'. With so many critics poised to underline the improvidence and insobriety of the peasantry, it is certain that, had there been any substantial conversion of the food of the people into inebriating liquor, more downright comment than these uncertain references would have been widespread.

It is a little surprising, then, to find the lord lieutenant, in late October 1845, considering the desirability of prohibiting 'distillation from potatoes',[101] and an editorial call[102] 'to stop distillation and brewing from grain or potatoes'. In so far as this movement was more than a diversionary tactic to save interference with the grain export trade, it can refer only to what was clearly a small-scale and harmless piece of temporary opportunism: 'Mr Dixon of Belturbet is distilling from damaged potatoes, and buying them up all round the country.'[103]

We can, for the purpose of the balance sheet of potato use, ignore its contribution towards the liquor trade, legal or illegal.

Wastage of potatoes

The loss of the modern potato crop due to shrinkage and disease in storage, and to other sources of waste, is put as high as 15%.[104] In the pre-famine crop, storage losses due to blight were not a factor, and the pig ate up both the peelings and the small and damaged potatoes which today normally go to waste. Rats and other vermin were a problem, of course,[105] and watery varieties like the Lumper were basically poor keepers even over the 10½ months we are catering for. Nevertheless, an allowance of 5% for wastage may be excessive; we adopt that figure primarily because it gives a perfect balance to our potato accounts.

Potatoes for seed

At a rate of 16 cwt of potato seed per acre (see note 5 above), the planting of 2,500,000 acres requires two million tons of potatoes.

The potato balance sheet

The various significant items in the balance sheet of the disposal of the pre-famine crop in Ireland are brought together in table 7.

The least confident figures – those for export and wastage – luckily play the least role in this balance sheet. The major elements have been checked for two relatively self-contained communities for which data (including the area under potatoes) are available. These are the co-operative group at Ralahine, Co. Clare, whose gallant experiment in the years 1831-3 still makes moving reading[106] and the people of the Aran island of Inishmore, for which the population structure is given in the census of 1841 and potato acreage in the constabulary reports of 1845.[107] It would be tedious to repeat the details of the computations here, but they tend to confirm the essential accuracy of table 7.

Table 7

UTILISATION OF THE POTATO CROP IN PRE-FAMINE IRELAND

	Amount in 1000s of tons	*Proportion* (percentage)
Human food	7,000	47%
Animal food	5,000	33%
Export	250	2%
Wastage	750	5%
Seed	2,000	13%
Total production	15,000	100%

Discussion

Dr O'Loan, who proposed the vote of thanks, posed the proposition – how near might we have been to dealing effectively with blight at the time of the famine had there been a little more enlightenment on the part of those posing as leaders in agriculture for a century prior to the famine?

Dubourdieu, commenting in his *Statistical survey of Antrim* (1802) on the common farm practice of treating wheat seed with lime or arsenic (two basic fungicides) against smut, says, 'It certainly seems extraordinary that so small a quantity of any substance as a grain of wheat can imbibe, should have so strong an influence during growth – the operator must certainly take the smut for a living animal?' That this lack of enlightenment prevailed in 'enlightened' circles over Europe is reflected in the contemporary description of the incidence of potato blight and consequent hunger in Switzerland (1845-8) in Jeremias Gotthelf's novel *Käthi, die Grossmutter*.

In discussing the introduction of the potato into Europe and this country Dr O'Loan referred to the evidence of two Irish poems reproduced in translation in McKay's *Anthology of the potato*. One was by O'Neachtain dated 1705. In both the potato is repeatedly referred to as 'An Spánach', indicating that the popular understanding of those who spoke and wrote Irish at the time was that the potato came from Spain – this in contrast to the Sir Walter Raleigh story of later times.

He referred to an early record of potatoes having been introduced into Germany through the offices of a Belgian papal legate under the name of 'tartaffel' (dialect Italian for potato). This was obviously the origin of the German 'Kartoffel'; Cruffels, the name of an old variety in cultivation in County Antrim a century ago was probably of similar origin; the sound is probably what some Antrim coast hooker skipper caught or remembered of the word picking up stores at some North Sea or Baltic port. The famous variety 'Skerries' had been introduced into the Braid valley as a couple of tubers in a barrel of flax seed from Riga and grown in the townland of Skerry.

Dr Nowlan seconded the vote of thanks.

Carmel Frost: We have been fortunate to have been able to learn, so easily and enjoyably, of the results of Mr Bourke's considerable research on the use of the potato crop.

The figure of 5% for waste is not, in my opinion, excessive. It agrees well with the losses due to shrinkage, sprouting and diseases other than blight, which have been reported in recent years. Drew and Deasy (*JDAF*, xl (1943)) reported a 5-11% loss in weight in three varieties after six months' storage in a clamp. The maximum level of disease was 5%. Wilson (*European Potato Journal*, v, no. 2) found a loss of 5% by shrinking alone when main crop potatoes were stored in a clamp until the end of May. Because of the lower incidence of mechanical damage, losses in store in pre-famine days might have been less than today.

The notes on the paper indicate that in 1951 44% of the crop was used as animal food, 15% was lost. A study by the Agricultural Institute suggests that in 1962 the total of animal feed and waste was 65%. Can we afford to grow a crop, two-thirds of which is used as a by-product or goes to waste? The use of potatoes for feeding animals is hardly justified nowadays.

The reason that farmers accept this situation may be historical. The low production standards still prevalent in many areas, and the feeling of the inevitability of blight may be due to his loss of faith in this crop. Many no longer consider potatoes as a crop to be grown for profit. Recent advances in cultivation techniques and the control of blight make this attitude indefensible.

Dr Neenan (written contribution): The difficulty of estimating yields and consumption in 1845 must have been great. Woodham-Smith has suggested that the human population may have been greatly underestimated in the 1841 census. What credence should we give to Dowdall's estimates of consumption? An intake of 12 lb. per day means the eating of 50-80 potatoes per day.

The figures for numbers of livestock are interesting; perhaps the lecturer would explain the correction made to the numbers of cattle in the 1841 enumeration. The time of the census is of importance if there is a seasonal breeding cycle in pigs. The figure of 12 lb. per pig is equivalent to 7-8 cwt of balanced feeding stuff. In 1841 diets were not balanced, the fattening period was longer and the housing probably poorer than at present. Unless there is a compensatory effect due to a seasonal variation in number, the estimate of 12 lb. appears low.

On the other hand, unless all potatoes were cooked, the daily intake of cattle was rather high.

Dr Bourke: thanked Dr O'Loan and Dr Nowlan for their kind remarks and interesting comments in proposing and seconding the vote of thanks. He was also grateful to Miss Frost not only for her own contribution but also for the points raised through her by Dr Neenan.

The present paper did not stand in isolation; it was just one piece of a large and complex jigsaw which covered the whole agricultural economy of 1845. For instance the sections of the paper which dealt with the oatmeal period, the oatmeal zone and the feeding of horses interlocked with a corresponding study of the use of the Irish oat crop, which in turn was related to the acreage under the crop and the national yield. The measure of agreement was remarkably high and justified confidence in the various statistics involved. The grand total of the acreages as calculated for the different crops (including hay and grass) corresponded closely with the available total of usable farming land; and the transition, both in acreages and yields, across the famine to the first official agricultural statistics of the era 1847-51 could be shown to be reasonable. The details would be found mainly in the speaker's works, referred to in notes 3 and 41, where a number of related matters which had come up during the discussion were treated in detail.

There was one point raised by Dr Neenan which deserved a few moments' consideration, since the prestige and wide circulation of Mrs Cecil Woodham-Smith's book involved a risk that her readers might be deceived into rejecting the enumeration of population which was carried out in the census of 1841.

What Mrs Woodham-Smith had written (*The great hunger*, p. 31) was as follows:

> It seems possible, moreover, that the census figure may be too low. Though the numerators of 1841 were largely members of the Irish Constabulary, superior to their predecessors and a 'highly disciplined body of men', much time, local knowledge and courage were needed to track down the communities of evicted and unemployed who existed in caves, sod huts and under tree-roots. An intelligent relief officer wrote that the census of 1841 was 'pronounced universally to be no fair criterion of the present population'. He had tested it in Co. Clare and found the population to be one third greater than had been recorded; therefore in 1845 when famine came the population might well have been above nine millions.

This conclusion is at variance with the consensus of informed opinion which has always considered that the 1841 enumeration of population had profited from the lessons of earlier censuses and could be accepted as accurate, whatever might be the deficiencies of agricultural data which were being collected for the first time. On reading it on the first publication of the book in 1962, Dr Bourke was convinced that it must be based on a misunderstanding of the evidence. In making written application to examine the original report in the State Paper Office [now the National Archives], he had justified his request in the following terms: the test carried out in County Clare could not conceivably have extended to the entire county, with its population of over a quarter of a million people; it was almost certainly confined to a small area containing no more than some thousands of people; his hope was that the original report would specify the area and prove his theory that it was a seaside district with access to seaweed for manure and possibly waste land to reclaim. If this were so, the evidence was not of an overall rise in population but of a *redistribution* arising from the well-documented flight from inland to the seashore, originating in the first place in the rise of the seaweed traffic as manure for the potato crop and supplemented later, after the onset of the famine, by reason of the availability of seafood.

The original document, a copy of a letter dated 5 December 1846 from Captain E. Wynne, inspecting officer of West Clare to Captain T. Larcom, proved to be even more specific than Dr Bourke had dared hope (National Archives, CSORP, 1846, W.22248):

> The census of 1841 being pronounced universally to be no fair criterion of the present population and consequent destitution, I tested the matter in the parish of Clondigad, Barony of Islands, where I found the present population more than a third greater than that of 1841. This I believe to be the case in all the districts along the coast, and to be caused entirely by the seaweed traffic, which has done an infinity of mischief. Squatters from all the southern counties have settled down and converted the county into one monster cottier farm.

Clondigad or Clondagad, on the estuary of the River Fergus, had returned in 1841 a population of 5,088 people, made up of 810 families. It was, according to Lewis's *Topographical dictionary* (second edition), a parish of 16,978 statute acres of which 4,711 acres were good arable and pasture, and the remainder improvable bog and mountain. There was 'a small rudely constructed quay at Ballycorig' which would have facilitated the gathering of seaweed.

Captain Wynne's complaint was thus not against the 1841 census as such, but against the use of its fine detail to quantify the 1845 population situation in those seaside parishes where the number of inhabitants had recently mushroomed, mainly because of the seaweed boom. There were several such districts in County Clare, notably in Kilmurry Ibrickan (Society of Friends, *Transactions*, p. 179); they were the scene of particularly severe suffering during the famine years.

Mrs Woodham-Smith was seriously in error in assuming that the rapid rise of population in these areas was representative of the country as a whole or that it cast doubt on the figures for total population collected in 1841.

CHAPTER 5

The average yields of food crops in Ireland on the eve of the great famine*

In order to analyse the food situation in Ireland in the early 1840s and to assess the disruption caused by damage to the potato crop in 1845 and the immediately subsequent years, it is necessary to know, *inter alia*, the average yield of the potato, oats and wheat crops in the years preceding the great famine. The first official statistics of crop yields in Ireland[1] were collected in 1847, at a time when the agricultural scene was radically disrupted by famine conditions. For earlier years there are many individual estimates in contemporary farming journals, but, quite apart from the considerable labour of collecting and analysing these figures,[2] there are problems of interpretation and judgement to be faced.

The first difficulty in assessing the evidence on yields of farm crops in Ireland prior to 1847 is the ambiguity of measures such as the 'bushel', the 'barrel' and the 'acre'. 'You want a book in your pocket to tell the different weights at the different markets you go to ... All the weights and measures differ in every district you go through. It is the most perplexing thing in the world.'[3]

The problem of the agricultural units of measurement of the period has been analysed in an earlier paper,[4] but even with the help of that partial guide, a number of yield estimates given, for instance, in the *Devon report* of 1845, remain ambiguous; in some cases, an examination of other evidence given by the same witness clarifies which units are being used.

Apart from uncertainty of units, many figures for pre-famine yields are unacceptable because they are unrepresentative or biased. Those calculated from small plots, often given special attention, are clearly unacceptable. Propagandists for prosperity under the union, and advocates of favoured varieties, or of special cultural or manurial practices, tended to give optimistic estimates. Where the clergyman was not 'a turbulent divine, who will have his rights', the yields agreed for tithing purposes were artificially low;[5] for this reason, data from the tithe applotment books, especially in a troublesome area like Tipperary,[6] are highly suspect.

Advocates of one crop as against another are also poor witnesses for the present purpose; in particular, enthusiasts for the turnip were apt to quote

* From *Journal of the Department of Agriculture and Fisheries*, lxvi (1969), pp 3-16.

low yields for the potato to the advantage of the favoured root. Naturally there is little information as to the produce of obscure smallholdings on the bogs or in the mountains; indeed most published yield estimates are those of the more prosperous and vocal cultivators.

It is convenient, if a little illogical, to quote first what are considered to be the best estimates of average yield of the major Irish crops in the early 1840s, and afterwards to review the available evidence in the light of these estimates:

Potatoes	6 tons per statute acre
Oats	13.0 cwt per statute acre
Wheat	12.5 cwt per statute acre
Barley	17.0 cwt per statute acre

Official crop returns from 1847

We shall consider first what relevant deductions may be drawn from the excellent series of agricultural statistics available for the period from 1847 to the present day. The data for potatoes, oats and wheat have been summarised in figures 1 to 3, which show, by means of five-yearly averages, the main trends in acreage and yield in the whole of Ireland. The causes of most of the marked peaks and troughs are indicated; the normal effect of war is to increase the acreage because of food requirements, and to decrease the mean yield because of the extension of cultivation into less suitable land, coupled with a shortage of imported fertilisers and of farm labour.

For our present purpose, the main interest lies in the earlier part of the yield curves; in this section, there is, on each of the graphs, a marked drop after the first ten years. Does this depression of yield over the period *c.* 1855-70 represent a real phenomenon, what caused it, and which section of the early yield curve, if either, approximates to the pre-famine situation?

Hancock,[7] who took a cheerful view of conditions in post-famine Ireland, suggested, without apparent conviction, that some minor changes in 1855 in the procedure for collecting yield estimates were responsible for the sharp downward trend in the figures. Formerly the estimates were made in November by the constabulary alone; henceforth they were made in January or February, and they were forwarded by the constabulary by way of the poor law guardians. 'The tendency,' says Hancock, 'of taking the opinion of the guardians has been to lower the rates of produce.'

However, it is not just the yields of potatoes, oats and wheat which showed a marked drop about this time, but also those of crops like barley and flax which were sold out of the farm for commercial use and of which the produce was, in effect, measured each year. Hancock himself admits,[8] at a time when the average potato yield was just above 3 tons per acre,

> I have been informed by persons of great experience that the produce of potatoes per acre has never since the famine at all equalled what it was before 1846,

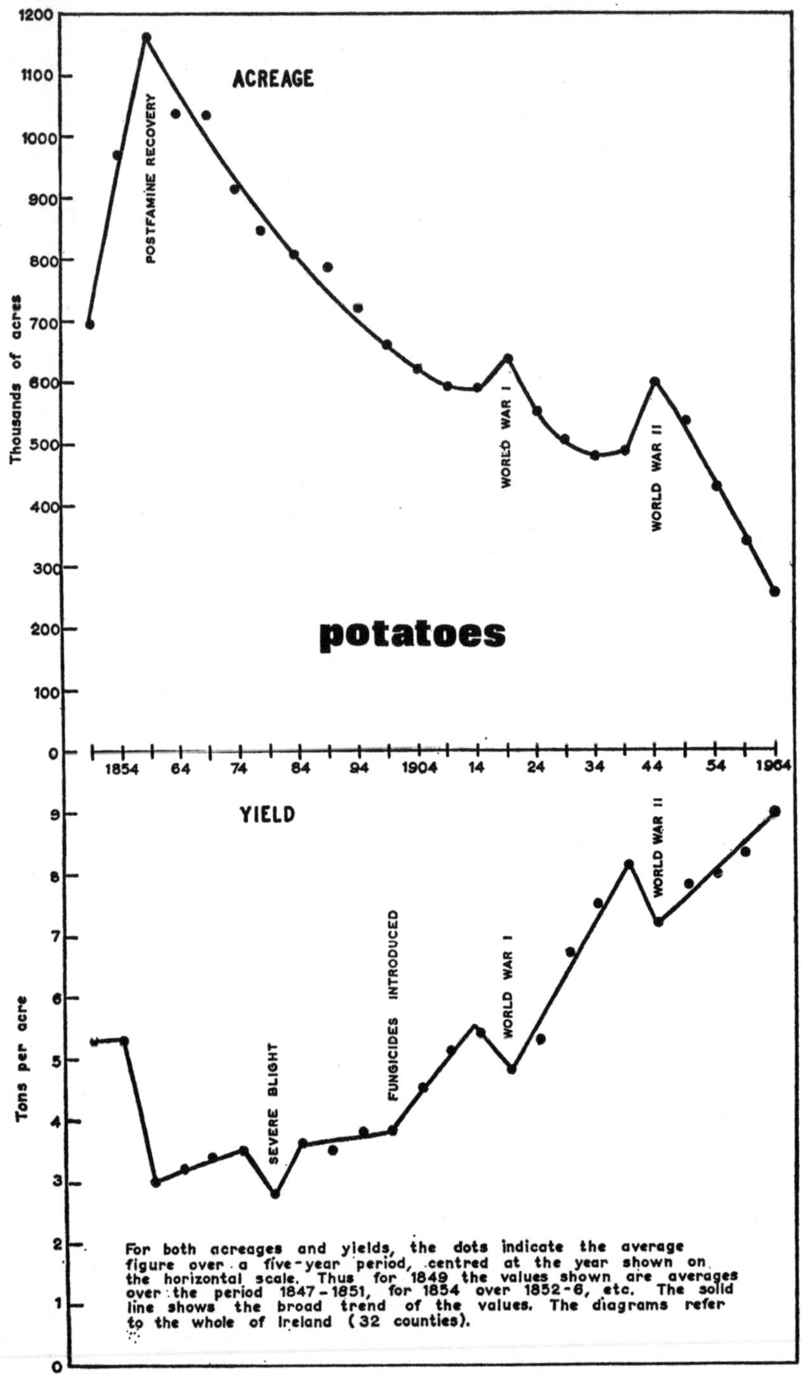

Fig. 1 Trends of acreage and yield of potatoes in Ireland, 1847 - 1966.

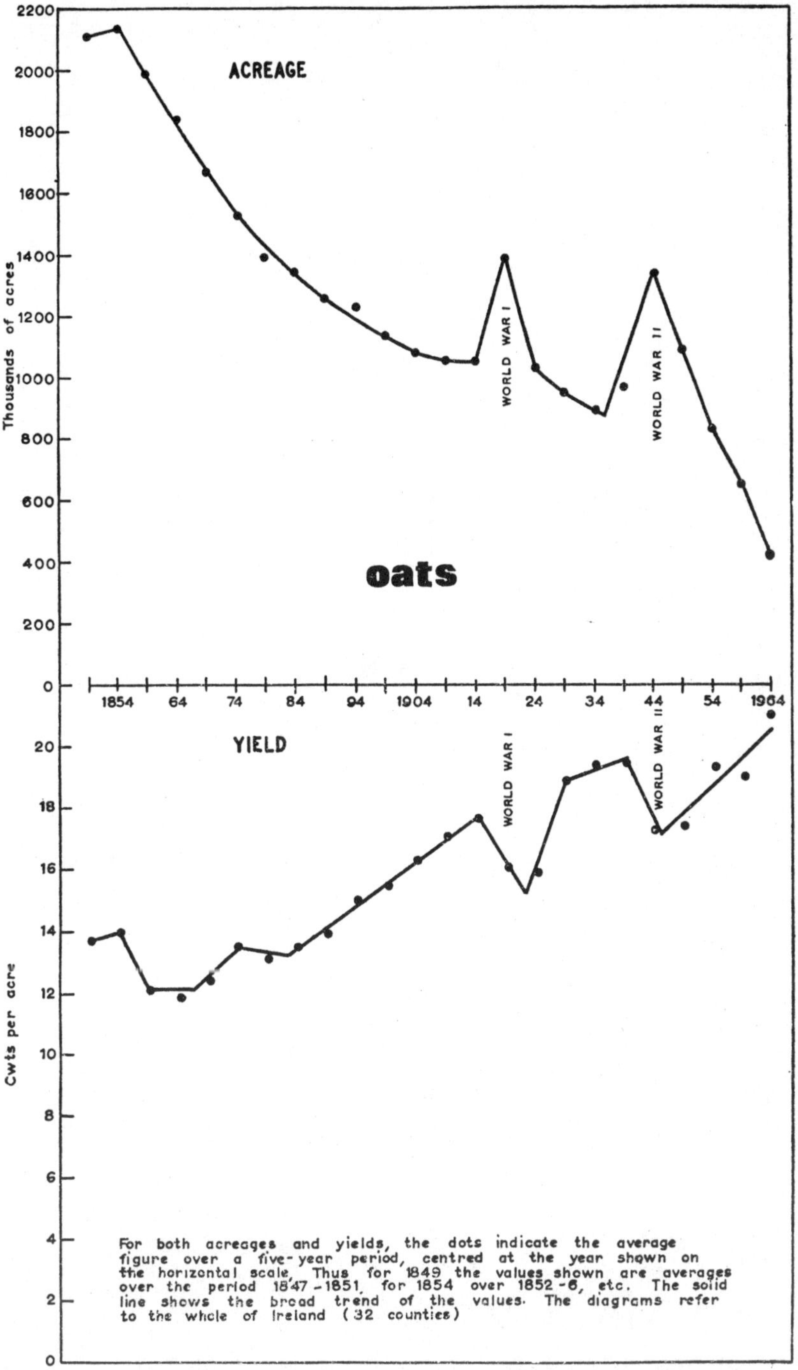

Fig. 2 Trends of acreage and yield of oats in Ireland, 1847 - 1966.

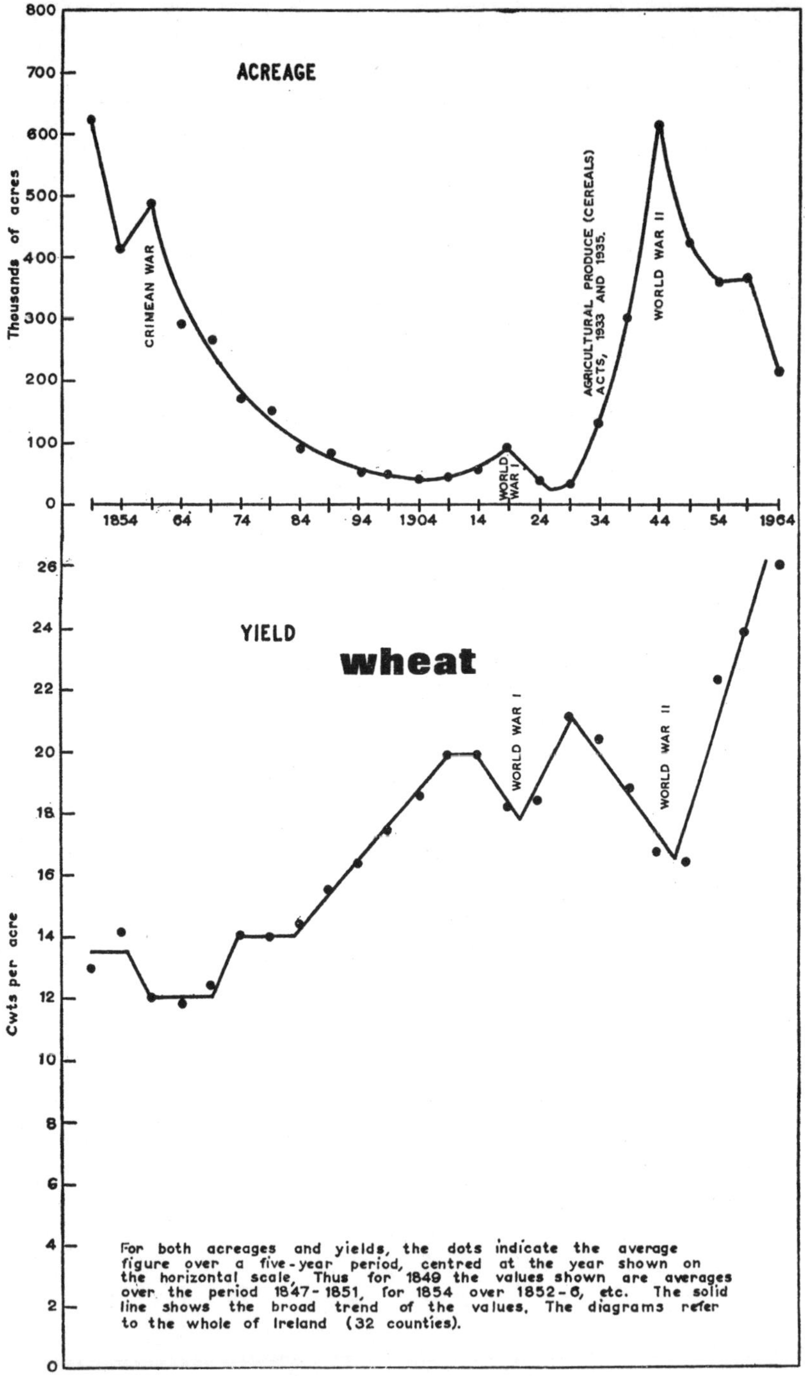

Fig. 3 Trends of acreage and yield of wheat in Ireland, 1847 - 1966.

being on an average about one-half. This circumstance my informants ascribe to something in the potato plant as inscrutable to our present knowledge as the potato disease itself.

In his classic study of Irish crop yield statistics, Barrington[9] accepts the reality of the post-famine collapse in general yields, and examines in detail the various factors, including weather and varieties, which might have been responsible. He concludes that the fall was due in part to less intensive methods of manual cultivation, with depletion in the supply of agricultural labour and with the plough replacing the spade, and in part to the decline in the intensive manuring which had been a feature of the pre-famine potato economy.[10]

We consider that the latter was the major factor, and one which explains better why the momentum of pre-famine yields was carried over into the earlier post-famine years, until the accumulated nourishment in the soil became exhausted. There followed a trough in yields, until the land act of 1870, which insured to the tenant compensation for improvements effected by him,[11] gave a stimulus to put new heart into the land, and until the rapid increase in cattle and the availability of artificial fertilisers provided the means of doing so. This is considered to be, on the whole, a more rational chronology of the wax and wane of soil fertility in the nineteenth century than that suggested, without detailed analysis of yield fluctuations, in an earlier paper.[12]

The section of the post-famine yield curve which may give some clue as to pre-famine conditions is, therefore, that referring to the years immediately following 1847. In the case of oats and wheat, the only complication is difference in acreage; a decline in the area under a crop, especially when those who drop out are the poorest and hold the worst land, tends to cause a rise in the mean yield. In the case of the potato crop, there is the additional major factor of losses due to blight which first appeared in Ireland in 1845. That the extent of these losses was considerable may be illustrated by comparing the rise of potato yields, after spraying with fungicides was introduced about 1900, with the simultaneous increase in other crops. Between 1895-9 and 1910-14, potato yields increased by 41% in comparison with an average rise of 16% in wheat, oats, barley, turnips and mangels.[13] This spectacular improvement, as a result of only partial protection against blight, suggests that the mean loss due to the disease in earlier years was well in excess of 20%.

Keeping in mind the altered circumstances, we shall review the range of yields in the earlier post-famine years.

The average extent of the oats crop in the five years 1847-51 was 2,100,000 acres. The range of annual mean yields was fairly narrow, from 13.3 to 14.7 cwt, with an average value of *13.7 cwt per acre*. Over the same five years the wheat crop covered 620,000 acres on the average. As might be expected with a crop which is rather marginal in the Irish climate, yields fluctuated considerably from season to season, ranging from 11.0 to 16.5 cwt, with an average value of *12.9 cwt per acre*.

Our pre-famine estimates for these two crops are close to, but somewhat below, the above values. The wheat crop was grown mainly in the south-east of Ireland where the impact of the famine was less severe; the scaling down of yield of wheat has been assessed at a rather lower value than in the case of oats. For barley, there is no reason to assume a pre-famine yield appreciably below the mean return for the period 1847-51, i.e. *17.3 cwt per acre.*

The post-famine yields of potatoes are almost totally irrelevant to the pre-blight situation. There was a very small acreage (284,000) in 1847, but in this dry season, blight caused little damage; the yield of 7.2 tons per acre was not exceeded until 1929, i.e. it stood as a record for over 80 years. In two good years subsequently (1853 and 1855) when the crop had recovered to nearly a million acres, the yield was over 6 tons per acre. Over the five years 1848-52, it averaged 4.8 tons per acre. By the period 1860-80 the mean yield had fallen to about 3 tons per acre, and during four of these years it reached 2 tons or less. About the turn of the century, the introduction of spraying led to a distinct improvement, particularly in wiping out the severe losses in wet years. Afterwards there were no yields below 3 tons, but, for a long time, none above 6 tons either. The modern era in potato returns began about 1927, from which date mean yields of 7 to 10 tons have normally been achieved.

Evidence before the Devon commission

The most abundant estimates of crop yields in Ireland in the 1840s are scattered throughout the evidence in the *Devon report* of 1845. The usable data have been assembled, converted to modern units, and classified in the following table.

SUMMARY OF EVIDENCE ON CROP YIELDS GIVEN BEFORE THE DEVON COMMISSION

(a) *Potato yields per statute acre:*

Estimate	*No. of witnesses*
4 tons or less	2
4.1 to 6.0 tons	12
6.1 to 8.0 tons	40
8.1 to 10.0 tons	16
More than 10 tons	5
TOTAL	75

The extreme estimates ranged from 1.9 to 12.3 tons, and the average was 7.4 tons.

(b) *Oats yields per statute acre:*

Estimate	*No. of witnesses*
6.1 to 8.0 cwt	1
8.1 to 10.0 cwt	5
10.1 to 12.0 cwt	10
12.1 to 14.0 cwt	23
14.1 to 16.0 cwt	20
16.1 to 18.0 cwt	21
18.1 to 20.0 cwt	14
20.1 to 22.0 cwt	6
22.1 to 24.0 cwt	2
TOTAL	102

The estimates ranged from 7.7 to 23.1 cwt, with an average value of 15.3 cwt.

(c) *Wheat yields per statute acre:*

Estimate	*No. of witnesses*
6.1 to 8.0 cwt	2
8.1 to 10.0 cwt	7
10.1 to 12.0 cwt	15
12.1 to 14.0 cwt	34
14.1 to 16.0 cwt	26
16.1 to 18.0 cwt	11
18.1 to 20.0 cwt	9
20.1 to 22.0 cwt	2
TOTAL	106

The estimates ranged from 6.2 to 21.6 cwt, with an average value of 13.9 cwt.

(d) *Barley yields per statute acre:*
Here there are only nine usable figures, much too small to form a representative sample. For what it is worth, the estimates ranged from 13.6 to 24.7 cwt, with a mean value of 18.3 cwt.

It must be taken into account that very few labourers and only a limited number of smallholders gave evidence before the Devon commission, which was mainly concerned with the tenure of land; the vast majority of these yield estimates were made by the more prosperous section of the community, and reflect the yields obtained under better conditions, when they were not just optimistic opinions designed to put a better face on agricultural conditions. They appear to be closer to the general picture in the case of barley and wheat than in the case of oats and potatoes. The yield values we have adopted for these four crops represent, in comparison with the average values of the Devon commission estimates, an approximate scaling down by 5%, 10%, 15% and 20%, respectively.

It would be impracticable to review here the evidence of individual witnesses before the Devon commission, but a few relevant points may be quoted.

Dr John Duke of Mohill[14] estimates that a good potato crop grown on the best land would average 7.5 tons per statute acre, 'but the people have not half that', due to shortage of manure and to late sowing.

Steuart Trench[15] gives a detailed account of potato cultivation on reclaimed bogland at a height of 1,000 feet in the Slievebloom mountains, which gave yields of from 4.6 to 8.3 tons per statute acre. Figures for reclamation of waste land in County Tyrone[16] include a yield of 4 tons per statute acre in the first year (with burning and liming, but no manure), rising to 8 tons in the second year when manure was used.

The earl of Mountcashell[17] gave the following breakdown of yields per statute acre in County Cork:

	Potatoes (tons)	*Wheat* (cwt)	*Oats* (cwt)
Grade 1 land	8.4	20.0	17.5
Grade 2 land	8.4	15.0	15.8
Grade 3 land	7.0	12.5	10.5
Grade 4 land	5.6	10.0	8.8
Grade 5 land	4.2	–	7.0
Grade 6 land	2.8	–	5.3

Evidence before the poor law inquiry

The produce obtained by the poorer grower is better represented in the evidence given before the poor law inquiry of 1836. A number of estimates on the potato crop, and a few on the oats crop, will be found in Appendix (F) to the *Poor inquiry*.[18] They do not lend themselves to tabulation, since they are presented, not as the opinions of individual witnesses, but in the form of a range of values covering the composite estimates of the assembled people. The range of values per statute acre for the potato crop is normally given as falling in the interval 4-8 tons, and frequently in the interval 5-6 tons. A Dublin estimate[19] gives a range of 3.9 to 4.7 tons for the Apple variety, and 5.4 to 6.2 tons (and occasionally up to 9.3 tons) for the more prolific Lumper. Evidence of the potato yields from conacre land of different grades may be broadly summarised in the formula that land let at £x per acre yielded 4/5x tons of potatoes. In all these statistics, the quoted values are for total yield of potatoes, including those considered to be fit only for seed or pigs.

The few estimates of oats yields before the poor law inquiry range from as low as 6.5 cwt to 16.2 cwt, i.e. consistently lower than those suggested to the Devon commission.

Other evidence

The contemporary statistician, Dowdall,[20] assumes an average potato yield of six and a quarter tons per statute acre, choosing this precise figure, equivalent to 1,000 stone, for ease of calculation. As a basis for this estimate he divides the potato growing land of Ireland into three categories:

– rich but limited land, such as the Golden Vale, the plains of Boyle and the alluvial valleys of Kerry, Mayo and Wicklow, giving average yields of about 9 tons.

– good land, rented at 30s. to 40s. an acre, giving average yields of 6 tons or slightly more.

– other land, representing the greatest area, and rented at about 20s. an acre, giving yields of 4 to 5 tons.

Dowdall[21] also gives some analysis of the variation of wheat yields in different parts of Ireland, and suggests an average production of 8 barrels (of 20 stone) to the Irish acre, equivalent to 12.3 cwt per statute acre. For oats he gives, without discussion, a mean yield of 11 barrels (of 14 stone) to the Irish acre, i.e. 11.9 cwt per statute acre.

'A gentleman of the first intelligence and experience', in the *Leinster Express* of 20 March 1847, assumes values as high as 17.5 cwt per statute acre for both wheat and oats, but also refers to a statement by Mr Labouchere in the house of commons in which the oats yield was taken as 10.5 cwt.

The produce of the wheat crop, in particular, varied with the quality of the land and the seasonal weather. In County Carlow, the average yield was placed as low as 10.8 cwt, but on good land, well-manured, 18.5 cwt was frequently obtained. 'In that great wheat year, 1812, Mr Alexander, near Carlow town, had 27.8 cwt and one or two individuals had 37 cwt to the statute acre. No crop since that remarkable season had come anywhere near such an average of produce.'[22]

The *Report on agriculture*[23] of 1836 quotes values for oats of 13.1 cwt, occasionally rising to 16.4 cwt; for wheat, 12.5 cwt and up to 14.0 cwt; and for barley 20.0 cwt. A moderate average potato crop is given in the *RDS Prize essays*[24] of 1835 as 6.7 tons per statute acre, and a corresponding crop of wheat as 12.2 cwt.

There is much information on Irish crop yields in the opening years of the nineteenth century in the county statistical accounts produced under the patronage of the RDS, but it is of doubtful relevance to our immediate problem.

It should be emphasised that the yield figures that we have proposed represent a nation-wide average, and are depressed, in the case of oats and, more particularly, of potatoes, by the low produce of inferior land and the difficulties of cultivation experienced by the poorer growers. Thus, as against a mean potato yield of 6 tons, it could be said[25] that a produce of double this amount was 'by no means an inferior but rather a superior one'. In good and well-cultivated land it was not exceptional 'to see 20 to 25 tons of Cups, and the same of Lumpers (provincially called Horsepotatoes) to an (Irish) acre'.[26] The maximum pre-famine potato yield from a statute acre in Ireland is given as 32.2 tons;[27] this is consistent with a figure of 34.4 tons in England.[28] Both values compare well with the modern best figure, according to the Department of Agriculture, of 35.3 tons obtained with the variety Arran Banner in Donegal, which suggests that the maximum yield potential of the potato has not altered much in over a hundred years.

Trend of yields

The average Irish potato yield about 1779 is given by Young[29] as 6.5 tons per statute acre. About thirty years later Wakefield[30] calculated it to be 6.1 tons. The best evidence of potato yields on the eve of the famine suggests a figure of 6 tons. It is remarkable to find so small a difference over a period of nearly seventy years. It would seem that the decline in average fertility of land arising from the extension of the crop was almost exactly compensated by the development and extended cultivation of inherently prolific varieties.

No evidence of any marked trend in the produce of oats has been found. There was, however, a considerable improvement in the yields of wheat in Ireland during the first half of the nineteenth century;[31] produce per acre had risen by about 20% and increased exports of wheat and flour were attributed to higher yields rather than to any increase in acreage.

This trend of wheat yield to gain in comparison with oats yield continued at a rather uniform rate during the second half of the nineteenth century. The data, as presented in figure 4, provide the basis for the differential of 0.5 cwt between our adopted pre-famine yield figures for wheat and oats.

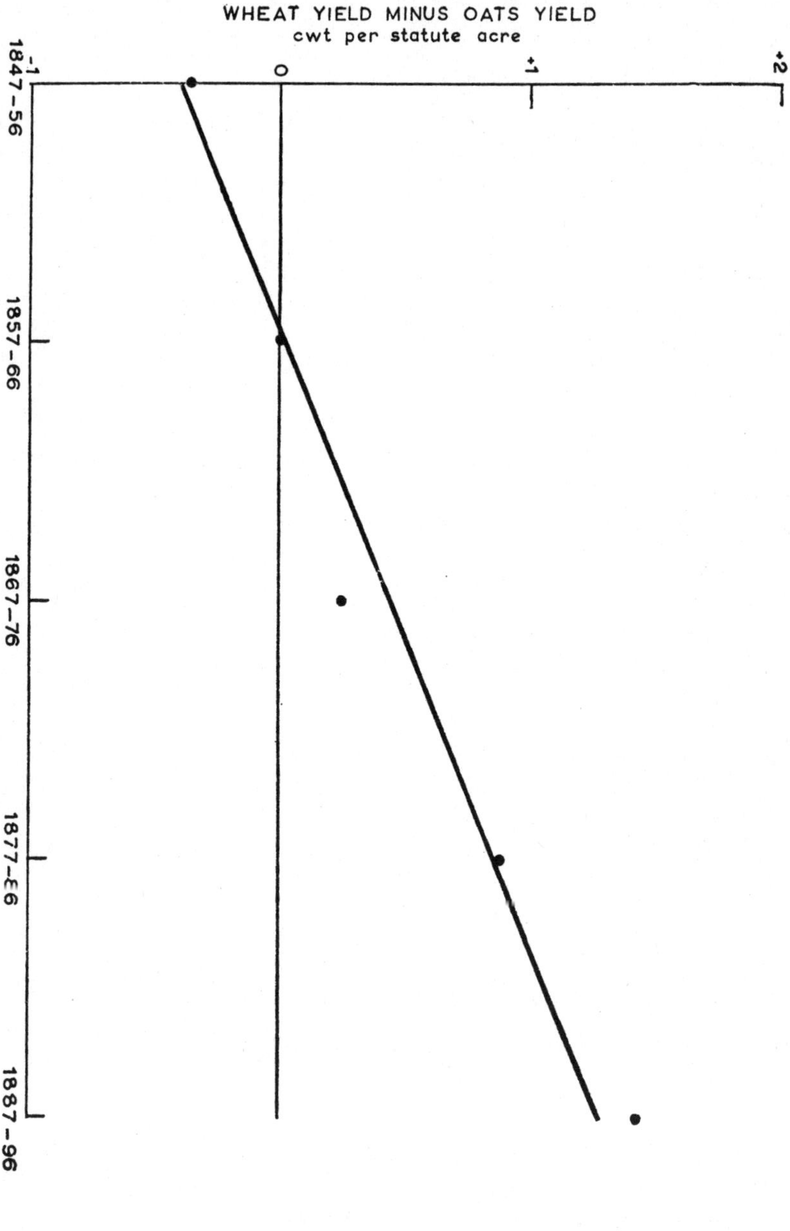

Fig. 4 Trend of excess of average wheat yields over oats yields in the nineteenth century. (means of ten year periods)

PART II

The famine

CHAPTER 6

Potato blight in Europe in 1845: the scientific controversy*

Potato blight in North America, 1843-5

Two years before the first great European epidemic of potato blight (*Phytophthora infestans* [Mont.] de Bary), the disease had broken out in the USA in the hinterland of the great east coast ports. Figure 1 (below, p. 142), which illustrates the rapid spread of the disease in the years 1843-5, is based largely on Stevens,[1] with some extra information in respect of Canada.[2] Americans had thus the earliest opportunity to speculate on the cause of the outbreak. In a pamphlet published in Boston, Bosson[3] attributed the disease to an exhaustion of the vital forces of the potato, similar to the deterioration which he observed in the royal families of Europe, where successive generations of inbreeding had culminated in 'a race of dwarfs and idiots'. Not everyone subscribed to this sturdy republican diagnosis. Bosson reports that J. E. Teschemacher of Boston had suggested that fungi were responsible for the disease, a theory which, in Bosson's view, had 'the merit of novelty, if little else'. Indeed the idea of a fungal cause of the disease was summarily dismissed in the USA as an amusing aberration. Teschemacher had submitted an account of his views to the New York State Agricultural Society in December 1844, but his paper was completely ignored, nor had the author taken the precaution to keep a copy. In the following year, when the agricultural section of the annual report of the US commissioner of patents reproduced European publications which initially seemed to favour a fungal explanation of the disease, Teschemacher, now anxious to establish priority, was chagrined to have to confess that his evidence had disappeared 'amongst things lost or forgotten'.[4]

Ailments of the European potato crop prior to 1845

By 1845 over two and a half centuries had elapsed since the Spaniards first brought the potato to Europe from South America. Although the potato had always been subject to direct damage by extreme weather conditions

* From *British Mycological Symposium*, xvii, *Phytophthora*, ed. J. Lucas *et al.* (Cambridge, 1991), pp 12-24.

– sustained drought, excessive rainfall, severe frost – it was not until the 1760s that a specific major disease of the crop was recognised. This was the 'curl', later to be identified as a virus disease, but attributed at the time to a gradual 'degeneration' of the seed, a diagnosis which had at least the merit of providing a ready-made explanation of later diseases, in which each new ailment was seen as the consequence of progressive degeneration.

It was again generally blamed for the 'taint', a dry rot of the potato tuber caused by *Fusarium spp.* which caused concern in Britain and Ireland in the early 1830s and later affected continental Europe. It reached its greatest intensity in Germany in 1841, and inspired the Bavarian government to commission a world-famous botanist, ethnologist and explorer, C. F. P. von Martius, to investigate and report on the problems besetting the potato. This he did in a classic study[5] which was at once recognised as a major contribution.

One of the pioneer features of von Martius's work was that he made it quietly clear that he was satisfied that dry rot was caused by a parasitic fungus. No one of von Martius's scientific and social standing had previously advanced so unorthodox an opinion, which, to some, smacked of heresy. In those pre-Pasteur days, long before the germ theory of disease began to find favour, the accepted wisdom was that spores, bacteria and germs were not a cause but a consequence of disease; they appeared by spontaneous generation after the organism had fallen ill. A few idiosyncratic thinkers took the contrary view, but the organised ranks of science, and, in particular, the learned societies, as always staunch supporters of orthodox opinion, stood firm in their distrust of novelty. Thus von Martius's report created something of a sensation. It was welcomed by progressive thinkers in many countries; Berkeley, for instance, translated it into English and had much of it published in the *Gardeners' Chronicle*. It would shortly encourage some emboldened fungalists to come out of their closets and declare themselves.

One further consequence of the dry rot outbreak in continental Europe in the 1840s may well have led to the accidental introduction of an even more serious disease. In a move to make the crop more healthy, the provincial government of West Flanders voted funds for the importation of fresh potato varieties from North and South America, and these imports were the subject of field trials in the years 1843-5. It was in West Flanders that potato blight was first reported in 1845.

First theories as to the cause of blight

The broad timetable of the European blight epidemic of 1845 is illustrated in figure 2 (below, p. 142).[6]

The outbreak first came to attention in Belgium in the last week of June. Local pundits had a head start in speculating as to its cause. Theories were already being put forward in the Low Countries as early as July. The disease did not manifest itself in the environs of Paris until mid-August, and specimens of affected foliage were first exhibited to a learned society there on 20 August. Simultaneously with publication of the news of the arrival of the epidemic in southern England in the *Gardeners' Chronicle* of 23 August, the scholarly editor, Professor John Lindley, committed himself firmly to the view that the cold and cheerless summer of 1845 was to blame. The weather theory, which had already been advanced by several Belgian commentators, was widely adopted in England thanks to the prestige and influence of Lindley; thus the Royal Agricultural Society awarded all three of its prizes for essays on the potato disease to protagonists of a meteorological cause.

While the majority of the earliest commentators held the weather to be the culpable factor, some argued that blight was merely a further downwards step in the progressive deterioration of the potato; others that it was due to insects or worms. A small group opted for a poisonous 'miasma' borne on the air, but differing as they did as to its origin, published individual pamphlets in support of industrial pollution,[7] volcanic exhalations,[8] gases from the recently introduced sulphur matches,[9] or 'some aerial taint originating in outer space'.[10]

A remarkable feature in retrospect is the fact that the true explanation was advanced at the very earliest stages in a series of newspaper articles written independently by a number of Belgian commentators, so that for a short time, until massive opposition overwhelmed it, it looked as if the truth might prevail.

Writing in *L'Organe des Flandres* of 31 July and 1 August, the Abbé Edouard van den Hecke, who was grand vicar to the bishop of Versailles and a keen amateur mycologist, reported on his examination of diseased potato leaves under high magnification. He discovered a fungus of the Botrytis family and was particularly struck by the unusual mechanism by which the spores were projected to a distance. He believed the fungus to be the true cause of the disease but modestly sought confirmation by others. Meanwhile he advised the early removal and destruction of affected potato foliage.

Professor Martin Martens of the University of Louvain, in a contribution to the *Journal de Bruxelles* of 14 August, also gave the apparent cause of the disease as a fungus which attacked the leaves, especially on their lower faces. He too advised the removal of diseased tops. He repeated his opinion in a letter dated 10 September, although he admitted there were difficulties. However, in a paper read to the Royal Academy of Brussels some months later, when the fungal theory was under severe attack, he prudently distanced himself from a cause which he confessed he had 'to a certain degree adopted' in his earlier writings.

On 19 August the *Journal de Liége* published a letter, written on 14 August, from Anne-Marie Libert, a cultured lady of leisure and a self-taught mycologist of international repute. She gave a clear and detailed description of the fungus responsible for the disease, but mistakenly believed it to be identical with one, *Botrytis farinacea*, described some years earlier by Fries. She suggested, in view of the devastation which it was causing, that the specific name should be changed to *vastatrix*.

At a meeting of the Agronomic Society of Thorout, held on 18 August and reported in the *Nouvelliste des Flandres* of 25 August, Dr René van Oye said that the one true determining cause of the potato disease was a fungus which, reproducing itself with astonishing rapidity and profuseness, had infected all the potato fields, and that the disease was clearly contagious.

In these early commentaries there had thus been a broad measure of agreement among some prominent Belgian savants, who put forward their opinions in the main with seemly restraint. The tone would become more strident at times in the immediately following stage.

The background of the dramatis personae

The subsequent phase of the controversy on the role of the fungus in the potato disease can be better understood against the background of the careers of three of the principal protagonists who now entered the field.

Two Belgian orphans, Charles Morren and Joseph Decaisne, grew up as close neighbours and schoolmates in Brussels; both embarked on scientific careers which soon diverged. After earning a doctorate in natural philosophy and mathematical science in 1829, Morren went to Paris on a travelling studentship, only to be recalled when Belgium became independent to assume the professorship of physics at Gand in replacement of his departing Dutch predecessor. His subsequent career was one of unbroken success. While at Gand he widened his scope by taking a medical degree, although he never practised as a doctor. Finding the climate of Gand uncongenial, he transferred to the professorship of botany at Liége. In 1842 a special new professorship of botany, agriculture and economic forestry was created for him, which enabled him to offer public courses popularising agricultural science which were designed particularly for extensive landowners.

Over all these years Morren's output of technical papers was prodigious and often controversial, for he hurled himself joyfully into many disputes. He sat on numerous commissions, many of them governmental, served on university examination boards, and edited several scholarly periodicals to which he was often the main contributor. He prided himself on revising his university courses each year to take account of the latest developments. Inevitably there were those, particularly in academic circles, who looked on Morren's high-flying career with less than complete enthusiasm, and who would not be broken-hearted should he come a cropper in one or other of his manifold activities.

Meanwhile Morren's old boyhood schoolmate Decaisne had been pursuing a rather less spectacular scientific career. By 1845 he was employed as assistant naturalist at the Museum of Natural History in Paris. This post, as Semal, Joly and Lamy[11] stress, was more important than its title might suggest, but it clearly represented a lower level of attainment than Morren's academic honours.

Also in Paris, working as a freelance mycologist, was Jean François Camille Montagne, who too was an orphan from infancy. (Orphans abounded in the post-Napoleon years.) Montagne had served in the French armed forces, first as a boy sailor and later as a military doctor. Retired from the army in 1831 at the age of forty-seven, he devoted the rest of his life to mycology. He was driven by two ambitions; first to fill a lacuna in French expertise which forced naturalist explorers, who brought home to France botanical specimens from the ends of the earth, to send them abroad to Sweden, Germany or England for identification and description, and secondly, to earn for himself election to membership of the French Academy of Sciences. He is credited with working on his speciality for ten hours per day over twenty years, and with introducing, describing and depicting nearly 2,000 specimens. For all his industry, he gathered a mere seven votes when he first tried for membership of the Academy in 1837. Clearly he could do with a spectacular addition to his mycological credits if he was to attract the support of the scientific electorate.

The entry of the big guns

On 18 August Morren issued his first broadside on the subject of the potato disease in the form of a letter to *L'Indépendance Belge* newspaper in which it was given first-page billing in the issue of 20 August. It was written with all of Morren's accustomed assurance and in his most trenchant style. He dismissed out of hand all earlier speculations with the exception of those of the two pro-fungal exponents (van den Hecke and Martens) which had first been published. The true cause of potato blight was a fungus of the Botrytis kind, similar to that which von Martius associated with dry rot of the potato. It was just one further example of the series of parasitic plants such as caused ergot of rye, rust of wheat and smut of oats and maize. In a learned paper which he would submit to the Royal Academy of Science of Brussels when that body resumed its meetings in the autumn, he would depict all phases of the development and reproduction of the fatal mould. Meanwhile he was publishing the present simplified account to counter the propaganda of certain persons whose blind hatred of what they called the theory of agriculture led them to mock that deeper knowledge which alone could enlighten practice and put an end to a deplorable empiricism.

The article concluded with ten items of practical advice on how to counter the disease, beginning with a repetition of van den Hecke's suggestion of removing and burning all diseased foliage. Affected tubers should also be destroyed and maximum sanitation practised. A mixture of copper sulphate, lime, salt and water should be used to dip potato seed and to disinfect the soil. Autumnal sowing was also suggested.

Morren made further contributions to the same newspaper on 2, 4 and 9 September. He combined and edited the content of all these articles in a major brochure[12] which was published in Brussels on 22 September in French and Flemish. In view of French interest in the work, a revised version of the brochure[13] was published in Paris on 1 October. In the middle of all this activity, Morren[14] managed to prepare his promised scientific article which was completed on 24 September and read to the Brussels Academy on 4 October.

Of all these publications, the one which created the greatest impact was the initial article of 18 August. It was, with remarkable speed, distributed, translated and reprinted throughout western Europe. It was reproduced even in North America.[15] More significantly, it appeared as early as 21 August in the official French publication *Journal des Débats* and was there seen by Montagne who was himself hard at work on specimens of diseased potato foliage which he had received three days earlier from a grower in the outskirts of Paris, and who was, no doubt, relieved to learn that Morren's scientific paper was not imminent. He had written a letter to his scholarly friend, Berkeley, in England, which the latter received on 26 August, enclosing specimens and recounting the description of the fungus which he planned to publish in Paris very shortly. In this letter he expressed some uncertainty as to the basic cause of the disease, but he recognised that it was closely connected with the fungus.

On the same day that he received Montagne's letter, Berkeley wrote to the *Gardeners' Chronicle*[16] saying that he had so far failed to locate the disease in Northamptonshire and that, in the absence of direct evidence, he was inclined to go along with Lindley's view in the previous issue that the continued wet weather was the primary cause of the malady. However, by the date of the following issue,[17] the disease had made a dramatic appearance all around Berkeley's home at King's Cliffe, and he wrote that having now seen the disease in situ he had no doubt that it was caused by the fungus *Botrytis infestans*, Mont., a title which Montagne had registered a few days earlier and which Berkeley was the first to utilise.

The counter-attack

Meanwhile the storm clouds were massing around Morren's head in Belgium. Already in his second letter to *L'Indépendance*,[18] Morren commented on the controversy which his earlier letter had aroused. The discussion, he said, had taken a rancorous turn in some journals. He himself would refrain from responding to insults, or malicious insinuations, or to comments inspired by evil passion. Quoting Linnaeus, he intended, he said, to devote the years which remained to him to useful work, and to waste no time in replying to his enemies. Errors in natural history could not long be defended; truth could not long be concealed. It was to time that he would entrust his reputation.

One of the earlier critics was Dieudonné,[19] who in a report commissioned by the public health authority of Brussels had denounced Morren's thesis which, he said, would hang for ever like a sword of Damocles over the heads of potato growers, if common sense, observation and long experience did not enable them to judge it aright. In order that the fungus might not become the terror of the farmers, this unfortunate and depressing thesis must be exposed. Even more barbed criticism came from some who had earlier rushed to clamber on to what they had mistakenly thought to be Morren's bandwagon but who found it advisable, in view of the violent reaction in many influential quarters, to declare themselves as born-again antifungalists. Typical of these was Boset[20] who admitted that he had first been deluded by Morren's thesis which he later recognised to have been modelled on 'the vagaries of von Martius'. In a bitter personal diatribe he condemned Morren as an armchair scientist who rushed into print in pursuit of precedence and publicity, a man notorious for his anxiety to add his torch of wisdom to the communal fire, a controversialist too eager to break a lance in all kinds of scientific tournaments.

Morren's vow of silence was not proof against such taunts and he was quickly stung to reply in kind. Thus, for example:

> not a fortnight ago some one wrote in all solemnity: 'The sun will soon dispose of M. Morren's fungi and make short work of all these microscopic fabrications.' Today it is my turn to answer: the only microscopic factor involved is the range of vision of some people. If the sun, which has spared both the fungus and the disease, has disposed of anything it is the inanity of the harebrained.[21]

Heavily beleaguered as he was in Belgium, Morren was heartened by news of support from abroad, first the declaration of the 'learned M. Berkeley'[22] and secondly the avowal of Dr Montagne, who, 'like all true savants', had recognised that the disease was caused by a fungus.[23] It was true that the doubts which Montagne had earlier expressed in his letter to Berkeley appear to have melted away in the blazing conviction of Morren's first article which he had read in the *Journal des Débats* of 21 August. Certainly there was a tone of utter conviction in the presentation of Montagne to the Société Philomatique of Paris on 30 August in which he laid claim to priority in describing and naming the fungus.[24] Indeed he gave fulsome praise to Morren's article in which, he said, the deleterious effects of the parasite had been perfectly depicted, and the cause and nature of the malady fully explained. Had Morren gone on to name and describe the microscopic fungus which was responsible for all the damage, there would have been nothing left to add. As it was, Montagne proceeded to propose the name 'only too well deserved', of *Botrytis infestans* and to add a description in Latin of the fungus.

No sooner had Montagne, well satisfied with a job well done, finished his presentation than two members of his audience rose to speak in turn. The first was Decaisne, the one-time schoolmate of Morren, and the other was Duchartre, editor of the *Revue Botanique*. Their purpose was not to congratulate, but to denounce the concept of a fungal parasite; indeed this early passage of arms was merely the first engagement in a running battle, directed primarily against Morren, which they kept up for months. It culminated in Decaisne's pamphlet[25] which was designed to be a counter blast to Morren's tracts.[26] In the concluding paragraph, Decaisne argued that Morren's thesis, which had done so much to spread panic among the population, was based on nothing more than observational error, and that, no matter what tortuous arguments he advanced, Morren would soon find himself alone if he persisted with his hypothesis.

And indeed Montagne, seeing that he risked losing favour with the French academicians who, with one sole exception (A. Payen), were strongly opposed to the fungal theory, tried at once to retreat into a neutral corner, and later took up a mildly antifungal stand. At the Société Philomatique meeting he expressed to his critics his regrets that the terms in which he had spoken could be interpreted as support for Morren's thesis, and protested that his sole purpose had been to describe and register the fungus, irrespective of whether it was the cause or consequence of the disease.

Montagne wrote forthwith to Berkeley describing the controversy into which he had unwittingly been drawn, and recalling the doubts which he had expressed in a previous letter, and to which he was now reverting. Berkeley, in his kindly way, replied that he could understand his friend's uncertainty; he acknowledged the difficulties of the case and himself remained open to conviction. Never given to dogmatic claims, he continued, in his 1846 paper, to state his opinion with a moderation unusual at the time:

> After an attentive consideration of the progress of the disease and of almost everything of value that has been written on the subject, and after duly weighing the peculiar difficulties with which it is attended, I must candidly confess, that, with a becoming share of philosophical doubt where such authorities are ranged upon the opposite side, I believe the fungal theory to be the correct one.

Such convoluted restraint was wide open to misinterpretation by a foreigner; certainly Montagne understood from Berkeley's letter that the latter had modified his original views. He hastened to convey the happy tidings to Duchartre who gave prominence in the *Revue Botanique*[27] to the news of the defection of the 'talented English mycologist', who was now disposed to seek the prime cause of the disease elsewhere than in the fungus, and to the claim that, in Duchartre's view, Morren now stood in absolute isolation. Curiously Berkeley[28] made almost the same comment: the fungal theory 'is now peculiar almost to Dr Morren, unless M. Payen is to be reckoned also as its advocate'. In fact, Payen, like Berkeley himself, was a firm believer but no missionary; he was satisfied to eschew controversy and wait for time to prove him right. Active propagandists for the fungal theory, now in low repute, were hard to find, and there were few new adherents. A remarkable exception was the Scot, David Moore, curator of the Dublin Botanic Gardens, who had at first subscribed to the weather theory but who, as a result of his own painstaking experiments, became a public convert to the fungal hypothesis at a time when it was being generally derided.[29]

And afterwards...

(a) The fungal theory

By the end of 1845 the vocal adherents of a fungal cause of the potato disease had dwindled to a beleaguered handful. At the 1846 meeting of the British Association in Southampton, the one point of virtual unanimity about the potato disease was that a fungus was not responsible. 'That the fungi were the cause had now been disproved by the best chemists,' said Dr Lankaster and Dr Solly agreed that the fungal theory 'had lost ground, latterly, very materially'.[30] In Britain it could be written that

> the notion that the fungi which have been detected are the cause of the disease has been abandoned by most of the writers on the subject, and they are all but proved, in most persons' estimation, to be the effect: amongst practical men it has been, all along, treated as a chimera.[31]

It was the same in France: the argument that fungi caused the disease was 'almost completely abandoned'.[32] The idea was derided even in contemporary popular ballads:[33]

> Some cock their glasses up to their eye,
> And mushrooms in the cells descry,
> But we, my Lords, have looked as well,
> And think such notions all a sell;
> Decaisne in France, in Germany Kützing,
> Have sought the rot all manner of roots in,
> And proved that those have looked with a loose eye
> Who said 'twas caused by fungi and fuci
> (Sure, never since the days of Plato
> Was there such a row about a rotten potato).

Ten years after blight had first ravaged Europe, Berkeley was still writing with circumspection in the *Cyclopaedia of agriculture*:[34]

> There are two theories which, in the present position of the subject, seem to us at all tenable – the fungal theory, and that which ascribes the disease to a vicious

mode of cultivation pursued through many years. It is not our intention to decide between them, and although we are certainly disposed to lay the greater stress upon the former, which is gaining ground and gives full conviction to many minds, we acknowledge that there are great difficulties about it, and such as to make it far from becoming to speak dogmatically.

Berkeley was correct in saying that the pendulum of scientific opinion was slowly swinging in his direction, although the more diehard opponents such as Baron de Croeser were calling for the final abandonment of the fungal theory as late as 1860. In the very next year de Bary[35] published the first of the two famous papers in which the life cycle of the potato blight fungus was described, and its responsibility for the disease irrefutably established.

(b) The name of the fungus

It was soon realised that the blight fungus did not fit well into the Botrytis genus, and it was reclassified as Peronospera by Unger in 1847 and Caspary in 1852. Much later, in 1876, de Bary set up a new home for the fungus and renamed it as *Phytophthora*.

The specific adjective *infestans* survived, but only after fierce controversy. Its connotation of something aggressive, hostile and dangerous remained an embarrassing reminder to Montagne of his earlier acceptance of the parasitic role of the fungus. Indeed in a letter to Montagne reported by Duchartre,[36] Desmazières suggested that *fallax* be used in place of *infestans* as a permanent reminder of how an innocuous fungus had led so many scientists astray. In a move towards an acceptable compromise Harting[37] suggested the neutral *solani* but gained no support.

There was also a school of thought that would assign the credit for naming the fungus to Miss Libert and use her adjective *vastatrix*.[38] Berkeley[39] supported the attribution to Montagne, and although the argument was revived in recent years by Puttemans,[40] Montagne's name and adjective have survived.

(c) The principals

Berkeley had always remained on the outer fringe of the blight controversy, partly because of his courteous and pacific nature, partly because his scientific paper[41] was published at a time when acceptance of the fungal theory was at its lowest ebb. Consequently what came in time to be ranked as a major work earned little immediate recognition. In his prize essay on the potato disease Graham[42] referred dismissively to Berkeley's 'elaborate memoir', in which blame was assigned 'to a species of botrytis which, singularly enough, had never been observed before'.

Outside of Britain, the erroneous reports that Berkeley had abandoned the fungal theory persisted for years, despite a correction by Berkeley in a footnote to his 1846 paper, and a withdrawal and apology by Duchartre.[43]

The rumour was repeated as fact by Roze[44] in his great *History of the potato*. Prunet[45] takes the story further in claiming that Berkeley, in time, took his place among the advocates of antiparasitism. Jones, Giddings and Lutman[46] brought the legend to its finest flowering in suggesting that Berkeley had lent his authority to supporting 'all the ignorance and superstition of the time in opposition to Morren'. Even in England official recognition and honours came belatedly to Berkeley, but the passage of time (he lived to eighty-six years) brought his genius into clearer focus.

As for Decaisne who had so doggedly attacked Morren's thesis, there is a certain irony in the fact that he was, in the year 1863, joint editor of the French journal in which was published the second part of de Bary's justification of the views of Decaisne's old antagonist. But Morren alas, did not live long enough to savour the triumph of his views. He took seriously ill in 1854 at the age of forty-seven, and died four years later without resuming his labours. The Belgian *Biographie Nationale* attributed his early death to an excessive work load over almost thirty years. The hyperactivity which marked his whole life suggests some inner imbalance which prevented him from earning the recognition that his brilliant intelligence merited, and aroused the fierce opposition to his views which, without much doubt, contributed to his early death.

On a happier note, Montagne gradually re-established himself in good favour with the French scientific establishment, and was elected virtually unanimously to the Academy of Sciences in 1852. He died in 1866 at the age of eighty-two.

CHAPTER 7

Emergence of potato blight, 1843-6*

No outbreak of a plant disease, before or since, has received the public attention given to the epidemic of potato blight (*Phytophthora infestans* [Mont.] de Bary) which commenced in Europe in 1845. The detailed consideration of the disease in agricultural journals like the *Gardeners' Chronicle* is not surprising; it is more unexpected to find no fewer than 66 entries on the subject in the official Belgian gazette, *Le Moniteur Belge*, during the five-month period, August-December 1845, and a number of articles in the French *Journal des Débats*.

The first appearances of blight were mostly recorded in local newspapers, which sometimes were led by political or sectional allegiances to minimise or exaggerate its intensity and extent. In the professional press, there was quite an amount of sharp jostling as to which group was most competent to deal with the outbreak. The medical men felt that all disease fell within their ambit, so the *Lancet*, in common with the corresponding continental journals, gave considerable space to the epidemic. In Ireland, the *Dublin Medical Press*, feeling the first chill breath of socialised medicine, suspected that governmental concern about food shortage, famine and fever was merely a stratagem to ease the passage of a 'medical charities bill', and for a long time denied the gravity of the situation. The chemists argued that the potato rot was primarily a chemical change and thus came within their field of competence; for this they earned the scorn of the London *Medical Times*, which dismissed them as 'the Giessen-bitten boys of the present day', mesmerised by 'the talismanic name of Liebig'. Commercial concern, and, in particular, possible repercussions on the grain market, explain the continued interest of journals like the *Mark Lane Express*; but, in fact, every periodical from the *Bankers' Circular* to *Punch* featured blight to such an extent that the American *Monthly Journal of Agriculture* was moved to complain that the British papers of the time spoke of nothing except the potato disease and the railway mania. The botanists and mycologists were quite outnumbered in this rush into print; the plant pathologists had not yet been invented.

The epidemic broke out at an awkward time for the learned societies. Some, like the Société Royale et Centrale d'Agriculture of Paris, were

* Reprinted by permission from *Nature*, cciii (22 August 1964), pp 805-8. Copyright © 1992 Macmillan Magazines Ltd.

summoned back by ministerial demand from their summer holidays to urgent special sessions; the remainder made up for lost time when they reassembled in the autumn. Many set up special committees to examine and to experiment on the disease, and, in due course, to add to the voluminous and perplexed reports which were emanating from officially inspired commissions in Belgium, Holland, France and Ireland. But it was the pamphleteers who had the real field day. An eruption of brochures broke out all over western Europe, written by physicians, surgeons, botanists, noblemen, pharmaceutical and other chemists, geologists, excisemen, gardeners and accountants; even a plain housewife added her meed of wisdom. Many of these pamphlets put forward highly eccentric views, but few were without useful factual information.

Although the attack took Europe completely by surprise, blight had already been ravaging the potato crops of North America in the previous two seasons. Stevens[1] has charted the annual progress of the disease, from its beginnings in 1843 in the five states closest to the great ports of the east coast of the United States, to an expanded area in 1845 which closely approximates to the limits within which blight is a serious problem today. Fig. 1 is based primarily on Stevens's work, with the addition of a limited amount of extra information on the impact of the disease in Canada. The diagram bears quite a resemblance to charts of the ten-yearly progress of the Japanese beetle from its introduction near Philadelphia in 1916.

From what has been said, it will be clear that there is no lack of material on which to base a similar chart of the geographical progress of potato blight in Europe in 1845; indeed, the major problem is the sheer volume of the relevant data. Eye-witness accounts of the earlier stages in Belgium and neighbouring countries are given by Dumortier[2] and by Martens.[3] Bonjean[4] adds details of the onset of the disease in southern France, Switzerland and north Italy. Muenter[5] and others describe its progress in Germany. Decaisne[6] is one of the few to attempt a comprehensive verbal picture of the spread of the disease. In France[7] and in Scotland,[8] reports were collected and co-ordinated by a central committee. In Ireland, the constabulary were instructed by an order dated 16 September 1845 to submit periodic confidential reports on the progress of the disease; the original returns from more than 250 police stations are filed in the PRO, Dublin (National Archives). Data from all these sources and from very many others, including British, Irish, French and Belgian newspapers, are summarised in fig. 2.

Onset of potato blight

The disease was first noticed in the Courtrai area of Belgium towards the end of June 1845. By mid-July it extended all over Flanders, and had appeared in neighbouring parts of the Netherlands and France. The first newspaper references to the strange and alarming disease occurred in

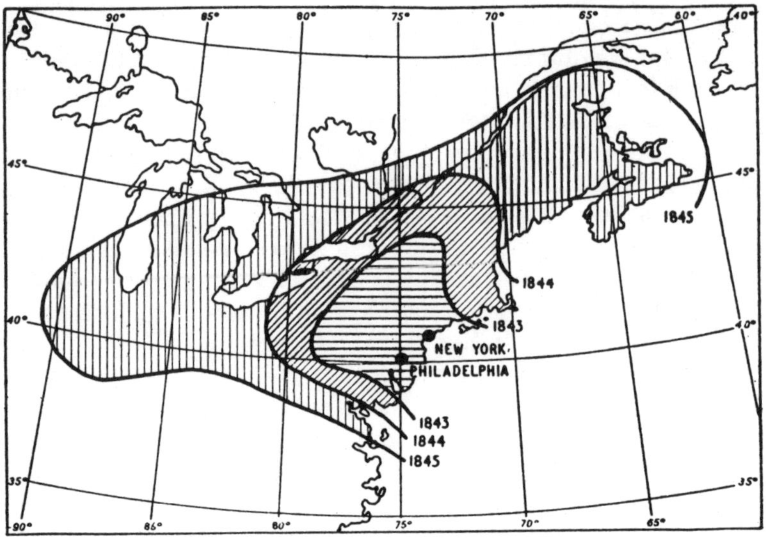

Fig. 1. Approximate extent of potato blight attacks in the United States and Canada during 1843–45 (after Stevens)

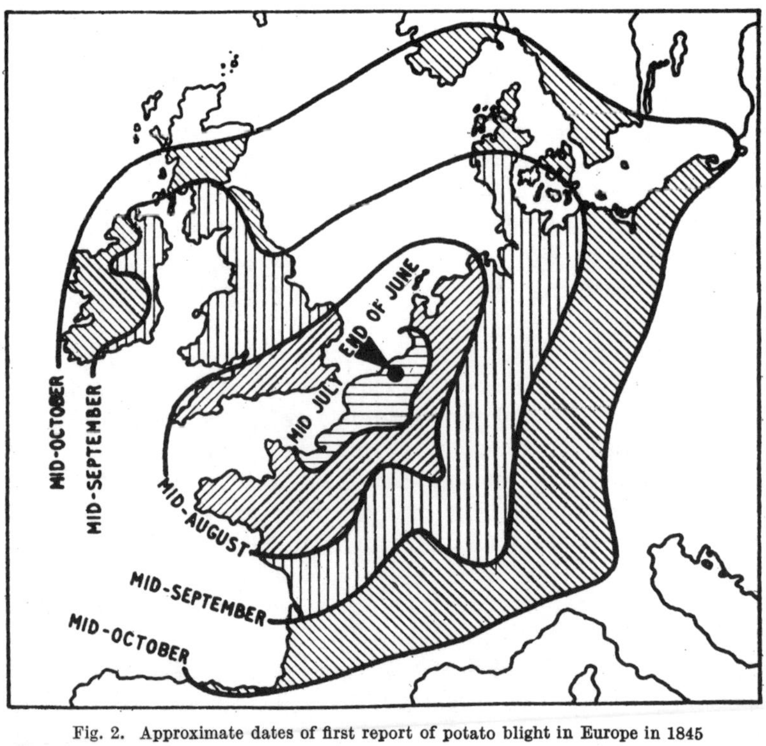

Fig. 2. Approximate dates of first report of potato blight in Europe in 1845

the second half of July. As early as 31 July 1845 *L'Organe des Flandres*, a newspaper published at Gand, printed an article by the Abbé Edouard van den Hecke, in which he suggested that the disease was due to a fungus which he described briefly, with particular reference to the remarkable mechanism by which it launched its spores. A previous suggestion as to the fungal nature of potato blight had been made in the United States by Mr J. E. Teschemacher of Boston, but had caused no reaction there. Van den Hecke's independent conclusion proved to be the first innocent shot in what soon developed into a violent controversy between those who considered the fungus to be the unique cause and those who dismissed it as a consequence of the disease. There were authentic grounds at the time for scientific doubt, but the issue was embittered by personal jealousy, international rivalry and even religious conviction. The standard-bearer of the fungal theory was Professor Charles Morren of Liége, who launched, in the Brussels newspaper *L'Indépendance Belge* of 20 August 1845, a vigorous manifesto which was reproduced all over Europe and in the United States. He was supported by the Reverend M. J. Berkeley in England and, more cautiously, by A. Payen in France; but the opponents of the theory were far more numerous and influential, and carried the waverers with them. The fungal theory quickly fell into disfavour with all except the faithful few, and did not emerge from the shadows until de Bary's time, some fifteen years later.

Spread of the disease

To return to figure 2, the extension of the disease from Belgium to Luxembourg seems at first to have been blocked by the Ardennes; it did not appear there until it had flanked the mountains from north and south. At a later stage, the entry of the disease into Switzerland appears similarly to have been made, virtually simultaneously in September, along the valleys of the Rhône and the Rhine.

The disease was found in the Paris area about mid-August. On 20 August, M. Elisée Lefebvre showed examples of blighted potato foliage and tubers to a session of the Société Royale et Centrale d'Agriculture. In Paris also, Dr C. Montagne hastened to comply with the botanical canons by describing the fungus in proper detail to a meeting of the Société Philomatique on 30 August, and thus gained priority over a number of Belgian writers – van den Hecke, Anne-Marie Libert, René van Oye and Morren – who had already given less formal accounts of the fungus in popular newspapers.

By mid-August the disease had also extended to the lower Rhineland, to north-west France, to the Channel Islands and to southern England. In England, the alarm was first sounded by Dr Bell Salter of the Isle of Wight in a letter which appeared in the *Gardeners' Chronicle* of 16 August; the following week's issue confirmed the presence of the disease over much of southern England. It had not yet appeared in the midlands, for when Rev. M. J. Berkeley of King's Cliffe, Northamptonshire, received on 26 August some infected foliage from his friend Dr Montagne in Paris, he had not succeeded, despite careful search, in finding any traces of the disease in his area. A few days later it made its appearance, and he followed its progress in the field and checked its characteristics against Dr Montagne's specimen and description.

The advent of potato blight in Ireland was announced simultaneously, on 6 September, in brief paragraphs in the *Waterford Freeman* and the *Dublin Evening Post*. On 13 September, Dr John Lindley, impressed by the advanced stage of destruction of the potato crops in the London area, stopped the press to announce the grim news from Ireland in the *Gardeners' Chronicle*. In Ireland itself, however, the newspapers and journals, irrespective of their political allegiances, tended in the earlier weeks to play down the disease, and it was not until considerable tuber rot was noted at harvest time in October that the popular panic spread to the Irish newspapers.

In the later stages of a potato-growing season, it is difficult to distinguish the effects of blight on haulm which is ripening to decay. The outer boundary line in fig. 2 thus encloses, in large part, areas in which tuber blight was discovered at or soon after harvesting. It is difficult to place with absolute certainty in Scandinavia and central Europe. There is little doubt that the disease in Scotland was virtually limited to the area south of the Grampians and, in particular, did not extend to the highlands in 1845. Neither did it appear in the Shetland, Orkney or Scilly Islands, and it made little or no impact in Achill Island on the Irish west coast. The southern limit of the disease did not quite reach the Mediterranean, with the possible exception of the Genoa area about which there were conflicting reports.

Extent of crop losses in 1845

Losses in the potato crop in 1845 were most severe in the area of earliest attack. In Belgium, Holland and north-east France, the foliage of the main crop was destroyed in most cases while the tubers were no bigger than marbles. In the regions of late season attack where the potatoes were almost fully developed, the extent of loss by tuber rot depended on the wetness or otherwise of the season before and at harvest time. In rainy areas, losses were quite serious, particularly where panic digging took place while the fungus was active. Appreciable damage was suffered in parts of Switzerland, and the effect on the lives of the poor is vividly described in the well-known novel, *Käthi, die Grossmutter*, by Jeremias Gotthelf (Albert Bitzius), published in 1847. In Ireland, the effects of the disease were very variable; but the mean loss by tuber rot was about 40% in a crop which had yielded remarkably well, so that the production of sound potatoes was about a quarter or a third below normal. In Bavaria and Prussia, where the autumn was dry, crop losses were slight. A contrary impression was created abroad by the decision of the Prussian government, by a decree dated 18 September 1845, to prohibit the export of potatoes but this was merely a temporary safeguard directed against heavy buying by Belgian and Dutch importers.

Pattern of blight progress in 1845 and 1846

Outside Belgium, the pattern of disease progress in 1845 (fig. 2) passed virtually unnoticed, and in each area which was attacked later in the season there was a tendency to interpret the data as showing a linear progression. Thus, in Britain, the apparent path from Belgium through England to Ireland was extrapolated backwards to include Germany and even Poland; the outbreak of blight was thus seen as 'coming from the east', and, with the path of the cholera pandemic of 1826-37 still fresh in the public mind, the disease was often described as the 'potato cholera'. In the south of France, potato blight appeared to travel from north to south, and its late season appearance was interpreted as support for the theory that the potato was suffering from a kind of cool weather degeneration. Writing about forty years later, Jensen of Copenhagen[9] recalled the sequence of successive blight appearances in 1845 from the Isle of Wight through England to Scotland, and from the Netherlands through Holstein to Denmark, and claimed that it was identical with the apparent progress of the disease in normal later years, as controlled by climatic factors.

In fact, however, the cycle of events as shown in figure 2 is completely untypical of the annual course of potato blight in Europe, nor is it explicable in terms of abnormal weather conditions. The summer of 1845 in north-west Europe was everywhere cold, sunless and wetter than normal, but, while it was a depressing season, it was by no means an unusual one. Growing seasons more favourable to blight development had occurred in every part of the region within the past 3-6 years. The only adequate explanation of the pattern of development of blight in 1845 is that the fungus had recently been introduced into Europe, and that the main concentration of inoculum in that year lay within the region in which the disease was obvious by mid-August.

This interpretation is reinforced by the sequence of events in 1846 when the apparent geographical march of the disease followed what was afterwards to be recognised as its characteristic climatic pattern.[7,10] It first appeared in the west, striking Ireland fully two months before it was noted in the previous year, and its apparent progress was eastwards or north-eastwards 'at about 50 miles per week'. In Ireland the crop was destroyed in most cases in early August at a time when tuber formation in the main crop, then sown later than nowadays, had barely begun. The sole food of a great part of the population was thus wiped out, and the year which followed marked the most intense stage of the great hunger so eloquently described in Mrs Woodham-Smith's book.[11] The Scottish highlands, which had emerged unscathed in 1845, suffered an early and severe attack of blight in 1846, and distress in this area was second only to that in Ireland.[12] In south-east England and on the neighbouring European mainland the disease not only appeared later, but also, since the summer there was dry and warm, such damage as the potato crop suffered was due more to drought than to blight.

In 1846, the disease made an appearance in new areas on the European mainland, in the Orkney and Shetland Islands, and even in Algeria.

A political consequence

The different courses of the disease in 1845 and 1846 had political repercussions which are of some historical interest. In 1845, the London area was attacked sooner and more spectacularly than was Ireland. We have seen that Dr Lindley, in his *Gardeners' Chronicle*, was already sounding the alarm for Ireland a month before the Irish journals commenced to treat the matter seriously. As a result, Peel's government in London took prompt action, required the constabulary to survey the Irish crops, and set up a scientific commission of three, including Lindley, to go to Ireland and report on the situation. Impressed by Lindley's estimate that five-sixths of the Irish potato crop would be lost, Peel placed an early order for maize in North America. The provision made was parsimonious by modern relief standards; but, since the actual loss was only about half the original estimate, the emergency measures blunted the sharper edge of starvation in the spring and early summer of 1846.

By the time the disease reappeared in Ireland in 1846, the parliamentary opposition which had berated Peel for exaggeration and unjustified panic was itself in power. Further, the disease was rampant in Ireland at a time when south-east England was virtually free. Russell's government, treating the earlier appeals from Ireland as cries of 'Wolf!', moved with tragic slowness and inadequacy. Meanwhile, in Ireland, Lindley's forecast was being more than justified, with a time-lag of a year. The result is a matter of history.

A new disease?

Although most observers in 1845, and particularly practical farmers, insisted that blight was a disease new to Europe, there was by no means complete agreement on the point. A new appearance was difficult to explain, irrespective of the theory advanced, and there was a rich source of error in the confusion of blight with earlier potato diseases, which was mined with particular industry by the academic commentators who lacked direct experience of the disease in the field. There were also those who felt that the first need was to dispel public panic and that this consideration justified the mild deception of identifying the disease with earlier outbreaks which had died down after a short period.

In the past, the potato had suffered from drought in dry seasons, from water-logging and consequent rot in wet years, and from frost damage in growth and storage when the weather was unusually cold. It was also subject to a number of minor ailments, like scab, which were more a nuisance than a matter of concern. Two diseases only had claimed major attention. The first was the 'curl', which we can now recognise as a virus attack. This was prominent from the last quarter of the eighteenth century and gave rise to a voluminous literature which has been fairly exhaustively reviewed by Atanasoff.[13] The development of new varieties and the regular replacement of seed potatoes from areas free of the complaint proved to be effective devices for the restraint of 'curl'. It led, however, to a continuous and uncontrolled exchange of potatoes which guaranteed the rapid extension and development of any new plant diseases.

The 'curl' differed so radically from blight that it is difficult to credit that anyone could confuse them; yet there was a small group who wielded Occam's razor with fanatical zeal and argued that 'curl', blight and other maladies of the potato were merely different aspects of a single disease.

The 'taint' or 'dry rot', now recognisable as a fungal infection caused by *Fusarium spp.*, appeared to a troublesome degree about 1830 and caused serious concern in Germany towards the end of the same decade. Again there was a voluminous output of articles, prize essays and pamphlets, culminating in the famous study by von Martius in 1842.[14]

Again, the course of the disease was quite distinctive, and only a small group of contemporary observers took the line that dry rot and blight were two aspects of a single malady, the respective characteristics developing according as the season was dry or wet. They were sufficiently vocal, however, to create a confusion regarding the time when blight first appeared in Germany and elsewhere in Europe. This confusion has persisted to the present day and has led to the supposition, which is in reality an extension of the cholera fallacy, that the disease might have travelled from Europe to North America.

The fact is that if blight existed in Europe prior to the 1840s, it passed completely unnoticed either by von Martius, who carefully recorded even the minor ailments of the potato, or by the hundreds of other commentators who wrote on the potato. All the evidence points to the conclusion that blight had arrived in Europe only shortly before the epidemic of 1845.

Date of introduction of potato blight into Europe

Accepting that the fungus had been recently introduced, the question arises as to whether the spread of blight in 1845 to a large part of Europe could have occurred in the course of a single season. The possibility cannot be entirely ruled out. It was a summer in which shallow thundery depressions penetrated into the continent and gave rise to a recurrent wind pattern which favoured the transport of spores eastwards as well as westwards in moist sunless weather.

A further favourable factor was the extreme susceptibility to blight of most of the potato crop of the time. No variety proved immune, but a few showed a fair resistance to the disease; it was from a build-up of these partially resistant potatoes that the crop continued to be grown successfully up to the time, towards the end of the century, when treatment with fungicides came into use. But the varieties then most widely grown, such as the 'Lumper' in Ireland, proved highly susceptible and went out of general use after 1846. No doubt there was much exaggeration in the frequent reports of fields which were blackened overnight or even in a matter of hours. But there is solid evidence that the disease worked its destruction with terrifying rapidity. This has recently been confirmed in a remarkable way by Professor van der Plank.[15] Using potatoes from a stock introduced by missionaries into Basutoland in 1833, which have since then survived in an ambient unfavourable to blight, he has tested the old varieties and found them to be intensely susceptible to the disease.

There is, however, some evidence that blight was already present in parts of Europe in 1844, when the summer was mainly dry. The areas for which a prior appearance are claimed with some plausibility are Belgium, the Lille district in France, the south-east corner of England (Kent and Sussex) and Dumfriesshire in Scotland. There are some reports in 1845 of appearances of the disease in Cheshire and in Dumfriesshire some weeks earlier than the orderly advance depicted in fig. 2 would suggest. Claims from South Africa, Poland and Portugal that the only crops in which blight appeared were grown from British seed potatoes of the 1844 crop would be decisive, if one could be sure that the disease in question was, in fact, blight. However, the accumulation of evidence does suggest strongly that the disease had already gained a foothold in 1844. There are isolated grains of evidence that the disease may have dated back locally to 1843 or even 1842, but they are far from conclusive. For 1841 and earlier, there is little risk in a dogmatic claim that potato blight did not then exist in Europe.

Source of blight

It may be deduced with some confidence that blight was not introduced from Europe into the United States; it may have come from the latter, where it was already widespread in 1843, to Europe or it may have arrived independently in the two areas from a common third source. Where this source was located remains a debatable point, on which further detective work is required. Modern commentators have suggested Mexico.[16] Recent work by Dr Niederhauser *et al.*[17] has shown that the blight fungus there comprises a highly specialised population of races and that it retains the power to mate and form oöspores freely. These characteristics give strong support to the claims of Mexico as the primary site of origin of potato blight; they are less convincing as evidence that Mexico was the immediate source of the less versatile fungus which invaded the United States and Europe.

The nineteenth-century theory was that blight came from the northern Andes region in South America. The direct evidence that the disease existed there prior to 1845 is not very satisfactory; but the region has recently proved to be one in which genes of hypersensitivity to blight occur in wild potatoes.[18] Certainly, the timing and method of disease entry are easier to demonstrate for the Andes area. The newly independent South American states opened up trade with Europe and North America, and this was greatly expanded with the guano boom which commenced in 1840. The problem of the dry rot may have induced the European growers to experiment with fresh stocks from South America, 'the home of the potato'. Certainly the guano ships brought South American potatoes to Europe, and among the newly introduced varieties which went down in the first attack in Belgium in 1845 were three which bore the significant names, 'Lima', 'Péruviennes' and 'Cordilières'.[19] The available evidence suggests that the disease may well have come from the Andes area; but there are several outstanding problems to be solved before a dogmatic answer can be given.

Acknowledgments
The investigation of potato blight and weather in the 1840s, on which this article is based, was partially supported, in the earlier stages, by a grant from the scientific activities fund of the Royal Meteorological Society and, more recently, by a travel grant, GA AGR 6407, from the Rockefeller Foundation.

CHAPTER 8

The scientific investigation of the potato blight in 1845-6*

The assessment of the contribution of Garret Hugh FitzGerald to the search for an antidote to potato blight, as put forward by Mr T. P. O'Neill in his article on the scientific investigation of the potato failure of 1845-6,[1] needs to be revised, if only to do justice to Robert Kane.

FitzGerald wrote to a local newspaper on 9 March 1846, suggesting, as a result of experiments he had made in search of a cure for potato blight, that seed potatoes should be steeped before planting in a solution of bluestone (copper sulphate).[2] In February and March of the same year he wrote letters on the subject for consideration to the relief commission, of which Robert Kane was the scientific member.

Copper sulphate is, of course, the common ingredient of Bordeaux and Burgundy mixtures, the fungicidal foliage sprays which, some forty years later, were found to control potato blight. For this reason, Mr O'Neill suggests that FitzGerald's name is worthy of inclusion in the annals of research into potato disease. He considers that Robert Kane was seriously at fault in not taking action on FitzGerald's suggestion.

Had Kane referred FitzGerald's communications to John Lindley, the latter would probably have published them in the *Gardeners' Chronicle*, for though Lindley did not accept the fungal theory he acted impartially as editor and published matter in support of that theory. It cannot be doubted but that such knowledge, combined with the later observations in that journal that the pall of copper smoke from the mines near Swansea in Wales prevented the disease from affecting the potatoes within the radius of its influence, together with Charles Morren's observations, would have led to the perfecting of a mode of treatment long before Millardet made his discovery in 1882. For almost forty years after 1846 the effect of copper fumes and copper sulphate on the fungus was forgotten, but it is possible that, had the suggestion made by FitzGerald received due attention, the losses occasioned by blight during those four decades might have been avoided. The crises of 1863 and 1880 in Ireland might have been averted, and it is possible that, though the discovery would not have been made in time to save the 1846 crop, yet the despair which came with the failure to find any means of dealing satisfactorily with the

* From *Irish Historical Studies*, xiii (1962), pp 26-32.

disease would not have been so overwhelming in 1847.[3]

A reconsideration of these points can most conveniently be presented in the form of answers to four questions.

1. Was FitzGerald's suggestion of a bluestone steep an original one?

As Mr O'Neill mentions, the practice of steeping wheat seed in a bluestone solution as a preventative of the disease known as bunt was developed in France early in the nineteenth century. This procedure was soon adopted by some wheat growers in Ireland,[4] and indeed the potato commissioners themselves, in their third report, dated 7 November 1845, recommended that it should be followed for all *grain* seed.[5]

The success of chemical steeps in countering cereal diseases made it likely that a similar seed treatment would be advocated for other plant diseases. This happened, for instance, when the Irish potato crop was attacked in the early 1830s by the 'taint',[6] a dry rot caused, most likely, by fungi of the *fusarium* family. Following the potato failure of 1832, B. H. Hickey experimented with immersing the seed potatoes in a solution of bluestone and salt.[7] He claimed that the treated seed vegetated while the controls failed. The Irishman's ideas were quoted with approval in a British agricultural journal of the time.[8]

When potato blight first came to notice in Europe in 1845, it was almost inevitable that the old remedy should again be proposed. The new disease struck early in the Low Countries, so it was natural that priority in mentioning bluestone in connection with potato blight should go to a Belgian. Dr Charles Morren of Liége, in one of the earlier European pamphlets on potato blight,[9] suggested the use of a mixture of bluestone, lime, salt and water. His recommendations first appeared in a letter to the *Indépendance* of Brussels, and were reproduced, in English translation, in the *Gardeners' Chronicle* of 13 September 1845,[10] within a few weeks of the first notice of potato blight in England. Mr O'Neill mentions Morren's advocacy of a mixture containing bluestone as a soil disinfectant, but the Liége professor also recommended it as a dip for potato seed: 'the seed for next year ought to be steeped like corn, etc., with lime, copper sulphate, and common salt, diluted in water, in order to kill the fungus, if any, on the potato'.[11]

In the following week's issue of the *Gardeners' Chronicle*, Morren's advice was repeated in the editorial article.[12] This double publication of the bluestone steep suggestion, in a British agricultural journal of wide circulation, took place about six months before FitzGerald's letter appeared in the *Limerick Chronicle*; furthermore, it mentioned both the ingredients of the future Bordeaux mixture, i.e. bluestone and lime.

2. Was adequate consideration given at the time to the suggestion of a bluestone steep?

Exactly one week after FitzGerald's suggestion appeared in the *Limerick Chronicle*, it was reproduced prominently in the *Gardeners' Chronicle*, with an acknowledgment of the source.[13] John Lindley included it in an editorial article in which he listed 'the kind of experiments which it may be advisable to try in the present emergency'. We do not know who brought FitzGerald's letter to Lindley's attention, but obviously it had not been neglected.

There is a clear link with Robert Kane in the Irish experiments which were carried out in 1846 to test FitzGerald's suggestion. Kane was professor of natural philosophy to the Royal Dublin Society, and David Moore was curator of the society's Botanic Gardens. In August 1846, Moore described[14] how he tried steeping seed potatoes in a sulphate of copper solution before planting them, 'with a view to destroying the spores of fungi which might be latent in them'. The treatment failed to prevent the disease, although Moore thought that it may have had some effect in delaying its appearance.

FitzGerald's reiteration of the bluestone suggestion was, therefore, adequately publicised and independently tested; and no stigma of inaction attaches to Robert Kane.

3. What merit was there in the idea of a bluestone steep for potato seed?

Chemical dips, though not using copper sulphate, are nowadays a recommended treatment for potato tubers as a protection against dry rot. To this extent, Hickey's suggestion of 1835 had some merit. With modern knowledge of the life cycle of the potato blight fungus, it is clear that surface disinfection of seed tubers provides no effective protection against this disease. It is true, as Mr O'Neill mentions, that G. H. Pethybridge repeated FitzGerald's experiments in 1911-12, but he stressed that he did this solely to counter a revival in some newspapers of the discarded theory of the value of 'disinfecting' seed tubers against potato blight.[15] His verdict was even more damning than Moore's: 'steeping seed potatoes, therefore, in such solutions is, as might perhaps be assumed from *a priori* considerations, worse than useless'.[16]

Doubtless FitzGerald honestly believed in his remedy, but his experiments took place during the winter half-year and mostly in a warm place indoors, i.e. in environmental conditions unfavourable to the blight fungus. Possibly his later silence on the subject was due to the fact that, like Moore, he may have found that the cure did not work in outdoor conditions during the summer of 1846.

The only real interest of the Morren-FitzGerald proposals was that they mentioned copper sulphate in connection with potato blight, but it was still a far cry to the development of a fungicidal mixture for application to the potato foliage which would not damage the plants.

4. Was an opportunity lost in the eighteen-forties to discover a fungicidal spray against potato blight?

Speculation about the 'ifs' of history is a fascinating, if unrewarding, study, which rarely leads to an unquestionable conclusion. An exception is that put forward by Mr O'Neill; the bluestone suggestion was, in fact, published in the same journal which treated most fully of the incident of the copper fumes; yet it did not lead to the discovery of an antidote to the potato disease.

To us who know the solution, the few authentic clues stand out clearly from the welter of irrelevant facts, inaccurate observations and wild theories which fill the agricultural journals of the time. But in 1846 only a minority held that potato blight was caused by a fungus, and the main features of the life cycle of the fungus were not established until the results of de Bary's famous studies were published in 1861-3. The investigators of the time were groping in the dark, and the odds were heavily loaded against their grasping the essential facts out of the confusion of contradictory evidence.

It is easy to see now that the really significant item was the report that potatoes grown in the immediate vicinity of the copper smelting works at Swansea remained free of the blight.[17] But, at the time, the report was denied by some,[18] and others queried it on the grounds that it would be singular if copper factory fumes which scorched pasture and injured livestock should be good for the potato plant.[19] A further complication was the report from Ireland that the potato crop near a vitriol works in Ireland was free of disease when the foliage elsewhere was destroyed,[20] an observation which suggested that acids and not metallic salts were the key to the effect of factory fumes.

Had an effective fungicide been found, it would have been necessary to apply it to the foliage and not the tubers. There were a few early but rather tentative suggestions in this direction. The Reverend Edwin Sydney, who doubted the fungal theory of potato blight, recalled that a light dusting of flowers of sulphur over the leaves was an effective remedy against the fungus *Erysiphe* and some forms of *Botrytis*.[21] David Moore, who at first rejected the fungal theory but soon became an enthusiastic convert, satisfied himself that the fungus attacked the potato leaves, and, in seeking a preventative, noted that *Erysiphe communis* was a similar mould to that causing potato blight, and that sulphur dusting of the foliage was effective against the former.[22] A Mr Errington recommended that the potato crop be dusted with freshly slaked lime, 'so thickly as to thoroughly whiten the whole plant'.[23] So near – and yet so far.

Even after de Bary's researches had shown the way more clearly, there seemed little hope of developing a suitable fungicide. This was the opinion, as late as 1880, of William Carruthers FRS, who gave expert evidence before a parliamentary inquiry into the potato disease:[24]

> *Q. 250.* Should you think there is a probable solution to the question; by endeavouring to find anything that will tend to kill the spore when deposited on the leaf, previous to the descent of the rain which might develop it?
> I think not. I know of nothing.
>
> *Q. 251.* But is that probable?
> I do not think it probable. I do not think we can hope for it.

Some two years later serendipity succeeded where plodding science had failed, and Millardet made the chance observation which was to lead to the application of Bordeaux mixture as a remedy for both vine mildew and potato blight.[25] Almost twenty years more elapsed before potato spraying was firmly established in Ireland.

In retrospect, the progress towards an effective cure may seem devious and dilatory, but history has many a similar tale to tell. The long interval between the observation that milkmaids were resistant to smallpox and the application of Jenner's discovery of inoculation is a classic case.

CHAPTER 9

A contribution to the early history of the black leg disease of the potato*

A voluminous, if confused, body of literature on the diseases of the potato in Europe was published in the century, *c.* 1760-1860, which preceded de Bary's authoritative clarification of the major aspects of the situation. Much of this literature has been reviewed by Appel.[1] Certain diseases can be clearly identified from the early accounts;[2] these include virus disease (the 'curl' which was noted in the latter half of the eighteenth century), *Fusarium* rot (the dry rot or 'taint' of the decade 1830-40), blight or 'potato murrain' (from the year 1845) and scab.

There remain several less distinctive diseases which are difficult to identify with any confidence. Some of the descriptions suffered both from careless observation and inadequate reporting. But the major problem arose from the simultaneous presence in the potato crop of two or more undifferentiated disorders; by coupling the head of one with the body of another and the limbs of a third, the early writers often produced a composite monster which defies pathological analysis.

The purpose of the present note is to suggest that the bacterial soft-rot disease known as black leg may be added, with some confidence, to the list of the potato maladies occurring in the first half of the nineteenth century.

It has been suggested by Davidson[3] that black leg may date back to the eighteenth century. In the course of his criticism of the attempt of Atanasoff[4] to particularise the kinds of virus responsible for the 'curl', he quotes the following abstract of a paper presented by Müller,[5] as given in English translation by Atanasoff:[6]

> In spring at the coming out of the potato plants and during the first period of growth the potatoes promise a rich crop, but as soon as the plants reach their full development and just before blossoming some of the vines wilt suddenly, the foliage grows poorly, etc., some plants send out flowers but prematurely. At this time the seed tubers are full of fibers and sprouts, and are unusually watery and their interior rotten, most of these seed tubers rot completely soon after.

On this, Davidson[7] comments:

* From *Journal of the Department of Agriculture and Fisheries*, lxiii (1966), pp 1-7.

Does not this description apply to Black leg rather than to Stipple-Streak? At all events surely no plant affected with streak, not to speak of 'Streak plus Crinkle or Mosaic' could ever 'promise a rich crop'.

One may admit the possibility of this being a case of black leg without regarding the evidence as at all conclusive.

A more convincing case starts with a letter from Mr T. P. Elliot, Florence Court, Co. Fermanagh, Ireland, which was published in the *Gardeners' Chronicle* of 4 October 1845:[8]

The ravages of the potato-murrain have not appeared here yet; but there has been a disease in this locality for the last three or four years which has done much mischief; instead of commencing above ground, it seems to commence with the decay of the old set. The tubers as soon as they are formed, are attacked with dark-coloured ulcerated blotches, which soon spread over the whole tuber, and end in putrefaction; meanwhile the plant becomes languid, the leaves have a sickly yellow colour; yet the plant still exists, and forms more tubers, which are also attacked and carried off; the plant becoming more and more unhealthy, most frequently dies a month or six weeks before the healthy plants arrive at maturity. Nor does the evil rest here; such tubers as escape the ravages of the disease in summer, are attacked after they are dug during the whole winter; so that before the planting season again arrives, the stock is in many cases completely destroyed. The disease is quite local, it is not known beyond six or eight miles from here in any direction. Various remedies have been tried, such as having sets from a great distance, planting in drills instead of beds (which is the common mode of planting here), planting in ground which has not been broken up for a long time, planting very thinly, etc.; but almost all the trials have been attended with failure. One method, however, so far as it has been tried, seems to remedy the evil; that is greening or sunning the sets; for the last two years those planted in the garden have undergone that process, and there has been no failure; previously, they were as much diseased in the garden as in the field. The experiment has been tried this season in the field, and from a partial examination seems to have answered equally well; but the crop will be dug in a day or two, when you shall know the result. Enclosed are some diseased stems, with the late growth of tubers attached.

To this, Dr Lindley made the following editorial comment: 'We are sorry to add that this disease is our English murrain in a mild form.'

This entry is the sole evidence for the persistent myth that potato blight was known in Ireland prior to 1845.[9] The story was added to a little by Cooke,[10] who claims that the correspondent of the *Gardeners' Chronicle* 'testifies' to the occurrence of potato blight 'in districts [*sic*] of Ireland for 2 or 3 years previous to its general outbreak'.

Jensen[11] claims to follow Cooke but in fact still further strengthens the story; the correspondent is now quoted as *certifying* that blight had *raged* in *several* parts of Ireland for two or three years before its general appearance. Meanwhile, in a later article, Cooke[12] made the more moderate statement that blight 'was stated to have been observed in Ireland' about 1842. This is the first citation of a specific year. Prunet[13] follows Cooke's second thoughts and claims that blight was known in Ireland in 1842. The uncritical summaries of Cooke and Prunet are the main references followed by Jones *et al.*;[14] they repeat the historical blunders of the earlier authors, including the statement[15] that blight was present in Ireland in 1842. Stevens[16] expands this to a claim that the disease was 'well established' in Ireland in 1842.

Lindley's diagnosis that blight was present on the specimen plants forwarded to him by 4 October 1845 is not in question. It is elsewhere confirmed that the new disease had appeared in County Fermanagh by mid-September of that year;[17] a report, dated 20 September 1845, from the constabulary post at Arney, Florence Court, says that 'the rot or disease is very general, and in one case I have seen nearly a whole field destroyed by it'.

But all the evidence is against identifying as blight the disease which is reported as attacking the potato in County Fermanagh in previous years. Wilde,[18] in a thorough review of potato failures in Ireland in earlier years, produces no evidence that suggests that blight was not new to Ireland in 1845. Again the experience in 1845-6 of the rapid spread of blight in a dense plant population[19] of highly susceptible varieties[20] makes it impossible to accept that earlier it would have remained dormant in a limited area, particularly during the poor summer of 1843. This point was made at the time by Townley[21] who describes a potato disease in virtually the same words as those used in the Florence Court case, and differentiates it from blight by the fact that the attack 'is not general but partial, a plant here and there is affected by it, while others continue healthy'.

If the disease at Florence Court prior to 1845 was not *Phytophthora infestans*, what was it? Many of the symptoms suggest black leg, but others, for instance the dark-coloured ulcerated blotches, are not characteristic. The matter would remain in doubt but for the decisive evidence of Niven,[22] who was an early director of the Dublin Botanic Gardens. His pamphlet is one of the saner and more scientific of the contemporary commentaries on the disease; he differentiates clearly, for instance, between the symptoms of dry rot and blight. He goes on to refer[23] to a separate disease:

> in which decay sets in at the bottom of the stem near the root; it is similar to that sometimes called 'black leg' in the cruciferous or cabbage family. The decay at the bottom of the stem causes, not blotching, but flagging of the leaves as the first consequence, and then a yellowing or premature ripening as the second. It may, in some instances, even be found accompanying the present epidemic, but more generally separate from it...I think the two have been confounded.

This evidence establishes beyond reasonable doubt that black leg of the potato was known in Ireland prior to 1845, and reinforces the diagnosis of the disease not only in the Florence Court case in Ireland, but in other contemporary cases in England and on the European continent,[24] which have been put in evidence as early cases of blight. It also puts back the date of first knowledge of black leg by over fifty years, for Whitehead *et al.*[25] give

1899 as the year of first indisputable identification of the disease, and 1907 as the year of the first report from Ireland.

Acknowledgments
Thanks are due to Mr E. C. Large and Dr J. M. Hirst for comment on some of the early literature, and to Dr I. Sestoft, Copenhagen, for analysis of Fjeldstrup's lengthy paper which is in Danish. Deductions from the data are the sole responsibility of the author.

CHAPTER 10

The Irish grain trade, 1839-48*

As a step towards a fuller understanding of the food situation in Ireland on the eve of and during the great famine it is necessary to analyse the exports and imports of grain and grain products in those years.

There are a number of major obstacles to doing this. To begin with the available statistics on the Irish grain trade are neither orderly nor complete. The most extensive of the relevant series covers each calendar year during the period 1839-48. Monthly figures are available only for the year 1846 and apply to exports only. Other official returns refer to isolated periods of varying length.[1]

Again obvious errors are to be found in some of the returns. There are, for instance, substantial differences between two sets of statistics for grain exports in the second half of 1846.[2] Some years earlier, the comptroller of the corn returns had himself expressed reservations about the accuracy of the statistics of Irish grain exports; he felt that conversion from the Irish unit of the barrel into bushels was not made in a uniform way. For all that he was not prepared to say that the quantity of grain actually exported from Ireland was greater than that shown in the Custom House books.[3] We have, in any case, no alternative but to accept the official returns as the best available estimates of the extent of the grain trade; that they are not in major error is suggested by the fact that the figures for the average outflow of grain in the pre-famine years fit well into a pattern of independently calculated statistics on land use, crop yields, average grain production and domestic consumption.[4]

A further problem, analogous to that mentioned by the comptroller of corn returns, is the fact that the statistics of the trade in whole grain are expressed in quarters of eight bushels. It is therefore necessary to fix conversion rates into standard weights for each kind of grain. The normal range of grain measures in the 1840s has been well summarised as follows:

> An imperial bushel of fine wheat will weigh 63 lbs., whilst much of the inferior sorts will not exceed 53 lbs. Fine oats will weigh 42 lbs.; ordinary oats only 36 lbs. per imperial bushel. Fine barley weighs 55 lbs., good 52 lbs., and ordinary 48 lbs. per imperial bushel.[5]

* From *Irish Historical Studies*, xx (1976), pp 156-69.

An earlier paper[6] showed that the closest to an official Irish table of grain equivalents was that used by T. A. Larcom for converting returns in the immediate post-famine years:

Quarter of wheat = 470 lb.
Quarter of oats = 313 lb.
Quarter of barley = 404 lb.
Quarter of rye = 454 lb.

The same paper cited a value, taken from the *Irish Farmers' Journal*,[7] of 53 lb. to the bushel of maize (Indian corn). This figure is almost certainly on the low side, for it was part of the justification of a high retail price for maize meal. Indeed in a contrary submission in the *Gardeners' Chronicle*[8] it was claimed that a bushel of maize would contain 'at least 58 lb.'. A figure of 56 lb. per bushel is quoted more than once in official documents[9] and is almost certainly representative. This gives

Quarter of maize = 448 lb.

The final problem, which is taken up in the following section of this paper, is that of combining trade figures which refer in part to unmilled grain and in part to the corresponding meal.

The remarkable rise in exports of wheaten flour in the second quarter of the nineteenth century is attributable to the introduction of steamships on cross-channel routes; in earlier years flour had often arrived in England in poor condition after a lengthy and disturbed voyage. The number of grain mills in Ireland, which was particularly rich in water power, increased rapidly with the coming of steamships.[10]

For comparative studies it is necessary to express the flour trade in terms of unmilled wheat and to add the result to the figures of the wheat trade proper; similarly the statistics for oatmeal and other meals must be converted into equivalent amounts of unmilled grain. In practical terms, we need to know what weight of each cereal was required in order to make one hundredweight of the corresponding meal. Modern equivalents are no certain guide since milling processes, at least in the case of flour, have changed considerably.[11]

Cereal products and their contemporary grain equivalents

(a) Flour and wheat

Over two hundred years ago the bakers of Dublin, in reply to complaints of overcharging, arranged for a demonstration of the grinding and dressing of wheat in the presence of the lord mayor and distinguished guests.[12] For grinding a total of 840 lb. of wheat, a toll was charged which, with waste at grinding, amounted to 51 lb. There was a further loss by natural drying of 5 lb. while the grain was stored awaiting further processing. The residue of 784 lb. was sieved or dressed, and produced:

flour for household bread	567 lb.
bran	155 lb.
short bran	60 lb.
lost in dressing	2 lb.
total	784 lb.

In the final stage of the demonstration barm, salt and water weighing 292 lb. were added to the 567 lb. of flour, and gave, following loss of weight in baking, 741 lb. of bread.

The grade of flour involved in the demonstration was claimed to correspond to the lowest of three classifications of bread: 'white' for the nobility and gentry, 'wheaten' for the middling sort of people, and 'household' for the poorest sort.

An arranged 'demonstration' of this sort is not, perhaps, the most convincing evidence of normal practice. However, another old estimate[13] puts the losses in converting wheat to flour as high as one-third, which is in close agreement with the Dublin bakers' figures, if one includes milling dues amongst the losses. In contrast to these low estimates of convertibility a later Irish witness[14] considered that a loss of only one-eighth occurred in converting wheat into 'flour of all kinds'. The last three words may be significant, but even so the estimate seems optimistic.

Two representative British returns[15] gave the following figures:

bushel of 59 lb. of wheat		*bushel of 60 lb. of wheat*	
first class flour...	42 lb.	fine flour...	25.5 lb.
second class flour...	5 lb.	'second' flour...	22.5 lb.
third class flour...	2 lb.	pollard...	1.0 lb.
bran...	9 lb.	bran...	10.5 lb.
waste	1 lb.	loss...	0.5 lb.

Apart from the classification of grades of flour, in which there was clearly a wide range of choice, these and other British figures[16] are reasonably consistent, and agree with statistics given a little earlier by George Frean, an experienced Plymouth miller and biscuit-maker, who found[17] that a quarter of wheat of 480 lb. gave:

336 lb. of very fine flour
56 lb. of coarse flour, suitable for biscuits
76 lb. of bran, unfit for human food
12 lb. of waste in cleaning, grinding and dressing

Whether the British values were fully applicable to Ireland can be questioned. Irish flour-making was said to be wasteful, and it was claimed that the wheat was often adulterated with straw, chaff, seeds, and other foreign matter on delivery at the mill, so that double cleaning was necessary.[18]

In round figures, assuming a convertibility slightly less than the British, we may take it that a hundredweight of flour of different grades was equivalent to 140 lb. of wheat.

(b) Oats and oatmeal

The same Irish witness to the poor law inquiry[14] who gave an optimistic value for the extraction of flour from wheat considered that a loss of only one-third was involved in converting oats into oatmeal. At the other extreme, there were claims[19] that 'each stone of oats would produce half a stone of sifted meal' and that 'a ton of oats will not produce more than half a ton of meal'. A contemporary critic[20] considered the latter estimates of losses to be too great and thought it probable that allowance had been made for coarse sifting to remove flummery (a practice almost obsolete) and for the deduction at the mill of grinding dues. He suggested that a cast, as it was technically called, of 8 stone of meal to the barrel of 14 stone of oats was not too high an average, even for the lower grade oats retained for home consumption, and that oats for export might be expected to give 9 stone to the barrel.

Contemporary figures for Britain[21] indicate that a bushel of 40 lb. of oats provided 22.5 lb. of oatmeal, in close agreement with modern Irish experience that dehulled groats of oats represent 8/14ths of the original grain weight and that they are converted into oatmeal with a further loss of only 1%.

In round figures we may take it that a hundredweight of oatmeal was equivalent to 200 lb. of oats.

(c) Maize and maize meal

Here the whole grain was ground or chopped into meal with only trifling incidental losses. The reduction in weight as a result of grinding and separation at the mill averaged 2%.[22] A further small loss could occur if kiln-drying was required but this applied to most grains with an unduly high moisture content.[23] In converting maize meal statistics to equivalent grain weight it suffices to add 2%.

(d) Other grains and meals

Small amounts of barley and rye meals appear in the trade returns.

Martin Doyle[24] considered that 14 lb. of Irish barley gave on average 12 lb. of barley meal. This claim is rather better than a British estimate of 37.5 lb. of meal to the bushel of 48 lb. of barley.[21] We adopt an intermediate value, in which a hundredweight of barleymeal is equated to 135 lb. of barley. For ryemeal we take a hundredweight to be equivalent to 144 lb. of the grain.[21]

The converted grain trade statistics

Table 1 (below) brings together the various equivalents for grain and meal as developed earlier in this paper and expresses them in the form of conversion factors which can be applied directly to the statistics included in the various grain trade returns.

In table 2, these conversion factors are applied to the detailed returns for 1846 to provide a synthesis of the trade in terms of the total amounts of each grain. It would be impracticable to reproduce here the corresponding tables for each of the years 1839 to 1848, but the main features of the grain trade in these years is summarised in table 3.[25]

It is not proposed to discuss the tables in detail but a few comments may be added.

Oats was easily the biggest item in the export grain trade in the pre-famine period and maintained a steady level from year to year. Its annual amount in each of the years 1839-42 was very close to the net outward flow of all grain. The figures for 1843 reflect an excellent growing season and a harvest which was 'all the farmer could wish'.[26]

The pre-famine figures for wheat are interesting as showing that up to 1842 the imports were often of the same order as the exports and once even exceeded them. The lack of uniformity from year to year of the net export figures is consistent with the fact that wheat was grown in Ireland purely as a commercial crop. The acreage under wheat fluctuated considerably from year to year as the price varied[27] and the yield was more sensitive to seasonal weather than in the case of oats. The succession of good harvests and steady wheat prices in the years 1842-5 is reflected in the upward trend of the export returns.

The figures for barley do not take account of processed grain in the form of malt and liquor, but the totals are in any case small. Barley and rye played a negligible role in the food situation.

The statistics for imports of maize show that there was an annual trickle of Indian corn coming into the country long before the famine. The slight upward trend in maize imports in 1845 is not attributable to Peel's famous order which did not begin to arrive until February 1846.[28] The extent of 'government interference' with the grain trade was trifling in comparison with the overall figures; Routh was not exaggerating when he described the official imports as 'almost only a mouthful'.[29] Their importance was mainly as evidence of a change of policy and as a catalyst which served to release other supplies.[30]

The stemming of the outflow of grain in 1846 and the enormous net inflow in 1847 reflect the extent of relief operations.

Annual totals of the grain trade are not of themselves sufficient to trace the rise and fall of starvation, and the other available figures do not add much to the precise detail. Over the critical period from the potato crop failure in 1846 to the first availability of homegrown food from the 1847 harvest – say September 1846 to June 1847 – total grain exports were of the order of 130 to 140 thousand tons, depending on which returns are accepted.[31] Imports over the same period reached 659,000 tons,[32] i.e. about five times as much in total.

The problem, however, was that the exports were bulked in the earlier part of the period while the main flow of imports came later, so that the most critical period for starvation was in the months immediately following the 1846 harvest. Writing to Trevelyan on 29 September 1846, Routh reckoned it 'a most serious evil' that 'the exports of oats have amounted since the harvest to 300,000 quarters'.[33] Mrs Woodham-Smith quotes Routh as giving a figure of '60,000 tons',[34] but a more accurate equivalent would be 42,000 tons. The monthly returns[35] for the period July-September 1846 give the export of oats and oatmeal over those three months as equivalent to 39,000 tons, a figure which presumably includes some preharvest exports; the value for September alone was 22,000 tons. The quarterly return[36] for the period 5 July to 10 October 1846 gives the figure for the three months as 45,000 tons.

Few statistics are available to help in a similar breakdown into shorter periods of the import figures. However, if the returns of imports during the first eleven months of 1846 and during the full year[37] are accepted – and they are certainly free of internal inconsistency – they provide some rather surprising information (table 4). The figure of total grain imports almost doubled during the last month, which means that the great surge of relief supplies had already begun to reach Irish ports as early as December 1846. In that month too, nearly 80% of the relief food, even in the case of maize, was imported from Great Britain.

Grain exports and the famine

Finally it is desirable to make a brief reference to the traditional belief that the Irish people could have been sustained in comfort, without outside aid, on the food that was exported during the famine years. Although the statistics presented here differ in many respects from those considered by Mr T. P. O'Neill in his pioneer paper[38] on the Irish food problems in the 1840s, they support the general conclusions which he reached. It is beyond question that the food deficiency arising from the loss of the potato crop in 1846 could not have been met by the simple expedient of prohibiting the export of grain from Ireland, even if the difficult practical problems of acquisition, storage, milling and distribution could have been surmounted at short notice. Grain exports in 1846 totalled 285,000 tons, which is the approximate food equivalent of a little over one million tons of potatoes; the shortfall in the potato crop of that year was well over ten times that figure. Again it is a major error to think that all the grain crops of Ireland were grown for export; in normal pre-famine years nearly 80% of the domestic oats production was retained in Ireland.[39]

In 1847, the first year for which official agricultural statistics were published, total oats production was 1.6 million tons, of which only a small fraction was shipped out (table 3).

In the course of the critical famine years, little evidence is to be found in the Irish newspapers – with the sturdy exception of the *Clare Journal* – of any public demand for the closing of the home ports against the export of food. O'Connell would have intervened only to stop the quite minor exports of provisions to foreign countries, i.e. those outside the United Kingdom: 'I don't mean to suggest any prohibition of the exportation of provisions between England and Ireland, and in fact it is possible that we may get far more from England than we send there.'[40] In the long run, O'Connell's hope that Ireland would receive more than it gave was amply fulfilled – but not before a tragic delay of several months had intervened.

It is here that the nationalist argument, stripped of gross exaggeration, still retains a small hard kernel of truth. The grain crop of 1846, if entirely retained in Ireland, could have made an appreciable contribution to bridging the starvation gap between the destruction of the potato crop in August and the arrival of the first maize cargoes in the following winter.

But, even as a supplement to a major relief operation and as a measure which would have called for an enormous organisation (as well as a political and economic volte-face by Lord John Russell), the retention in Ireland of all home-produced food could have served only as a temporary device to win time. Now that the Irish economy could never again be based entirely on an ailing potato crop, the problem of the emergency feeding of a swollen population would have had to be faced again and again in each succeeding year. There was a social malaise which went deeper than, and had long preceded, the immediate food shortage, and its cure would have been slow and painful even had the dreadful solution provided by starvation, fever and emigration been even partially circumvented.

Table 1
CONVERSION FACTORS FOR IRISH GRAIN STATISTICS

To convert the trade item in the first column into its equivalent in tons of the corresponding grain multiply by the factor in the second column.

Grade trade item	*Conversion factor to tons*
Wheat (qtr)	0.2098
Flour (cwt)	0.0625
Oats (qtr)	0.1397
Oatmeal (cwt)	0.0893
Barley (qtr)	0.1804
Barleymeal (cwt)	0.0603
Rye (qtr)	0.2027
Ryemeal (cwt)	0.0625
Maize (qtr)	0.2000
Maize meal (cwt)	0.0510

Table 2 Statistics of Irish grain trade for 1846

IMPORTS	amount	equivalent in tons of grain	total tons of grain
Wheat from G.B. Wheat, other Flour from G.B. Flour, other	109,235 qtr 90,853 qtr 292,209 cwt 43,404 cwt	22,918 19,061 18,263 2,713	WHEAT 62,955
Oats from G.B. Oats, other Oatmeal from G.B. Oatmeal, other	1,167 qtr 9,630 qtr 22,580 cwt 2,259 cwt	163 1,345 2,016 202	OATS 3,726
Barley from G.B. Barley, other Barleymeal from G.B. Barleymeal, other	20,463 qtr 16,078 qtr 11,659 cwt —	3,692 2,900 703 —	BARLEY 7,295
Rye from G.B. Rye, other Ryemeal from G.B. Ryemeal, other	2,042 qtr 1,366 qtr 626 cwt —	414 277 40 —	RYE 731
Maize from G.B. Maize, other Maize meal from G.B. Maize meal, other	172,237 qtr 393,109 qtr 102,550 cwt 64,947 cwt	34,447 78,622 5,231 3,312	MAIZE 121,612
EXPORTS	**amount**	**equivalent in tons of grain**	**total tons of grain**
Wheat Flour	186,730 qtr 723,562 cwt	39,176 45,223	WHEAT 84,399
Oats Oatmeal	958,851 qtr 554,307 cwt	133,951 49,500	OATS 183,451
Barley Barleymeal	92,854 qtr —	16,751 —	BARLEY 16,751
Rye Ryemeal	— —	— —	RYE Nil

Table 3 Summary of Irish grain trade, 1839-48, in thousands of tons of grain equivalent

YEAR	WHEAT		OATS		BARLEY		RYE		MAIZE		ALL GRAINS		NET GRAIN FLOW OUTWARD
	export	import	export	import	export	import	export	import	export	import	export	import	
1839	56	26	266	3	11	10	—	—	—	1	333	40	+ 293
1840	37	38	285	2	17	4	—	—	—	1	339	45	+ 294
1841	47	34	355	—	14	4	—	—	—	1	416	39	+ 377
1842	43	42	317	3	9	7	—	—	—	4	369	56	+ 313
1843	89	14	371	—	20	—	—	—	—	1	480	15	+ 465
1844	94	23	314	1	16	5	—	—	—	1	424	30	+ 394
1845	167	12	329	1	17	7	—	1	—	7	513	28	+ 485
1846	84	63	183	4	17	7	—	1	—	122	284	197	+ 87
1847	39	199	98	12	9	25	—	21	—	632	146	889	− 743
1848	65	116	235	1	14	8	—	8	—	306	314	439	− 125

Table 4 The main grain imports into Ireland in 1846 in thousands of tons

The first figure in each case refers to the months January to November inclusive; the following figure in brackets refers to the complete year. Apparent discrepancies in the units figures are due to rounding to the nearest thousand.

1846	from Great Britain	from other countries	total
Wheat	2 (23)	16 (19)	18 (42)
Flour	– (18)	2 (2)	2 (21)
subtotal	2 (41)	19 (22)	21 (63)
Maize	8 (34)	63 (79)	70 (113)
Maize meal	– (5)	3 (3)	3 (9)
subtotal	8 (40)	66 (82)	73 (122)
total	10 (81)	81 (104)	94 (185)

CHAPTER 11

Apologia for a dead civil servant*

In the service of Peel

In the course of an essay on corruption in developing countries which is reproduced in his stimulating book *Writers and politics*, Dr Conor Cruise O'Brien had this to say about the less desirable attributes in a civil servant:

> Personal bribe-taking, though obviously a serious vice in an official, can be less grave than a form of corruption much more general at various periods among servants of the empire: that vicarious form of corruption which consists in being an unquestioning agent of collective rapacity. Thus Sir George Trevelyan was, according to the conventional view, an upright civil servant. It would have been far better for the Irish people who were unfortunate enough, during the famine of the 1840s, to have their fate decided and sealed by Sir George, if he had been a drunkard and a bribe-taker with some compassion in his heart and less complacency about 'iron laws' which enriched those whom he served.

The intended object of this severe criticism is clearly not George but *Charles* Trevelyan, who was the permanent civil servant in charge of the Treasury at the time of the famine. It is tempting to speculate in passing on the measure of toleration which Dr O'Brien would be prepared to extend to a corrupt alcoholic with a heart of gold if such were to be found today in the employ of the Department of Posts and Telegraphs. One must, however, note in fairness that the essay was written several years before the author assumed ministerial responsibility; in fact, very shortly after Mrs Cecil Woodham-Smith, in *The great hunger*, had broken new ground by casting Trevelyan in the role of principal scapegoat for the British government's mishandling of the famine crisis.

The pillorying of Sir Charles, ungrateful though it be to 'by far the ablest man connected with Irish relief', has value as a cautionary example of how easily one can be led to transfer guilt from a responsible minister of government to a public servant who faithfully implements and defends his master's policy without regard to his own opinions or preferences. Luckily for the defence of Trevelyan's memory, he served as head of the Treasury under two successive prime ministers, and some clues appear in the official records as to his reactions in carrying out two divergent policies in very different phases of the Irish famine.

* From *The Irish Times*, 5-6 May 1977.

When a new and virulent disease was detected in the potato crops of Europe in 1845, the earliest report came from Belgium. It was over a month later that blight first came to notice in southern England, and not until late in the growing season that it was at last reported in Ireland. The prime minister, Sir Robert Peel, was first alerted at the beginning of August by news that the potato crop was stricken in the Isle of Wight; shortly after, he read a grave report from an extensive potato grower in Kent who foresaw 'a shocking calamity for the poor' if the disease was not contained.[1] In the following weeks, as reports of the disease spread further west and north, anxiety grew in London lest the scourge should cross the Irish Sea, but the reports from Ireland were uniformly reassuring. The potato crop was extensive and was expected to yield heavily.

The first confirmation early in September of scattered outbreaks of the disease in Dublin and Waterford caused no public concern in Ireland; as Andrew Kettle recalled, 'the blight came on like a thief in the night in the autumn of 1845'.[2] It was, many felt, too late in the growing season for the disease to make serious inroads into a flourishing crop. The news was, however, received with consternation in England; Professor John Lindley, editor of the influential *Gardeners' Chronicle*, stopped the press on 13 September to bring the fateful tidings and to speculate on where Ireland would be in the event of a universal potato rot. The government hastened to instruct the constabulary to make regular reports on the state of the potato crop in every part of Ireland. When the initial batch of police reports proved conflicting, Peel decided to seek scientific advice at the highest level and, in the middle of October, appointed a triumvirate of professors – Lindley, Playfair and Kane – to inspect and report on the Irish crop.

By now alarm had begun to replace complacency in Ireland when a number of tubers were found at digging time to have rotted in the ground. As the weeks passed by concern gave way to panic when it was discovered that potatoes which had appeared sound at harvest were 'melting away' in storage. From the second week of October to the last week in November the Irish newspapers reflected an atmosphere of terror and despair. The potato commissioners could find no basis for hope in their reports to Peel. Lindley concluded that his earlier estimate that one-sixth of the potato crop might be saved was unduly optimistic.

Having taken every possible step to arrive at a true account of the situation, Peel acted with decision. As a long-term measure he proposed to his cabinet that the corn laws should be repealed; as an immediate precaution he ordered a supply of maize from North America as backing to his relief employment measures.

This unconventional and courageous act helped to bring Ireland safe through the next nine months, but led to the ruin of Peel's political career. It can, of course, be validly judged only against the background of accepted contemporary wisdom rather than the very different opinions of the era of the welfare state. What 'the enlightened principles of political economy' dictated should be done by government in case of food shortage had been discussed most eloquently by Edmund Burke exactly fifty years earlier. The British harvest of 1795 had been a miserable failure after a season of prolonged drought and there were calls to the government to take action. In November Burke placed in the hands of the prime minister, William Pitt, an economic pamphlet, *Thoughts and details on scarcity*, which comprised a thundering denunciation of governmental interference in the food trade.

The opening sentence set the tone: 'Of all things, an indiscreet tampering with the trade of provisions is the most dangerous, and it is always worst when men are most disposed to it, that is, in the time of scarcity.' It was bad policy for government to attempt to feed the people: 'if once they are habituated to it, even but for one half year, they will never be satisfied to have it otherwise. And having looked to government for bread, on the very first scarcity, they will turn and bite the hand that fed them.' Such acts were worse than impolitic, they were immoral: 'It is not in breaking the laws of commerce, which are the laws of nature, and consequently the laws of God, that we place our hope of softening the Divine displeasure, to remove any calamity under which we suffer or which hangs over us.'

From these implacable 'principles of general policy', which Karl Marx was to quote ironically in *Capital*, Burke was not prepared to admit of deviation except in exceptional circumstances. He would, without much doubt, have conceded that such circumstances faced Peel, confronted as he was with the best available advice that an entire food supply was being wiped out.

Happily (in the short term) for Ireland, but unhappily for Peel's political future, the professors' judgement was soon proved faulty. They could not know that the new potato disease did not spread from tuber to tuber in storage. Only those potatoes which had contracted the disease in the soil or at harvest time were liable to rot in the clamps; those tubers which were sound when pitted continued healthy. By late November 1845 it became clear that, while about one-third of the potato harvest had indeed 'melted away', the process had come to a halt. In the words of Jonathan Pim, 'the disease appeared stayed, no one could say how'. From an abundant potato crop, about three-quarters of a regular year's food supply was safe. The disaster was on a much smaller scale than had appeared certain when Peel had committed himself irrevocably to his counter-measures.

These counter-measures were in consequence highly successful. The relief officers under the general direction of Trevelyan tackled a difficult and unfamiliar task with commendable industry and devotion and sincerity. Trevelyan drove his team as hard as himself; when Routh, who headed the relief commission in Ireland, complained that he was grossly overworked: 'I cannot write more, as I am an invalid today and intend to remain quiet to recruit,' Trevelyan replied drily by return: 'I hope to hear tomorrow that you have got rid of your indisposition – we have not time to be ill nowadays.'[3]

What troubled some of the workers in the field was not so much the heavy burden of relief work as what they felt to be the moral problem of affording governmental help which could not be justified by abnormal circumstances. Burke had expressed this as a matter of conscience, and quite honourable men became increasingly troubled in their minds about the morality of the government's measures as winter gave way to spring without many signs of distress in excess of that which was 'normal' in Ireland.

The unhappily named Commissary-General Pine Coffin wrote to Trevelyan from Limerick on 11 April 1846: 'I am so thoroughly persuaded of the general truth of the principles laid down by Burke in his *Thoughts and details on scarcity* that I have always sought to excuse rather than commend the interference of government on the present occasion.' Shortly afterwards his colleague Dobree in Waterford also drew the Treasury's attention to the correctness of Burke's views.

Trevelyan replied to both in a message sent to Routh on 29 April 1846: 'Our measures must proceed with as little disturbance as possible of the ordinary course of private trade, which must ever be the chief resource for the subsistence of the people, but, *coûte que coûte*, the people must not, *under any circumstances*, be allowed to starve.'[4] 'Whatever the expense' is no common phrase to find underlined in a Treasury directive: certainly there is no sign here of heartless complacency about the 'iron laws' of commerce.

In reviewing the first season of relief early in June 1846, Trevelyan claimed that there was a party interest in playing down the extent of the loss of the previous season's potato crop and the consequent distress. 'If the government machinery had never been set up or were now to be withdrawn, the persons who hold this tone would be shocked by the result.' He did not know that before the month was out a political decision by his new masters would forthwith begin to dismantle the machinery which he had hitherto operated to such good effect.

In the service of Russell

Ireland did not shriek when Peel fell from office on 25 June 1846; quite the reverse, in fact, for a majority of Irish MPs had voted to bring him down. They were led by Daniel O'Connell, who was 'only too proud to serve under such a leader' as Lord John Russell, the new prime minister. Had he been able to foresee the events of the coming twelve months, he would surely have revised the verdict.

O'Connell cannot fairly be criticised for not foreseeing that blight, which had struck only a late glancing blow at last year's crop, would shortly wipe out the new season's potato plants almost before they had begun to yield. A plant disease of such virulence was quite unknown to Ireland, and Professor Lindley was almost alone in continuing to fear disaster. The seeds of destruction had unwittingly been sown at harvest time in 1845 when large numbers of affected tubers were discarded in the fields; a mild winter permitted many of these to survive long enough to act as potential infection foci in the new season. Nor was this the only way in which the weather conspired in setting the scene for the disaster of 1846. A wet spring delayed the planting of the potato crop, and quick growth was further hampered in mid-June by one of the longest and most intense early heat waves known in Ireland.

This hot, dry spell was caused by a continental anti-cyclone which continued to dominate the weather of western Europe and most of England throughout the summer of 1846, so that while the potato and other crops in that area suffered from drought, blight was completely kept at bay. In Ireland and in the Scottish highlands, however, the weather broke with recurrent thunderstorms in the second half of June; depressions skirting the Atlantic edge of the continental high pressure system brought a succession of rainy spells in July.

The foliage of the potato varieties most widely grown in Ireland at the time proved to have little or no resistance to the new disease. In the last few days of July and the first week of August 1846, the Irish potato crop succumbed completely and fatally to blight. At this time the total weight of marble-sized tubers beneath the blackened tops was little more than one-tenth of a normal crop. Lindley's forecast had come true with a time-lag of a year. The potato yield represented only about a month's food.

What O'Connell might reasonably have been expected to realise was that the switch from Peel to Russell threw away any insurance Ireland had against renewed hunger. The new government was inhibited by the circumstances under which it had assumed power, and by its conviction that all the measures taken by its predecessor in respect to Ireland were either 'crimes or blunders'. A contemporary analysis in the *Irish Farmers' Journal* put the point clearly and reasonably:

> Last year Sir Robert Peel was loaded with all sorts of obloquy and abuse, for raising a famine cry to enable him to carry out his measures of free trade – for giving ear to the alarms sounded forth by interested persons – for waste of public money in endeavours to ascertain the cause of the disease, to provide remedial means, and to preserve for the public use as much as possible of the failing food.
>
> Towards the end of October 1845 the destructive disease in the potato was proceeding with a rapidity that, had it continued at the same rate of progress throughout the winter, the entire crop must have been destroyed long before the spring of 1846. There were, however, many men whose minds are too powerful to

be led by circumstances or persuaded by facts; men so sceptical that the plainest proofs require to be more plainly shown; men who think it wiser to run the risk of ruin rather than excite alarm; these men denied the general character of the disease, scouted at precaution, and laughed at the apprehension of famine. An unforeseen check to the disease in the decrease of the temperature of the weather on the approach of winter – a check equally unforeseen by both parties – turned the scale in favour of the no-famine side, and the no-famine party either ungenerously or ignorantly claimed a triumph for their opinions, and Sir Robert Peel was a cheat and the potato commissioners fools.

Had the present government, with the prescience of a Peel, upon the blighting of the potato stalks this season, immediately brought before parliament those comprehensive measures, for which we now all admit the necessity, they would at once have been met by derisive sneers as alarmists untaught by the experience of the miscalculations of the year 1845; and had it afterwards turned out that this blight of the stalk was only the effect of a passing breath, had the tenacity of life of the potato plant enabled it to send forth fresh leaves, as it did to a small degree, and to recover from this passing attack, we should then have had the whole pack open with clamorous yells and some sinister causes discovered of their vain alarm.

Unfortunately for the country, her majesty's ministers had either been over-taught by the experience of the last year, or had not sufficient reliance on those whose science of research might have enabled them to form a more correct judgment of the enduring nature of the disease, and in this the country has no right to blame them, for none would listen to a warning noise.[5]

Within a week of Russell's assumption of the seat of power in place of Peel there is a distinct change of tone in the official correspondence. On 8 July 1846 Messrs Baring Brothers, who had handled Peel's maize order, were told that there would be no further need for their services: 'I am happy to say that we do not require to make any further purchases,' to which the grain importers replied congratulating Trevelyan 'on the termination of your feeding operations'. Arrangements to wind up the relief organisation were pushed ahead.

Colonel McGregor, head of the Irish police, was filled with foreboding as he noted the fresh inroads of the potato disease in Ireland and realised the difficulties in stirring the new government to action. In a letter of foresight and compassion, which he wrote to Trevelyan on 15 August 1846, he clearly recognised the problem facing the latter: 'I apprehend, notwithstanding your experience, you will not have the same facilities for counteracting the coming calamity: yet, unless speedy measures be adopted the most serious consequences will ensue.' In other, less tactful words: I realise that your hands are now politically tied.

There is an ironic echo of the previous year's correspondence in the new-season's exchanges between Trevelyan and his anxious associates in Ireland.[6] Now it was the subordinates who begged for more effective government action, and Trevelyan who, in defence of Russell's inactivity, quoted back to them the principles laid down by Burke. He did this for instance to Routh when the latter expressed his concern about the exportation of the oats crop. A week later, like a good civil servant,

Routh in his turn explained to a delegation from Achill Island that the present government was determined to act more in accordance with the enlightened principles of political economy; if the delegates would read and consider what had been written on the subject by Edmund Burke, their illustrious countryman, they would be compelled to agree.

There was nothing in the English agricultural scene to confirm the tales of disaster which came from Ireland in the autumn of 1846. The Londoner of 1845 had not needed to travel far to see with his own eyes the ravages of which the new disease was capable; Mr Alfred Smee, surgeon to the Bank of England, had observed its progress during his professional journeys through the city, partly in gardens in Upper Clacton and partly in 'a little field in the Old Kent Road'.[7] But in 1846 potato blight no longer forced itself upon the attention of those who lived in the capital or in most of England, and the memory of its virulence soon died away. The initial reaction of London circles to reports of the fresh outbreak in Ireland was one of incredulity and exasperation: 'It is possible to have heard the tale of sorrow too often.'

To add to the inevitability of tragedy there was initially a complete absence of public clamour from Ireland to give urgency and direction to Russell's dilatory steps. The zeal with which Peel had been hounded and the enthusiasm which had so recently greeted the coming to power of Russell made it difficult for O'Connell and his supporters to criticise the new administration publicly, at least before giving it time to prove itself. In a private letter, O'Connell might plead that the government feed the people, '*no matter at what cost,* and without delay' – a curious echo of the same phrase used by Trevelyan in the previous year – but he had, in fact, never favoured the discontinuation of the shipping of grain from Ireland.[8] In public, the *Freeman's Journal* claimed that 'Ireland will acknowledge the promptitude with which Lord John Russell has provided against coming evil.'

In these circumstances there was little prospect that Trevelyan or any other civil servant could hope to soften government policy, even if the prime minister had been one to welcome advice from his entourage. Russell's character had been accurately if mordantly summarised by Sydney Smith:

> There is not a better man in England than Lord John Russell, but his worst failure is that he is utterly ignorant of all moral fear; there is nothing he would not undertake. I believe he would perform the operation for the stone – build St Peter's – or assume (with or without ten minutes' notice) command of the Channel Fleet; and no one would notice by his manner that the patient had died – the church tumbled down – and the Channel Fleet been knocked to atoms.[9]

In precisely this 'unflappable way' Russell took on the task of governing a starving people and, showing none of the urgency or troubled anxiety of Peel in the previous autumn, proceeded with apparent confidence to attack a problem of unprecedented magnitude with quite inadequate measures. As so often in later disasters all over the world, it would be left to the Quakers to be the pioneers of effective practical relief, unencumbered by theory or politics.

During his subsequent service in India, Trevelyan showed in his approach to periodic famine what Mrs Woodham-Smith considered to be 'a less rigid and more humanitarian attitude than he exhibited in Ireland'; his Irish experience had had, she surmised, a softening effect. It would be kinder and surely more accurate to say that, freed from the dead weight of Russell, Trevelyan resumed in India the more humane and flexible stance which he had shown in Ireland under Peel.

CHAPTER 12

Reassessing the famine*

It is difficult for an Irishman, even after the lapse of more than a century, to discuss the famine years with unemotional objectivity, but an effort should be made. As the Italian historian, Gaetano Salvemini, wrote: 'We cannot be impartial, only intellectually honest. Impartiality is a dream; honesty a duty.'

It should be said right away that there is not a tittle of evidence during these years which points to deliberate malintent towards the Irish people on the part of the British government or its representatives in Ireland. There is, on the contrary, ample proof, in all their deliberations and acts, of a sincere desire, within the then accepted ideas of the limits of legitimate government action, to alleviate the crisis brought on by the potato failure. This is not to say that successive British governments did not bear a heavy share of guilt, in common with many in Ireland, for failure to make a serious effort to correct, in earlier years, the instability in the Irish economic structure which led inevitably to disaster. The real lesson of the famine is not a sterile one of bitterness and hatred, but a warning that is never outdated – that the greed and shortsighted self-interest of groups with effective power, no matter with what veneer of respectability they may be disguised by current economic or political thought, must not be permitted to ride roughshod over the long-term welfare of the people as a whole.

But if no charge of deliberate murder or genocide may be brought home to the English rulers of the famine years, what of culpable homicide, of guilt by delay and inadequacy? Before reaching a final verdict, account must be taken of the dimensions of the problem with which they were faced, of the difficulties arising from an imperfect knowledge of these dimensions and the crippling effect of current concepts of the role of government.

The immeasurably greater problem which faced Russell in 1846-7, as compared with that with which Peel grappled fairly effectively in the previous year, can be easily illustrated. The smooth operation of the potato economy required an annual intake of 15 million tons of potatoes; of this amount only a little over one million tons was available in 1846.

* From *The Irish Times*, 19-20 October 1966. This article is largely a summary based on the author's formal papers on the quantification of the pre-famine socio-agricultural situation in Ireland.

The most pressing task, to be solved within the six-week period for which the remnant of the 1846 crop could be eked out, was to provide food for 4.7 million people who lived wholly or largely on the potato; within this group there were 2.3 million landless farm labourers and their dependants, almost wholly without resource. At the other extreme, there were less than three-quarters of a million people – i.e. less than 10% of the population, whose diet was not seriously affected by the potato failure.

But keeping the people alive would be only the first step. The potato was not merely the food of the people, and of the pigs and other livestock; it was the base on which the whole pyramid of Irish life had balanced precariously for a hundred years – and the base suddenly collapsed. A whole way of life would have to be rethought and reconstructed in the middle of disaster. It was a problem to which there was certainly no easy solution, and probably no adequate one.

The first prerequisite to solving any problem is to define it accurately. In place of reliable information, the authorities were confused by discordant estimates and grappled largely in the dark with an elusive enemy. The lack of the appropriate agricultural statistics was sorely felt from an early stage of the potato failure. In reply to criticism by Mr Stafford O'Brien in the house of commons, the government reply was that all efforts to collect such information had failed. Indeed it was felt by many in Ireland that statistical inquiries were 'a prying into the private affairs of individuals'.

In September 1846 Sir Charles Trevelyan of the Treasury asked for fundamental information on the extent and yield of food crops in Ireland both in normal seasons and in the current year.[1] The request caused consternation in Ireland. Sir Randolph Routh, chairman of the relief commission, replied that he had been trying without success to obtain just this kind of data ever since he had first come to the country. Colonel McGregor, head of the constabulary, was at first reluctant to take on the task of belatedly collecting crop information since 'I despair of our people being able to answer all your queries.' Nevertheless, the police made a remarkable effort at a statistical survey of the food situation, and, although the main returns came too late to be an effective help in relief work, it is largely on the basis of the material assembled by the constabulary that a quantitative analysis of the crop situation in the years 1845-6 is possible.

The crippling restriction placed on government activity by the principle of *laisser faire* is an aspect of the famine years which strikes an unsympathetic chord in the modern mind. But it is not entirely fair to judge Russell's actions other than against the background of the accepted economic tenets of his day. That private enterprise was sacrosanct was an opinion held with all the conviction of religious dogma. Nearly thirty years later it could still be claimed that 'it was at least doubtful whether the late purchase of Indian corn by Sir Robert Peel was not contrary to sound principle'.

It is easy to forget that the concept of the welfare state caused acute moral anguish in Ireland in quite recent times and that it is still regarded with righteous suspicion in the USA. Nor can we reassure ourselves that the cries of starving people could not today be drowned by fashionable catchcries, while the problems of hunger, illiteracy and disease in a large part of the world 'have strong and living roots in the system of exploitation known as the maintenance of Western Civilisation'.[2]

Let us suppose that Russell had been a man of a different mould, fully and immediately informed in August 1846 on the scale of the problem and free (if that be possible) of all confusion between moral principles and private interests. The question of the cost of relief we shall take to be quite secondary – '*coûte que coûte*, the people must not, *under any circumstances*, be allowed to starve', to quote the often harshly judged Trevelyan.

The first necessary step would be to prohibit grain shipments from Ireland and to divert this food to home use. Other food exports would make too small and impractical a contribution to the domestic food balance to warrant an even greater outcry from the deprived British public. The amount of grain thus made available would be considerably less than the 284,000 tons which was shipped out in the calendar year 1846; at a very outside figure we may estimate it at a quarter of a million tons, valued at about £2 million at a low market price. It would be scarcely feasible simply to confiscate these exports, if only because the co-operation of landlords and commercial interests would be essential for any continuing relief scheme, but no doubt the shippers and English corn traders could be left to bear their own losses.

GRAIN TRADE, IRELAND 1845/7
(in thousands of tons)

	Exports	*Imports*
1845	513	27
1846	284	189
1847	145	836

Immediate steps must then be taken to repress grain hoarding by severe penalties. The enormous problems of milling, distribution, storage and rationing must be solved in a few weeks, as well as the recruitment and instruction of a much-expanded commissary staff. With this organisation, the grain in hand, equivalent to less than a million tons of potatoes, might, with frugal use, solve the human food problem until the early new year.

All the effort so far could buy only a respite of a couple of months. The next problem would be to seek, in a restricted sellers' market, a total of at least a million tons of grain to bridge the gap to the next harvest. It would be difficult to fill even a part of this sudden extra demand with maize from North America; adequate shipping space would be a further problem, and, even if the Atlantic winds were favourable, there would be inevitable delays in delivery. On arrival in Ireland the recurrent problem of milling and storage, which had been so troublesome in the case of Peel's tiny maize cargoes, would arise again in greatly aggravated form.

But all this, should the miracle come off, would be only a beginning, even if the unsound potato economy could be immediately re-established upon a no longer dependable crop. Either the same rescue operation, on a varying scale, must be undertaken year after year, or some way must be found – possibly by assisted emigration – to solve the problem of the group of over two million people, made up of landless men and their families. Even after the dreadful bloodletting of the famine, the road to the beginnings of a juster social system would be long and arduous; to expect that an immediate, permanent solution could have been found for the far greater problem of the swollen pre-famine population is scarcely realistic.

It is difficult to disagree with the contemporary conclusion reached by the Quaker, Jonathan Pim: 'No human power, nor any amount of expenditure, could have wholly averted starvation, or prevented the loss of many lives.'[3]

When what was done was done, the total of refugees and dead was close to one-quarter of the whole population. And since those in charge were ordinary human beings coping with an extraordinary situation, there were inevitably the usual ingredients of waste, stupidity, selfishness, inefficiency and bungling. 'Times such as these call forth into strong relief both the kindness of humanity and the innate selfishness of the human heart,' wrote Pim. It is not unnatural that Irish bitterness should focus upon the blunders and omissions, and concentrate its sorrow and fury against the person of the 'Famine Queen', regardless of the unfairness of placing the main load of guilt on the shoulders of a young woman of twenty-six years, never particularly bright or well informed, and without effective power.

One could, however, look on the question from a different point of view. When what was done was done, more than six million people came out alive from an unprecedented catastrophe, and the number of survivors amongst those who lived wholly or largely on the potato was substantially greater than the number of victims. The measure of success attained by private and official relief operations was not inconsiderable. 'Never before had any civilised people experienced such suffering, never had there existed such a feeling of universal sympathy, accompanied by exertions for their relief on so gigantic a scale,' wrote Pim.

The amounts of money made available from official sources and by private subscriptions are impressive. Generous contributions came not only from England, but from as far afield as Russia, Turkey, India, Australia, America and the Seychelles Islands. But money alone could not solve Ireland's problems, and the difficulty was not confined to finding food to buy. To quote Pim:

> It was natural to expect, when subscriptions were raised on so large a scale, that the distress should quickly be relieved; and the generous donors in England were surprised and pained to find that on the contrary it continued unabated, or rather increased in intensity. Many thought that it only needed to convert the subscriptions into food, pour it into the distressed places, and all would be right again. But the real difficulty lay in the structure of society throughout a great part of Ireland...The machinery for relieving distress did not exist, it could not be created with sufficient rapidity, and therefore the people suffered.

To those, whether government agents or voluntary workers, who devoted themselves to the field work of relief, Ireland owes a great debt of gratitude. One Quaker relief worker wrote as follows:

> If I were merely to consult my personal ease, I would greatly prefer being a donor to being a distributor of relief. It is much easier for a man to put his hand into his purse than to labour from morning till night in giving out stirabout to crowds of half-clad, hungry people sinking with weakness or fever...I saw thousands today of the most miserable people I have ever seen. I saw more misery today than I have ever seen before.

Of the Quakers themselves, it is only necessary to say that their work was in the high tradition of Christian brotherhood which has distinguished the Society of Friends in many areas of distress and in many times.[4] No greater praise is possible. The Irish priests, sprung from the people and one with them in thought and sympathy, did heroic work. Starvation was something no doctor could cure, but against fever and disease the doctors of Ireland fought without sparing themselves.

Of the two groups whose image did not come untarnished through the famine years, a special word must in justice be spoken.

The clergy of the established church lived for the most part in isolation from the mass of the people. They were of two types. The first and smaller group was dominated by narrow denominational fanaticism. It saw nothing about it, even in the height of the famine, but the hated 'superstitions of Popery'; it smelled not the stench of the rotting potato crop, but the sulphurous aroma of hellfire and eternal damnation into which it considered the erring heathen to be sinking. Some few – and over the country as a whole they *were* few, and rejected by the body of their fellows – were reduced by blind bigotry to the stupidity of thinking that men might be bought for God with bowls of soup.

A handful of wet straws upon the fire set up so thick a cloud of anger and recrimination that it blotted out the stars. The stupid sectarianism of a few misguided opportunists obliterated in time the memory of the good deeds of the many humane and tolerant ministers and of their families. As Pim points out:

The exertions of many of the clergy of the established church are well known, and appreciated as they deserve to be; the efficiency of their labours was, in many cases, owing to the cordial and skilful co-operation of their wives and daughters. The peculiar position of the Roman Catholic clergy in this respect rendered them less able to take an effective part in administering relief; but many of these, also, as well as the ministers of other religious bodies, have not been wanting in the discharge of the great and perilous duties which devolved on them.

Of the Reverend Valentine P. Griffith, minister of the parish of Maghery, in Co. Donegal, the Quaker, William Bennett, wrote on 23 March 1847:

I have rarely received the impression of more heartfelt zeal and devotedness in the cause of the poor than was manifested by this gentleman and his family; but they seemed indeed almost cast down and overborne by the rising tide of famine and desolation at their very doors, and by the hopelessness of the future. Everything, they said, was getting worse and worse; and where would it end, except under the over-ruling hand of Divine Providence, save in famine and pestilence consummating the work of depopulation, they were unable to conceive. The stubbornest heart would break beneath the sight of the harmless multitude – men, women, and little children – pining away in want and misery – our fellow-creatures and countrymen – in this boasted land of wealth, civilisation and humanity.

Resentment against the many landlords who helped scantily or not at all, and particularly against those who aggravated the catastrophe by harshness and inhumanity, has diverted attention from the proportionately even heavier burden borne by those who did their duty and often much more than their duty. When William Bennett was travelling through County Donegal in March 1847 he found that he could 'distinguish a long way off – by the number of poor people surrounding them – the residences of those who are devoting themselves to endeavours to mitigate the severity of this awful crisis'. The problems of these scattered good Samaritans were well summarised by Pim:

It cannot be denied that some landed proprietors, both resident and non-resident, have not only been wanting in efforts to mitigate the prevailing distress, but have even aggravated it by a selfish and unfeeling line of conduct towards their miserable tenantry; but there are very many also who have done their duty nobly in the difficult position in which they have been placed. They saw and felt for the misery around them, and gave their time and largely of their substance for its relief. No one who has not witnessed it can conceive the difficulties of their situation. Few and widely separated amidst such a mass of suffering; cramped by the non-payment of rents; without any personal assistance, and in great part without pecuniary contributions from the numerous non-resident proprietors, many of whose estates furnished much beyond an average proportion of pauperism; weighted down by the constant sight of misery which they could not relieve; oppressed by an anxious sense of the responsibility of their position and by the weight of public business; alarmed for the future, and frequently reminded of the dangerous nature of their duties, by seeing neighbours one after another struck down by the fever everywhere prevalent, and which had proved peculiarly fatal to the higher classes – it is indeed wonderful how so many of the resident gentry have been supported through difficulties so unparalleled, which might well have appalled the stoutest heart.

The Very Reverend Richard Butler, Church of Ireland dean of Clonmacnois and vicar of Trim, was a good and kindly man. He had no illusions about the deficiencies of the measures taken against the famine, and, in a sermon preached on 17 October 1847, the day prematurely appointed for a general thanksgiving for the ending of the late calamity, he did not spare his congregation:

> It may be doubted whether equal justice has been done to the conduct of the poor...It is easy to say, with Pharaoh's taskmasters, 'Ye are idle; ye are idle.' It is easy to say 'Ye are worthless and ungrateful.' It is easy, *but it is not true*. Idle! When they go far and near to seek for work. Worthless! When they possess such family affection and self-denial that soldiers have saved their pay on the banks of the Sutlej and labourers have hoarded their hard-earned wages on the wharfs of New Orleans, and sent them home to this parish, to enable their fathers and their mothers, whom perhaps they were never to see again, to bear the hardship of the year. Ungrateful! *Have you earned their gratitude?* I do not mean the gratitude of classes, but of individuals. Those who have earned the gratitude of the poor do not speak of their ingratitude. Happy have they been if they have not felt over-paid by the gratitude they have received, and if the thankfulness of the poor has not made them sensible, painfully sensible, of the shortcomings of their bounty, and ashamed of the paltriness of their benefits.[5]

In the course of the same sermon, Dean Butler made a prophecy:

> The graves of many a magistrate and physician, and poor law guardian, and clergyman, both Protestant and Roman Catholic, will tell to future times how boldly and how truly the resident gentry of Ireland did their duty in the past year of famine and of fever.

It is a prophecy which has not yet been fulfilled. Perhaps one day, if only in the interests of our children, we shall excise from our history books the corroding canker of hatred, and extend the roll of honour of those who died for Ireland to include not only those who fell in armed combat, but also those – English and Irish; Catholic, Protestant, Presbyterian, Quaker – who gave up their lives for their fellowmen in peaceful service. With such a change of heart we might truly speak of a visitation of God.

Notes and references

Chapter 1

1 R. N. Salaman, *The history and social influence of the potato* (Cambridge, 1949).

2 A. Payen and A. Chevallier, *Traité de la pomme de terre* (Paris, 1826); R. S. McAdam, 'On the potato' in *Quarterly Journal of Agriculture*, v (1835), pp 321-43; *Census of 1851*, v (i), p. 237.

3 W. R. Wilde, 'On the introduction and time of the general use of the potato in Ireland' in *Proceedings of the Royal Irish Academy*, vi (1853-7), pp 356-72.

4 W. D. Davidson, 'The history of the potato and its progress in Ireland' in *Journal of Department of Agriculture*, xxxiv (1937), pp 286-307.

5 W. R. Wilde, 'The food of the Irish' in *Dublin University Magazine*, xliii (1854), pp 127-46; id., 'On the introduction of the potato in Ireland'; *Census of 1851*, v (i) p. 238.

6 Davidson, 'History of the potato'; Salaman, *History and social influence of the potato*; id., *The influence of the potato on the course of Irish history* (Dublin, 1943); G. Hill (ed.), *The Montgomery manuscripts* (Belfast, 1869); K. H. Connell, *The population of Ireland, 1750-1845* (Oxford, 1950), pp 125-35; id., 'The history of the potato' in *Economic History Review*, 2nd. ser., iii (1951). pp 388-9; M. Drake, 'Marriage and population growth in Ireland, 1750-1845' in *Economic History Review*, 2nd ser., xvi (1963), p. 312.

7 J. Townley, *The diseases, regeneration and culture of the potato* (London, 1847), p. 34.

8 J. Jackson, *A treatise on agriculture and dairy husbandry* (Edinburgh, 1840), p. 80; R. Mitchison, *Agricultural Sir John: the life of Sir John Sinclair of Ulbster*, 1754-1835 (London, 1962), p. 88.

9 *Edinburgh Review*, xxxvii (1822), p. 95; *Irish Farmers' Journal*, 1845, pp 841-2.

10 Anon, 'On Irish agriculture', in *Quarterly Journal of Agriculture*, iv (1832-4), pp 296-310 (p. 302); F. Barker and J. Cheyne, *An account of the rise, progress and decline of the fever lately epidemical in Ireland* (Dublin, 1821), i, 31-2.

11 J. Rutty, *An essay towards a natural history of the county of Dublin*, 2 vols (Dublin, 1772), i, 82; W. G. Wood-Martin, *History of Sligo* (Dublin, 1892), p. 64.

12 Davidson, 'History of the potato', p. 299.

13 J. Townley, *The diseases, regeneration and culture of the potato* (London, 1847), p. 2.

14 Salaman, *History and social influence of the potato*, pp 226, 228, 447-8.

15 Quoted in Salaman, *History and social influence of the potato*, p. 235.

16 J. M. Mogey, *Rural life in Northern Ireland* (London, 1947), p. 18; McAdam, 'On the potato', p. 343.

17 Anon., *An essay on the potato blight and garden allotment system* (Oxford, 1846), p. 17.

18 Townley, *Diseases, regeneration and culture of the potato*, pp 2, 10-11.

19 McAdam, 'On the potato', p. 343; Jackson, *Treatise on agriculture*, p. 80; *Report on agriculture III*, 1836, p. 209, q. 13427; ibid., *I*, 1836, p. 150, q. 3080.

20 Drake, 'Marriage and population growth in Ireland', p. 312; *Census of 1851*, v (i), pp 124, 138.

21 C. Farran, *Letters on the origin of the disease in the potato* (Dublin, 1846), p. 11; Barker and Cheyne, *Account of the fever in Ireland*, i, 33.

22 *Edinburgh Review*, xxxvii (1822), p. 95.

23 Cited in *Census of 1851*, v (i), p. 193.

24 R. Maxwell, *The practical husbandman, being a collection of miscellaneous papers on husbandry, etc.* (Edinburgh, 1757); McAdam, 'On the potato', p. 327.

25 W. Aitken, *The potato rescued from disease and restored to pristine vigour* (Edinburgh, 1837), p. 5.

26 Mitchison, *Agricultural Sir John*, p. 155; J. Sinclair, *On the culture and uses of the potato* (Edinburgh, 1828), p. 15.

27 J. Muenter, *Die Krankheiten der Kartoffeln, insbesondere die im Jahre 1845 pandemisch*

herrschende nasse Fäule (Berlin, 1846), p. v; F. A. Pinkert, *Die Kartoffelnot unserer Zeit und ihre Abhülfe* (Weimar, 1843), trans. in *Journal of Agriculture*, 1844, p. 540.

28 J. Mareska and J. Kickx, *Rapport sur l'épidémie actuelle des pommes de terre* (Gand, 1845), p. 3; H. M. Waidson, *Jeremias Gotthelf: an introduction to the Swiss novelist* (Oxford, 1953), p. 27.

29 E. Roze, *Histoire de la pomme de terre* (Paris, 1898); McAdam, 'On the potato', pp 328, 343; Payen and Chevallier, *Traité de la pomme de terre*, pp 2-3; L. J. E. Meunier, *Du sulfatage systématique de la pomme de terre* (Auxerre, 1904), pp 9-10.

30 Arthur Young, *A tour in Ireland*, Bohn edn (London, 1892), ii, 46; McAdam, 'On the potato', pp 341-3; *RDS Prize essays* (Dublin 1835), p. 3; C. P. Bosson, *Observations on the potatoe, and a remedy for the potatoe plague* (Boston, 1846), p. i; D. Bain, *Observations upon the potato disease of 1845 and 1846* (Edinburgh, 1848), pp 2-4.

31 The most comprehensive account will be found in *Poor inquiry (F)*, 1836, p. 284 (for full details, see under *Poor inquiry* in bibliography).

32 H. Dutton, *Statistical survey of the county of Clare* (Dublin, 1808), p. 43, footnote.

33 H. Townsend, *Statistical survey of the county of Cork* (Dublin, 1810), p. 88.

34 R. McKay, *An anthology of the potato* (Dublin, 1961), pp 24-42.

35 *RDS Prize essays*, pp 5, 19.

36 G. Rye, *Considerations on agriculture* (Dublin, 1730); M. MacNeill, *The festival of Lughnasa* (London, 1962), chap. 4; *Poor inquiry (E)*, p. 2.

37 C. E. Trevelyan, *The Irish crisis* (London, 1848), p. 13, note; *Census of 1851*, v (i), pp 124, 239; W. Aitken, *The potato rescued from disease and restored to pristine vigour* (Edinburgh, 1837), pp 5-6.

38 Connell, *Population of Ireland*, pp 133-4.

39 J. M'Sweeny, 'An essay on the climate of Ireland' in *Transactions of the Royal Irish Academy*, xvii (1837), p. 231; *Irish Farmer's and Gardener's Register*, 1842, p. 34.

40 W. Maunsell, *On the culture of potatoes from the shoots* (Dublin, 1794), pp 10, 73.

41 Cited in Davidson, 'History of the potato', p. 299.

42 Ibid.

43 *MFM*, 1811, p. 46.

44 *Limerick Chronicle*, 11 Feb. 1846.

45 T. C. Foster, *Letters on the condition of the people of Ireland* (London, 1846), pp 75, 558-9; Rye, *Considerations on agriculture*.

46 R. C. Gaskell, *The life of Charlotte Brontë* (London, 1857; 1924 edn), p. 38.

47 Aitken, *The potato rescued from disease*, p. 9; J. M. Bauer, *As far as my feet will carry me* (London, 1959), p. 174.

48 *Irish Agricultural Magazine*, 1798, p. 186.

49 Davidson, 'History of the potato', pp 298, 300-1.

50 *MFM*, 1812, pp 126-7.

51 Davidson, 'History of the potato', p. 269: *IAM*, 1798, p. 62.

52 *MFM*, 1811, p. 46; ibid., 1812, p. 216.

53 Dutton, *Statistical survey of Clare*, p. 53.

54 Maunsell, *On the culture of potatoes from the shoots*, p. 40; *IAM*, 1798, p. 108; R. D. Edwards and T. D. Williams (eds), *The great famine: studies in Irish history, 1845-52* (Dublin, 1956), p. 395.

55 Cited by Davidson, 'History of the potato'.

56 Townsend, *Statistical survey of Cork*, p. 415; G. V. Sampson, *Statistical survey of the county of Londonderry* (Dublin, 1802), pp 135, 407-8.

57 *Report on agriculture III*, 1836, p. 283, qq 14723-30; Barker and Cheyne, *Account of the fever in Ireland*, i, 35.

58 *MFM*, 1812, p. 126.

59 E. Wakefield, *An account of Ireland, statistical and political*, 2 vols (Dublin, 1812), ii, 718.

60 *Cork Constitution*, 2 Oct. 1845; *Poor inquiry (D)*, Supp., p. 214.

61 In this connection, the correspondence between Maria Edgeworth and David Ricardo in 1822 is of interest: N. Mansergh, *The Irish question 1840-1921* (London, 1965), pp 289-90.

62 *Poor inquiry (E)*, pp 1-37 on 'Food'; *Edinburgh Review*, 1822, pp 94-5.

63 A. Atkinson, *Ireland in the nineteenth century* (Dublin, 1833), pp 167-8.

64 J. Binns, *The miseries and beauties of Ireland* (Dublin, 1837), ii, 454; E. R. R. Green, *The Lagan valley, 1800-1850* (London, 1949), p. 159; *Londonderry Journal*, 18 June 1833.
65 Mitchison, *Agricultural Sir John*, p. 255; Sinclair, *Culture and uses of the potato*, Appendix; J. Buckman, *The potato blight, its causes and remedies* (Cheltenham, 1845), p. 14.
66 William Drennan, *Glendalloch and other poems* (Dublin, 1859).
67 W. Cobbett, *Rural rides*, Everyman edn (London, n.d.), ii, 291.
68 *Poor inquiry (H)*, pt. ii, pp 7-10; Binns, *The miseries and beauties of Ireland*, ii, 127; J. H. Andrews, 'Road planning in Ireland before the railway age' in *Irish Geography*, v (1964), pp 17-41; *Report on agriculture III*, 1836, p. 261, q. 14298; *Report on bogs*, 1813-4, App. ii, p. 183.
69 *Tyrawly Herald*, 13 March 1845; Andrews, 'Road planning in Ireland'.
70 *Report on agriculture I*, 1836, p. 261, q. 14289; p. 263, q. 14345; *Report on agriculture II*, 1836, p. 81, qq 6003-5; p. 149, q. 6995; p. 150, qq 7013-6; *Report on agriculture III*, 1836, p. 286, qq 14781-3.
71 *Report on agriculture III*, p. 259, qq 14256, 14261-3; p. 261, qq 14299-300; p. 264, q. 14352; p. 267, q. 14422; p. 279, q. 14644; *Devon report*, 1845, witness 166, q. 7.
72 J. Wiggins, *The monster misery of Ireland* (London, 1844), pp iii, iv, 164, 267.
73 *IFGM*, 1838, p. 52.
74 D. H. K. Lee, *Climate and economic development in the tropics* (New York, 1957), p. 34.
75 C. F. P. von Martius, *Die Kartoffel-Epidemie der letzten Jahre, oder die Stockfäule und Räude der Kartoffeln* (Munich, 1842); *Report of Belgian commission*, 1845; C. P. Bosson, *Observations on the potatoe, and a remedy for the potatoe plague* (Boston, 1846); Earl Cathcart, 'On the cultivated potato' in *JRASE*, xx (1884), 266-300; Roze, *Histoire de la pomme de terre*; O. Appel, *Beiträge zur Kenntnis der Kartoffelpflanze und ihrer Krankheiten* 1. *Arbeiten aus Kaiserlichen Biologischen Anstalt für Land- und Forstwirtschaft*, Berlin, v (7) (1907), pp 377-435; D. Atanasoff, 'A study into the literature on stipple-streak and related diseases of the potato' in *Mededeelingen van de Landbouwhoogeschool*, Wageningen, no. 26 (1922); W. D. Davidson, 'A review of literature dealing with the degeneration of varieties of the potato' in *Economic Proceedings, Royal Dublin Society*, ii (1928), pp 331-89.
76 *Census of 1851*, v (i), p. 238.
77 M'Sweeny, 'Essay on the climate of Ireland', pp 218-9, 230; *LC*, 5 July 1845.
78 G. Boate, *A natural history of Ireland* (Dublin, 1775), chap. 21, sect. v; *Census of 1851*, v (i).
79 *Report on agriculture III*, 1836, p. 271, q. 14508; *The Plough*, 1846, p. 515; R. Maxwell, *The practical husbandman, being a collection of miscellaneous papers on husbandry etc.* (Edinburgh, 1757), pp 173-4.
80 *Census of 1851*, v (i), pp 151, 169, 190, 206, 240.
81 Ibid., p. 239.
82 *Irish Farmers' Journal and Weekly Intelligencer*, vi, pp 28, 31.
83 Davidson, 'Review of literature', p. 336; J. Duncan, *Essays on the potato plant, its failure in 1845-6 and the remedy* (Wick, 1847), p. 2.
84 Maxwell, *The practical husbandman*, p. 174.
85 Salaman, *History and social influence of the potato*, p. 189; *MFM*, i (1812), p. 347.
86 W. D. Davidson, 'History of potato varieties' in *JDA*, xxxiii (1935), p. 64.
87 J. Dubourdieu, *Statistical survey of the county of Down* (Dublin, 1802), p. 105.
88 Sampson, *Statistical survey of Londonderry*, p. 129; Sinclair, *Culture and uses of the potato*, pp 30-1; Aitken, *The potato rescued from disease*, pp 18-9; *IFJ*, 1847, p. 74; *RDS Prize essays*, p. 45.
89 Rye, *Considerations on agriculture*; Maxwell, *The practical husbandman*; Dubourdieu, *Survey of Down*, p. 84.
90 Davidson, 'History of potato varieties', pp 61-3; Dutton, *Statistical survey of Clare*, p. 43.
91 Sinclair, *Culture and uses of the potato*, p. 12.
92 *MFM*, ii (1813), p. 324; Aitken, *The potato rescued from disease*, pp 6, 33; *Journal of Agriculture*, 1844, p. 401.
93 Townley, *Diseases, regeneration and culture of the potato*, p. 36; Appel, *Beiträge zur Kenntnis der Kartoffelpflanze*, pp 379-83; Atanasoff, 'Study into the literature on stipple-streak and related diseases', pp 3-7.
94 *MFM*, ii (1812), pp 67, 126; *GC*, 1846, pp 211, 260.

95 *MFM*, ii (1812), p. 256.
96 *Census of 1851*, v (i), p. 240.
97 *RDS Prize essays*; Aitken, *The potato rescued from disease*, pp 83-115; von Martius, *Die Kartoffel-Epidemie der letzten Jahre*.
98 Townley, *Diseases, regeneration and culture of the potato*, pp 76-82; J. M. Wilson, *The potato: an essay on its constitution, diseases, varieties, cultivation and uses* (Edinburgh, 1850), pp 26, 35; G. H. Pethybridge and H. A. Lafferty, 'Further observations on the cause of the common dry-rot of the potato tuber in the British Isles' in *Scientific Proceedings of the Royal Dublin Society*, xv (1917), pp 193-222; MAFF Leaflet 218 (1956).
99 Aitken, *The potato rescued from disease*, p. 19; Wilson, *The potato*, p. 26; J. C. Morton, *A cyclopaedia of agriculture, practical and scientific*, ii (London, 1855), Article on the potato, p. 687; *RDS Prize essays*, p. 33.
100 *QJA*, v (1834-5), p. 594; vi (1835-6), pp 359-60; Roze, *Histoire de la pomme de terre*, pp 244-7; A. Smee, *The potatoe plant, its uses and properties; together with the causes of the present malady* (London, 1846), p. 31; R. Thompson, 'Observations and experiments made in the garden of the society in 1846 relative to the potato disease' in *Journal of the Horticultural Society of London*, ii (1847), pp 179-82.
101 *RDS Prize essays*, p. 67; *IFJ*, 1845, p. 1148; *IFGM*, 1834, p. 431; *IFJ*, 1845, p. 198; Smee, *The potato plant*, p. 31; Thompson, 'Observations and experiments'; J. F. W. Johnston (ed.), *The potato disease in Scotland* 5 (Pamphlets 1 to 6) (Edinburgh, 1845-6), p. 163.
102 *GC*, 1845, p. 370; Townley, *Diseases, regeneration and culture of the potato*, pp 34-5.
103 *RDS Prize essays*, pp 48-9; Cathcart, 'On the cultivated potato', p. 297, footnote; Johnston (ed.), *The potato disease in Scotland* 5, p. 146.
104 Aitken, *The potato rescued from disease*, p. 92; Johnston (ed.), *The potato disease in Scotland* 5, pp 139, 177.
105 Maunsell, *On the culture of potatoes from the shoots*, p. 14; *RDS Prize essays*, pp 39, 45; *QJA*, v (1834-5), pp 345, 593; Aitken, *The potato rescued from disease*, pp 60-5; *GC*, 1844, p. 140.
106 *IFJ*, 1845, p. 229.
107 *FG*, 1844, p. 203; *IFJ*, 1847, p. 290.
108 *GC*, 1845, p. 170; Aitken, *The potato rescued from disease*, p. 52; *IFJ*, 1845, p. 147; *NG*, 7 March 1846.
109 P. M. A. Bourke, 'Emergence of potato blight, 1843-6' in *Nature*, cciii (1964), pp 805-8 (above, chap. 7); M. J. Berkeley, 'Observations, botanical and physiological, on the potato murrain' in *Journal of the Horticultural Society of London*, i (1846), pp 9-34; Townley, *Diseases, regeneration and culture of the potato*.
110 H. Niven, *The potato epidemic and its probable consequences* (Dublin, 1846), pp 8-9.
111 *GC*, 1844, p. 234; J. Jackson, *A treatise on agriculture and dairy husbandry* (Edinburgh, 1840), p. 78.
112 Berkeley, 'Observations on the potato murrain', p. 10; Niven, *The potato epidemic*, p. 13; *Farmer's Guide*, 1841, p. 91.
113 Davidson, 'History of potato varieties'.
114 Ibid., p. 59.
115 Maxwell, *The practical husbandman*, p. 165; Dubourdieu, *Statistical survey of Down*, p. 102; Sinclair, *Culture and uses of the potato*, p. 13.
116 *RDS Prize essays*, p. 24; *Northern Whig*, 23 Sept. 1845; Constab. reports, 1845, Ballymena, 24 Sept.
117 Rye, *Considerations on agriculture*; *Annals of Horticulture*, 1847, p. 177; Davidson, 'History of potato varieties', p. 60.
118 Maunsell, *On the culture of potatoes from the shoots*, p. 41.
119 Sampson, *Statistical survey of Londonderry*, pp 136, 167; Dubourdieu, *Statistical survey of Down*, pp 102, 104; W. Tighe, *Statistical observations relative to the county of Kilkenny* (Dublin, 1802), p. 479.
120 *MFM*, 1811, p. 183.
121 Townsend, *Statistical survey of Cork*, pp 212, 407.
122 *MFM*, 1811, p. 25, footnote, p. 46; Sinclair, *On the culture of the potato*, p. 13; *IFJ*, 1846, p. 573; *IFGM*, 1834, p. 430; Morton, *A cyclopaedia of agriculture, practical and scientific*, ii, 668.

123 Dutton, *Statistical survey of Clare*, p. 43; Townsend, *Statistical survey of Cork*, p. 407; *Annals of Horticulture*, 1847, p. 177.
124 *QJA*, v (1834-5), p. 345; *Poor inquiry (F)*, pp 216, 316.
125 *Poor inquiry (E)*, 1836, p. 35.
126 *IFJ*, 1846, p. 573; *Poor inquiry (F)*, pp 308, 316; *GC*, 1846, pp 147, 179, 204, 260; Aitken, *The potato rescued from disease*, pp 92-3.
127 Davidson, 'History of potato varieties', p. 64; Salaman, *History and social influence of the potato*, p. 163; *IFJ*, 1846, p. 573; *CC*, 26 July 1845, advertisement; *LC*, 27 Sept. 1845; *Poor inquiry (F)*, p. 290.
128 *NW*, 23 Sept. 1845; *IFJ*, 1846, p. 742; *Poor inquiry (F)*, p. 298; *MFM*, ii, 1813, p. 338; *Poor inquiry (A)*, p. 511.
129 Johnston (ed.), *The potato disease in Scotland* 3, p. 63; *RDS Prize essays*, p. 64.
130 Townley, *Diseases, regeneration and culture of the potato*, p. 39; *RDS Prize essays*, p. 62.
131 *NW*, 23 Sept. 1845; Morton, *A cyclopaedia of agriculture, practical and scientific*, ii, 670.
132 Dutton, *Statistical survey of Clare*, p. 43; Townsend, *Statistical survey of Cork*, pp 88-90; Dutton, *Statistical survey of Galway*, p. 354.
133 P. W. Joyce, *Old Irish folk music and songs* (Dublin, 1909), p. 218.
134 *Drummond report*, 1837-8, p. 81.
135 Letter from an Irish tenant to Lord Althorp, June 1833, cited in R. B. O'Brien, *Thomas Drummond, life and letters* (London, 1889), p. 208.
136 *LC*, 5 Nov. 1845.
137 *Poor inquiry (A)*, p. 373.
138 *LC*, 8 Nov. 1845.
139 *IFJ*, 1846, p. 222.
140 *Poor inquiry (A)*, p. 528.
141 *Poor inquiry (D)*, Supp., pp 171, 199; *CC*, 7 Oct. 1845; *LC*, 13 Nov. 1845; Morton, *A cyclopaedia of agriculture, practical and scientific*, ii, 668.
142 Davidson, 'History of potato varieties', p. 60; Young, *Tour*, i, 331; *MFM*, 1811, pp 46, 55, 183, 263; *IFGM*, 1838, p. 195; *QJA*, vi (1835-6), p. 144.
143 *GC*, 1844, p. 78; *Annals of Horticulture*, 1847, p. 178; *JRASE*, vi (1846), p. 353.
144 Aitken, *The potato rescued from disease*, p. 92; W. Rothwell, 'Potato disease' in *The British Cultivator and Agricultural Review* (1845), p. 334; Johnston (ed.), *The potato disease in Scotland* 3, p. 112.
145 *Poor inquiry (D)*, Supp. p. 246; H. Mayhew, *London labour and the London poor* (London, 1861), iii, 288-92.
146 Townsend, *Statistical survey of Cork*, p. 616; J. E. Handley, *The Irish in Scotland: 1798-1845*, 2nd edn (Cork, 1945), p. 64.
147 W. H. R. Jackson, *An address...on the landlord and tenant question* (Cork, 1848), p. 5.
148 *RDS Prize essays*, p. 10; T. Johnson and C. Boyle, 'The industrial and nutritive value of the potato in Ireland' in *JDA*, xviii (1918), pp 453-4; *IFJ*, 1845, p. 448.
149 *Poor inquiry (F)*, p. 227.
150 Davidson, 'History of potato varieties', p. 64; Connell, *The population of Ireland*, p. 137.
151 *Drummond report*, p. 81.
152 *Poor inquiry (H)*, pt. ii, p. 10; App. (E), p. 2; App. (F), p. 205.
153 *Poor inquiry (F)*, pp 264, 267, 251.
154 *Devon report*, 1845, w. 39, q. 31.
155 *Poor inquiry (F)*, pp 276, 279, 285; *Poor inquiry (H)*, pt. ii, p. 10.
156 *DMA*, 24 Oct. 1845; Constab. reports, 1845.
157 *Poor inquiry (H)*, pt. ii, p. 10; T. W. Grimshaw, *Facts and figures about Ireland* (Dublin, 1893), pt. ii.
158 W. R. Wilde, 'The food of the Irish' in *Dublin University Magazine*, xliii (1854), p. 128; F. Dowdall (article on Irish agricultural statistics) in *Dublin Evening Herald*, 10 Nov. 1846.
159 *Poor inquiry (F)*, p. 237. Similar comments are to be found elsewhere in the *Poor inquiry*, for example in App. (F), pp 236, 247 ('the increase of poverty...has diminished the consumption of oatmeal and augmented that of potatoes') and in App. (E), p. 35.
160 Doyle, *Cyclopaedia of practical husbandry*; *Farmer's Guide*, 1841, pp 57, 63, 66, 158-61; *IFJ*, 1846, pp 243, 259.

161 Maunsell, *On the culture of potatoes from the shoots*, pp 22, 74; Townsend, *Statistical survey of Cork*, p. 212.
162 *MFM*, 1811, p. 174; *Poor inquiry (F)*, p. 316.
163 *IFGM*, 1838, p. 77; Martin Doyle, 'Hints to small farmers' in *The works of Martin Doyle* (Dublin, 1830), p. 43.
164 T. Radcliff, *A report of the agriculture and live stock of the county of Wicklow* (Dublin, 1812), pp 20-34.
165 *QJA*, vi (1835-6), p. 171; *IFJ*, 1846, pp. 177, 742.
166 Dubourdieu, *Statistical survey of Down*, p. 103; *MFM*, 1811, p. 53.
167 *QJA*, v (1834-5), p. 191; *IFGM*, 1835, p. 251.
168 *IFGR*, 1842, p. 111.
169 *IFJ*, 1845, pp 147, 565, 281; *KE*, 8 May 1846; *IFJ*, 1846, p. 259.
170 *RDS Prize essays*, pp 22, 56, 65; *DUM*, xxii (1841), p. 522; *Poor inquiry (F)*, pp 205, 215, 220; *IFJ*, 1845, p. 282.
171 C. E. Trevelyan, *The Irish crisis* (London, 1848), p. 38; *IFJ*, 1845, p. 1117.
172 *RDS Prize essays*, p. 6; *MFM*, 1812, p. 346; Constab. reports, 1845, return dated 19 Sept. 1845 from Marble Hill, Galway.
173 *MFM*, 1812, p. 153; C. B. Newenham, *Good news: potatoes grown from peels* (Cork, 1848), p. 16.
174 See *Poor inquiry (D)*, p. 30, and supplement I.
175 G. de Beaumont, *L'Irlande sociale, politique et religieuse*, 2 vols (Paris, 1839), i, 207.
176 *Poor inquiry (E)*, p. 16.
177 Trevelyan, *The Irish crisis*, pp 10-11.
178 D. A. Chart, *Ireland from the union to Catholic emancipation. A study of social, economic and administrative conditions, 1800-1829* (London, 1910), p. 77; id., *An economic history of Ireland* (Dublin, 1920), p. 91. Estyn Evans argues (in *Irish heritage* [Dundalk, 1942] p. 77) that July was designated the 'blue month' in Ulster because of food scarcity, and the term is taken up by Salaman (*History and social influence of the potato*, pp 253, 278). The adjective 'blue' seems unlikely in this connection, either in terms of nineteenth-century English or as a derivative from Irish. In a private communication, Professor Evans said that he could not recall the origin of his earlier statement. Dineen's *Irish-English dictionary*, p. 737, gives the 'yellow month' as a description in Irish of both July and August.
179 *Poor inquiry (E)*, pp 1-37.
180 *Poor inquiry (E)*, p. 1; *Report on agriculture III*, 1836, qq 13936-41, p. 242.
181 *LC*, 1 Nov. 1845.
182 Sinclair, *Culture and uses of the potato*, App., p. 11; *DUM*, 1841, p. 522.
183 *Poor inquiry (A)*, pp 407, 381, 374.
184 *Poor inquiry (E)*, p. 16; ibid., (A), p. 381; Wood-Martin, *History of Sligo*, p. 71.
185 *Poor inquiry (E)*, pp 16, 7, 4.
186 Sinclair, *Culture and uses of the potato*, App., pp 10-11.
187 *Poor inquiry (E)*, p. 16.
188 *Poor inquiry (E)*, p. 5; *DUM*, 1841, p. 522.
189 Trevelyan, *The Irish crisis*, pp 13, 15, 17.
190 P. M. A. Bourke, 'The extent of the potato crop in Ireland at the time of the famine' in *JSSISI*, xx (1959), pp 8-9; Constab. reports, 1845.
191 *Census of 1851*, v (i), 1856, pp 229, 231, 234, 360; Bourke, 'The extent of the potato crop', pp 7-8.

Chapter 2

1 P. M. A. Bourke, 'The use of the potato crop in pre-famine Ireland', in *JSSISI*, xxi (1967-8), pp 72-96 (above, chap. 4); id., 'Meteorological studies in relation to plant diseases and pests' in S. Krishnamurti (ed.), *Advances in agricultural sciences and their applications* (Madras, 1965).
2 Bourke, 'Use of the potato crop'.

3 Department of Health, 1950.
4 E. Wakefield, *An account of Ireland, statistical and political*, 2 vols (Dublin, 1812), ii, 714.
5 D. Bain, *Observations upon the potato disease of 1845 and 1846* (Edinburgh, 1848), p. 1.
6 Connell, *Population of Ireland*, pp 153-6.
7 M. McArthur, 'Some factors involved in estimating calorie requirements, with special reference to persons engaged in agricultural labour in Asian countries' in *Journal of the Royal Statistical Society*, ser. A, cxxvii (1964), pp 392-408.
8 Martin Doyle, *The works of Martin Doyle* (Dublin, 1830).
9 J. K. Trimmer, *A brief inquiry into the present state of agriculture in the southern part of Ireland* (London, 1809), p. 47.
10 H. B. Thompson, *Ireland in 1839 and 1869* (London, 1870), p. 10.
11 *MT*, xiii (1845-6), p. 273.
12 *Edinburgh Review*, xxxvii (1822), p. 95.
13 Salaman, *History and social influence of the potato*, p. 321.
14 Finlay Dun, *Landlords and tenants in Ireland* (London, 1881), p. 50.
15 Bourke, 'The extent of the potato crop in Ireland at the time of the famine', pp 13-14.
16 *Edinburgh Review*, xxxvii (1822), p. 95; R. Ryan, *Prize essay upon the following subject of inquiry, 'What are the best means of rendering the national sources of wealth possessed by Ireland effectual for the employment of the population?' (proposed by the Royal Irish Academy, 1822)* (London, 1824), p. 12.
17 Ryan, *Prize essay*, p. 75.
18 Ibid., p. 29.
19 *GC*, 1844, pp 689, 756.
20 *Devon report*, 1845, w. 450.
21 Hall, *Ireland*, ii, 123.
22 Ryan, *Prize essay*, pp 17, 80.
23 *Poor inquiry (F)*, p. 2.
24 *Report on agriculture III*, pp 261-2; Ryan, *Prize essay*, pp 81-2.
25 Townsend, *Statistical survey of Cork*, p. 187.
26 *Devon report*, 1845, w. 620, q. 11.
27 Ryan, *Prize essay*, pp 29, 82; *Report on agriculture III*, p. 283, q. 14731.
28 *LC*, 11 July 1846.
29 J. Caird, *The plantation scheme, or the west of Ireland as a field of investment* (London and Edinburgh, 1850), p. 83.
30 Ryan, *Prize essay*, p. 22.
31 Ibid., p. 51; *Report on agriculture III*, p. 282, q. 14716; pp 261-2.
32 *IFJ*, 30 Dec. 1846, p. 1004.
33 Caird, *The plantation scheme*, p. 109.
34 E. Carroll, 'Observations on the conacre system' in *IFGM*, ii (1835), pp 9-10.
35 *Poor inquiry (F)*, pp 1-34.
36 R. S. McAdam, 'On the potato' in *QJA*, v (1835), p. 332.
37 Thompson, *Ireland in 1839 and 1869*, p. 36.
38 Caird, *The plantation scheme*, pp 107-8.
39 *Report on bogs IV*, 1813-14, App. 5, p. 37; App. 6, p. 61; App. 7, p. 133; Hall, *Ireland*, ii, 37.
40 *GC*, 1845, p. 449; Anon. (C. T. Barrington), 'The yields of Irish tillage food crops since the year 1847' in *JDA*, xxi (1921), p. 217.
41 Young, *Tour in Ireland*, ii, 40; Maunsell, *On the culture of potatoes from the shoots*, p. 20.
42 *MFM*, 1813, p. 70; *Report on agriculture III*, p. 261.
43 *IFGM*, vi (1839), p. 82; *MFM*, 1813, p. 33; Barrington, 'The yields of Irish tillage food crops', p. 216; Lewis, *Topographical dictionary of Ireland*, ii, 70.
44 *IFJ*, 1845, p. 1038; *Devon report*, 1845, App. 8, p. 31.
45 W. O'Connor Morris, *Memories and thoughts of a life* (London, 1895), p. 29.
46 *GC*, 1845, p. 247; Society of Friends, *Transactions* (Dublin, 1852), p. 148.
47 *Devon report*, 1845, w. 813, q. 8; w. 843, q. 4; w. 454, q. 8; w. 1119 (Daniel O'Connell), q. 6; w. 719, q. 22; w. 663, qq 7-10; w. 505, qq 11-14; w. 601, qq 4-5; etc.
48 Young, *Tour in Ireland* i, 139; E. E. Evans, *Irish folk ways* (London, 1957), p. 221; *IFJ*,

1845, p. 1091.
49 Doyle, *Cyclopaedia of practical husbandry*, p. 419.
50 Dutton, *Statistical survey of Clare*, p. 41, footnote; *Report on agriculture III*, p. 318.
51 *LC*, 8 Nov. 1845; *CC*, 19 Sept. 1846.
52 Bicheno, *Ireland and its economy*, p. 21.
53 *JA*, 1844, pp 219-226; *GC*, 1844, pp 93, 121, 338, 822; *IFGM*, vi (1839), pp 282-3.
54 Dubourdieu, *Statistical survey of Down*, p. 79; *IFJ*, 1845, p. 198.
55 Maxwell, *The practical husbandman*, pp 161-3, 166; Maunsell, *On the culture of potatoes from the shoots*, p. 19; Sinclair, *Culture and uses of the potato*, p. 31.
56 W. H. R. Jackson, *An address...on the landlord and tenant question* (Cork, 1840), p. 76; *IFJ*, 1845, p. 198; *Report on the potato crop*, 1880, pp 20, 41, 47, 51, 52, 56, 61, 113; Salaman, *History and social influence of the potato*, pp 232-3.
57 Lewis, *Topographical dictionary of Ireland*, ii, 151; *IFJ*, 1845, p. 229; *Devon report*, 1845, w. 500, q. 30.
58 NAAS, *Fourth annual review*, pp 17-20.
59 W. J. Fitzpatrick, *Life, times and correspondence of Dr Doyle*, new edn, 2 vols (Dublin, 1880) i, 429.
60 Wilde, 'The food of the Irish', p. 138.
61 *The Plough*, ii, 1846, pp 732-6; Anon., *The potato blight famine. Questions and replies between two travellers on its causes and results* (Dublin, 1847), p. 3.
62 J. Wolseley, *The difficulty met: a letter to the labouring poor of Ireland* (London, 1846), p. 6.
63 *SJ*, 12 Sept. 1845.
64 E. Newman, *Notes on Irish natural history* (London, 1840), pp 45-6.
65 Ryan, Prize essay, pp 88-9; J. K. Trimmer, *A brief inquiry into the present state of agriculture in the southern part of Ireland* (London, 1809), p. 1.
66 R. B. McDowell, *Public opinion and government policy in Ireland*, 1800-1847 (London, 1952), p. 237.
67 Ryan, *Prize essay*, p. 83.
68 Newman, *Notes on Irish natural history*, p. 1.
69 *JA*, 1848, p. 505.
70 Society of Friends, *Transactions*, p. 308.
71 Ibid., p. 327.
72 Caird, *The plantation scheme, or the west of Ireland as a field of investment*, pp 98, 134.
73 *GC*, 1846, pp 163-4, 227, 567, 629-30, 646; *IFJ*, 1846, p. 112; *MT*, 1846, p. 506; *IFJ*, 1846, p. 1004.
74 *IFJ*, 1846, p. 685; R. Kane, 'On the recent progress and the present state of industry in Ireland; and the Dublin international exhibition of 1865' in H. Parkinson and P. L. Simmonds (eds), *The illustrated record and descriptive catalogue of the Dublin international exhibition of 1865* (London, 1866), p. 54; Society of Friends, *Transactions*, p. 296.
75 J. Prebble, *The highland clearances* (London, 1963).
76 James Connolly, *Labour in Irish history*, 1922 edn., p. 163; R. D. Edwards and T. D. Williams (eds), *The great famine: studies in Irish history, 1845-52* (Dublin, 1956), p. xv.
77 W. F. Adams, *Ireland and Irish emigration to the New World* (New Haven, 1932), p. 413; Hall, i, 42.
78 *LC*, 25 June 1845.
79 *Poor inquiry (D)*, Supp., p. 294.

Chapter 3

1 *Agricultural returns*, 1847. *Returns of agricultural produce in Ireland in the year 1847*, pt. i, HC 1847-8 (923), lvii; pt. ii, HC 1847-8 (1000), lvii.
2 *Census of 1851. The census of Ireland for the year 1851*, pt. ii, HC 1852-3 (1589), xciii; pt. v (i), HC 1856 (2087-1), xxix; pt. vi, HC 1856 (2134), xxxi.
3 *Census of 1841. Report of the commissioners appointed to take the census of Ireland for the year*

1841, HC 1843 (504), xxiv.

4 *Agricultural returns*, 1847, pt. ii, p. iii.

5 See, for instance, note 8 below.

6 *Agricultural statistics, 1847-1926* (Dublin, 1928), p. v.

7 P. M. A. Bourke, 'Uncertainties in the statistics of farm size in Ireland, 1841-1851', *JSSISI*, xx, pt. 3 (1959-60), pp 20-26.

8 There exist two sets of official returns of farm size for each of the years 1841 and 1847, which differ in detail. For particulars, see Bourke, 'Uncertainties in the statistics'. The figures shown here are the revised data for 1841 and the original (and only complete) data for 1847.

9 *Agricultural returns*, 1847, pt. ii, p. iii.

10 These are, to some extent, arbitrary figures. However, as a numerical trial will readily show, the substitution of any other reasonable figures does not affect the argument.

11 To the extent that the difference between 1847 and 1851, thus roughly estimated, needs explanation, it arises in part from abandoned farm land not yet incorporated into other holdings (J. Caird, *Ireland and the plantation scheme* [Edinburgh and London, 1850], p. 114), and in part from the trend towards increased average size in the holdings above 30 acres (*Census of 1851*, pt. ii, p. iv).

12 Bourke, 'Uncertainties in the statistics'.

13 Here the term 'arable' is used in the narrower sense of tilled land, i.e. that under crops or in fallow. Pasture was defined on the census form as that portion of the farm fit for grazing which was not under tillage.

14 This was put forward as a rational hypothesis by Bourke, 'Uncertainties in the statistics', p. 25. It has since been confirmed by the discovery of a footnote to p. xii of the *Returns of agricultural produce in Ireland in the year 1855*, HC 1857 (2174 Sess.1), xv: 'The classification of holdings in 1841...did not include bog or waste.'

15 W. G. S. Adams, 'Some considerations relative to the position of the small-holding in the United Kingdom', in *Journal of the Royal Statistical Society*, lxx (1907), p. 412.

It is noteworthy that farm-size statistics for Great Britain follow the procedure adopted in Ireland in the 1841 census, i.e. the size of holding there is based on the 'crops and grass' area, ignoring wasteland, etc. (Adams, loc. cit.; D. K. Britton and K. E. Hunt, 'The agricultural statistics of the United Kingdom', *JRSS*, ser. A, cxiv (1951), 59-98 at p. 66).

There are, of course, other aspects of 'size of agricultural holdings' which have not been treated uniformly down the years, e.g. whether a group of parcels of land, in single ownership or control but divided either by geographical boundaries or otherwise, are to be considered as single or separate holdings (*Agricultural statistics, 1847-1926*, p. xlii). The problem we deal with here is, however, more fundamental and affects the statistics to a far greater degree.

16 The Irish acre = 1.62 statute acres. The exact proportion here depends on the extent to which returns were made in Irish, statute, and Cunningham acres (1.29 statute acres) respectively. Evidence of contemporary use suggests a ratio of 80:16:4. This is the basis for the figure 1.5.

17 *Returns of agricultural produce in Ireland in the year 1853*, p. xi, HC 1854-5 (1865), xlvii.

18 *Appendix to minutes of evidence taken before her majesty's commissioners of inquiry into the state of the law and practice in respect to the occupation of land in Ireland*, Appendix 94, pp 280-9, HC 1845 (672), xxii.

19 J. Pitt Kennedy, *Digest of evidence taken before her majesty's commissioners of inquiry into the state of law and practice in respect to the occupation of land in Ireland* (Dublin, 1847), pt. i, p. 396.

20 In addition to the categories listed in table 3, the original data give a breakdown of the larger holdings into sizes of 50-100, 100-200, 200-500, 500-1,000, 1,000-2,000, 2,000-3,000, 3,000-4,000, 4,000-5,000 and above 5,000 acres. In addition, sub-totals are given for each acre interval between 1 and 10 acres. From these detailed figures, the number of holdings in the category 'above 2 and not exceeding 10 acres' is found to be 319,504, which is in reasonable agreement with the figure of 310,436 as estimated in table 2.

21 Here and in table 4 the date 1845 has been assigned to the poor law returns which were

issued on 12 July 1845. The year to which the data refer is not stated, but in view of the amount of work involved in classifying the data, it seems very possible that the returns refer to 1844, if not earlier. The only statement that can be made with assurance is that they relate to the immediate pre-famine situation.

22 I am grateful to Dr R. C. Geary, director, Economic Research Institute, for examining this problem and for providing the reclassification of the 1845 data given in table 4.

23 Figures for numbers of holdings of up to 1 acre, which were not provided in the 1841 census returns, are available for the poor law returns, and also for 1847 and 1851. There are obvious difficulties in making a correct enumeration of the very smallest holdings, down to tiny gardens. For what they are worth, the returns of holdings of up to 1 acre for the three years are as follows;

1845... ...135,314
1847... ... 73,016
1851... ... 37,728

24 *Census of 1841*, pp xxxi, xxxii.

25 Ibid., pp 454-7.

26 Ibid., p. xcii.

27 *Agricultural returns*, 1847, pt. ii, p. 15.

28 *Agricultural statistics, 1847-1926*, pp xv, xvi; 'National farm survey, 1955/56-1957/8: livestock mortality, seasonality of birth, etc.' in supplement to *Irish Trade Journal and Statistical Bulletin*, xxxiv (1959).

29 H. Staehle, 'Statistical notes on the economic history of Irish agriculture, 1847-1913' in *JSSISI*, xviii (1950-51), 444-71.

30 *Census of 1851*, pt. v (vol. i), pp 360, 363.

31 W. F. Adams, *Ireland and Irish emigration to the New World* (New Haven, 1932), p. 413.

32 *Census of 1841*, p. xxxi.

33 T. W. Freeman, *Pre-famine Ireland* (Manchester, 1957), p. 71.

34 *Census of 1841*, p. 453; *Agricultural returns of 1847*, pt. i, p. vi; *Census of 1851*, pt. ii, p. xxviii, pt. vi, p. xi.

35 *Census of 1851*, pt. ii, p. xi.

36 The word 'cultivated' in the wider sense is still often employed officially (Britton and Hunt, op. cit., pp 63-4), and it, rather than arable, will be used, other than in quotations, in the remainder of this paper.

37 *Census of 1851*, pt. ii, p. vi.

38 *Poor inquiry (F)*, pp 226, 236, 250, 259, 268.

39 The figures, as given in the *Agricultural returns* for the four years 1851-4, are, respectively, 195,053, 143,617, 103,365 and 85,434 acres.

40 *Census of 1851*, pt. ii, p. xxviii.

41 See, for example, *Census of 1851*, pt. ii, p. xi, where the term is used in different senses in two successive tables.

42 *Census of* 1851, pt. vi, p. xi. The commissioners go on to compare the returns of 'uncultivated land' made by the enumerators in the years 1847-51, as being 'a better criterion' of the changes in its extent than a comparison with the figure given in the census of 1841. They feel happier in relating the 1851 figure for woods and plantations with that given in the census for 1841; both of these are, they claim, based on 'returns obtained through the constabulary from the landowners and occupiers, and will, therefore, admit of a fair comparison'. Here they are possibly over-optimistic, for there had been 'great difficulty in collecting information' on plantations in 1841, and gaps in the returns were filled from the ordnance survey maps (*Census of 1841*, p. xxix). The commissioners seem, in fact, surprised by the result of the comparison; the area under plantations, they say, '*would appear* to have decreased' (*Census of 1851*, pt. vi, p. xii).

43 A list of the years in which the different counties were surveyed is given in Freeman, *Pre-famine Ireland*, p. 317. The dates quoted here and later have been checked against the original records, by courtesy of the Ordnance Survey Office, Dublin. The earlier year (1829) is that in which the county surveys commenced in the north of Ireland. They continued, moving gradually south, over the next thirteen years. Kerry and Cork were the last to be surveyed in 1841-2, and the results were available just in time to be

used for the report of the 1841 census, which was published in 1843. Publication of the first series of six-inch maps was not completed until 1846.

44 See, for example, the quotation to which note 37 refers.

45 J. E. Portlock, *Memoir of the life of Major-General Colby* (London, 1869), p. 208.

46 C. Close, *The early days of the ordnance survey* (Chatham, 1926), p. 120.

47 *Report of the progress of the ordnance survey and topographical depot to 31 Dec. 1859*, pp 9-10, HC 1860 (2629), xxiii.

48 *Census of 1841*, p. xiii.

49 Carrickfergus is described as 'a county of itself, locally in the county of Antrim' in Lewis, *Topographical dictionary of Ireland*, i, 269.

50 See quotation to which note 42 refers.

51 *Instructions for the interior survey of Ireland* (Dublin, 1825).

52 This and the immediately following quotation are taken from an amending instruction, issued by Lt. Col. Colby on 21 June 1831, which will be found inserted between pages 22 and 23 of the (only) copy of the 1825 *Instructions* held in the Ordnance Survey Office, Dublin.

53 *Census of 1851*, pt. vi, p. xi.

54 The extent of the potato crop in the successive years 1845-7 was 2,516,000, 1,999,000 and 284,000 acres respectively: P. M. A. Bourke, 'The extent of the potato crop in Ireland'.

55 (F. Dowdall) Series of anonymous articles on Irish agricultural statistics in the *Dublin Evening Herald*, commencing 5 Nov. 1845. Summarised and attributed to Dowdall in *Thom's directory*, 1848, pp 165-7.

56 *Report on agriculture III*, p. 238, q. 13,852; p. 265, qq 14,374-9, HC 1836 (465), viii. P. M. A. Bourke, 'Grass and the Irish climate' in *Proceedings, grass conservation conference* (Dublin, 1963), pp 1-22.

57 Caird, op. cit., pp 18, 88-9.

58 This latter was a common cause of fluctuations in the total of cultivated land after 1851, and makes nonsense of any attempt to equate the differences between successive returns of cultivated land with the wax and wane of genuine reclamation. 'A tract of mountain-side which carried a few score sheep in one year may not happen to be grazed at the time of enumeration in a succeeding season, with the result that it is entered on the statistical forms in a different column on each occasion.' *Ireland, industrial and agricultural* (Dublin, 1902), p. 305. 'Another element that produces apparent fluctuation in the amount of waste land is that where livestock are very plentiful, lands which are almost waste are temporarily used during the fine summer months, when the acreage of the country in use is enumerated,' Grimshaw, op. cit., p. 523.

59 K. H. Connell, 'The colonization of waste land in Ireland, 1780-1845' in *Economic History Review*, 2nd ser., iii (1950-1), p. 59.

60 *Land reclaimed (Ireland)*, p. 3, HC 1846 (240), xlii; *Land reclaimed (Ireland)*, p. 3, HC 1849 (267), xlix. The second of these papers gives the total area of uncultivated land in Co. Donegal at the time of the original survey as 765,051 acres, which differs slightly from the corresponding figure of 769,587 acres quoted in the *Census of 1841* (p. 453). This difference is in the reverse sense of what might have been expected if (as appears to be suggested by Dr Connell [loc. cit.] in the third note to his table 2) the figures given in the 1841 census, although based on the ordnance survey maps, had been revised in some way to give the situation in 1841. No evidence of any sort has been found to support this suggestion.

61 R. D. Collison Black, *Economic thought and the Irish question, 1817-1870* (Cambridge, 1960), p. 188, note 2.

62 Kennedy, op. cit., pp 565-70. Dr Collison Black himself recognises this, and in a personal communication has said that he agrees with the views expressed here.

63 *Nineteenth annual report of the commissioners of public works in Ireland*, HC 1851 (1414), xxv.

64 Op. cit., pp 4, 22.

65 Grimshaw, op. cit., p. 524. Kennedy (op. cit., p. 566) reckoned that 10 million acres of the cultivated land in Ireland before the famine were in need of drainage.

66 Connell, op. cit., pp 50-2.

67 Loc. cit., p. 50.

68 The exact figure in question has been variously quoted. It depends, in fact, on one's angle of approach to the comparative data for 1841 and 1851 given in table 6. From the positive aspect of increase in the amount of cultivated land, it is 1,338,281 acres; from the negative aspect of decrease in uncultivated land it is 1,271,751 acres. Both of these approaches give a round figure of 1.3 million acres.

There is a third and radically different figure of 1,073,652 acres, first derived in a confused way by Grimshaw (op. cit., pp 523, 525), and recently quoted by Dr Collison Black (op. cit., p. 188, note 3). What Grimshaw did was equivalent, in terms of table 6, to adding the 1841 figures for 'uncultivated', 'water' and 'towns', and subtracting from the total so reached the 1851 sum of 'uncultivated', 'water', 'towns', and *incredibly, 'fallow and uncropped arable'*. The figure so reached of 1,073,652 acres, he equated in error with 'the decrease of waste land between 1841 and 1851' (op. cit., p. 523). If a correction is made by adding the 1851 figure of 195,053 acres in fallow, this approach (which is then equivalent to calculating the change in the sum of cultivated land and woods) also gives a round figure of 1.3 million acres.

69 *Dublin Evening Herald*, 19 Nov. 1845.

70 Not only did Griffith assist in the calculation of these figures, but he also presented before the Devon commission, at about the same time, figures on waste land which are consistent with those given in the *Census of 1841*. *Appendix to minutes of evidence taken before her majesty's commissioners of inquiry into the state of the law and practice in respect to the occupation of land in Ireland*, App. 96, p. 290, HC 1845 (672), xxii.

71 *Poor inquiry (H)*, pt. i, p. 11, HC 1836 (41), xxxiv.

72 G. O'Brien, *Economic history of Ireland from the union to the famine* (London, 1921), pp 123-8, 149-57.

Chapter 4

1 *Waterford Freeman*; *Dublin Evening Post*. [David Moore, curator of the Dublin Botanic Gardens, reported some weeks later that he had first noticed signs of the disease in the locality on 20 August: see E. C. Nelson, 'David Moore, Miles J. Berkeley and scientific studies of potato blight in Ireland, 1845-7' in *Archives of Natural History*, xi (1983), pp. 249-61, at p. 251.]

2 *Gardeners' Chronicle*, 13 Sept. 1845.

3 P. M. A. Bourke, 'The extent of the potato crop in Ireland at the time of the famine' in *JSSISI*, xx (1959), pp 1-19. In the Appendix, Note III to his *Irish agricultural production; its volume and structure* (Cork, 1966), Mr Raymond Crotty argues in a rather confused way in favour of what he terms 'the more traditional figure of one million acres' under pre-famine potatoes, a value which would accord with Mr Crotty's unorthodox theses of a constant 'corn/root ratio' before as well as after the famine, and of no substantial drop in tillage as a result of that disaster. The pertinent question of how a potato crop of 2.5 million acres fitted with grain and tillage requirements into the available cultivated land in 1845 is discussed quantitatively in P. M. A. Bourke's 'Potato, blight, weather and the Irish famine' (Ph.D. thesis, NUI, 1967, Appendix 4). The other point of substance in Mr Crotty's criticism, the usage of the pre-famine potato crop, is dealt with in the present paper.

4 *Limerick Chronicle*, 21 June 1845.

5 The question of the average pre-famine yields (and seeding rates) of major crops in Ireland is considered in Appendix I of Bourke's Ph.D. thesis (see note 3). It is curious that the determined figure of 6 tons per acre as a representative national potato yield in the pre-famine decade should differ so little from that of 6.1 tons calculated by Wakefield in 1812 or that of 6.5 tons found by Arthur Young in 1780. It appears that the decline in average fertility of land arising from extension of the crop and the competition for manure was almost exactly compensated by the development and extended cultivation of inferior but prolific potato varieties, with the 'Irish Apple' being ousted by the 'Cup' and it in turn giving way to the notorious 'Lumper' (chap. 1 above).

The average potato seeding rate in the early nineteenth century was found to be 16 cwt per statute acre, i.e. much the same as modern usage.

6 A broad reconstruction of the use of the potato crop in all Ireland in 1951 is given in Appendix 2 of Bourke's Ph.D. thesis (see note 3). It is based on published data for Northern Ireland and on information supplied by CSO, Dublin for the rest of the country, and indicates that in 1951 7% of potato production was exported, 11% reserved for seed for the home crop, 23% eaten as human food, 44% used as animal food and 15% lost in disease and other forms of wastage.

7 F. Dowdall, see chapter 3, note 55 above.

8 P. V. Sukhatme, 'The world's hunger and future needs in food supplies' in *JRSS*, ser. A, cxxiv (1961), pp 463-508 (p. 467).

9 R. Passmore, 'Estimation of food requirements' in *JRSS*, ser. A, cxxv (1962), pp 387-97 (p. 397).

10 K. H. Connell, *The population of Ireland, 1750-1845* (Oxford 1950), pp 147-50.

11 C. E. Trevelyan, *The Irish crisis* (London, 1848), p. 10.

12 *Poor inquiry (E)*, pp 1-37, HC 1836 (37), xxxii, 1.

13 Ibid., p. 30.

14 Ibid., pp 34-5.

15 *Sixth annual report of the poor law commissioners*. HC 1840 (253), xvii, 447. Appendix (D), report no. 21 (pp 238-42): R. Hall, *Report on workhouse dietaries*. Appendix (D), report no. 22 (pp 242-8): W. H. T. Hawley, *Report on workhouse dietaries*.

16 Hall, pp 238, 241 (see note 15).

17 Hall, p. 241 (see note 15).

18 Hawley, p. 244 (see note 15).

19 Hall, p. 239 (see note 15).

20 Hawley, pp 245-8 (see note 15).

21 *Poor inquiry (E)*, p. 21.

22 W. R. Wilde, 'The food of the Irish' in *Dublin University Magazine*, xliii (1854), p. 131.

23 *Irish Farmers' Journal* (Dublin), 1846, p. 112.

24 *Gardeners' Chronicle*, 1846, p. 11.

25 D. Bain, *Observations upon the potato disease of 1845 and 1846* (Edinburgh, 1848), pp 1-2.

26 Hawley, p. 245 (see note 15).

27 R. S. McAdam, 'On the potato' in *Quarterly Journal of Agriculture*, v (1835), pp 321-48, (p. 322); Dowdall, note 7.

28 (i) *Household budget inquiry*, 1951-52, p. xxviii, Central Statistics Office (Dublin, 1954).

(ii) M. McArthur, 'Some factors involved in estimating calorie requirements, with special reference to persons engaged in agricultural labour in Asian countries' in *JRSS*, ser. A, cxxvii (1964), pp 392-408 (p. 402).

29 *Census of 1841*. HC 1843 (504), xxiv, pp 438-9.

30 Allowance is made here for the average length of the summer 'oatmeal period' (or 'potato gap') between the exhaustion of the old potato supply and the availability of the new. 'There was in Ireland what was called a "starving season" for about six weeks before the new harvest' (Daniel O'Connell in a speech in the house of commons, 30 March 1846). For a detailed consideration see Bourke's Ph.D. thesis (note 3), chapter 1, pp 73-7 (above, chap. 1).

31 M. Doyle, *The works of Martin Doyle* (Dublin, 1830), p. 24.

32 *Devon report*, 1845, w. 1051, q. 24., HC 1845 (606), xix, 57; (616), xx, 1; (657), xxi, 1; (672), xxii, 1; (673), xxii, 225.

33 Society of Friends, *Transactions of the central relief committee of the Society of Friends during the famine in Ireland* (Dublin, 1852), p. 100.

34 E. R. R. Green, *The Lagan valley*, 1800-1850 (London, 1949), p. 125.

35 *Devon report*, 1845, witness 431, q. 55 (see note 32).

36 R. N. Salaman, *The history and social influence of the potato* (Cambridge, 1949), p. 279.

37 C. Wilmot, *An Irish peer on the continent (1801-1803)*, ed. T.U. Sadleir (London, 1920), p. 80.

38 Wilde, 'The food of the Irish', p. 128.

39 Above, chap. 1.

40 *Census of 1841*, p. 440.
41 Bourke, 'The agricultural statistics of the 1841 census of Ireland; a critical review', chap. 3 above.
42 *Devon report*, 1845, App. 94, pp 280-9 (see note 32).
43 Bourke, 'The extent of the potato crop in Ireland', p. 8 (see note 3).
44 *Poor inquiry (E)*, p. 1.
45 *Census of 1841*, pp 454-7.
46 Ibid.
47 Bourke, 'The agricultural statistics', chap. 3 above.
48 Dowdall, note 7 above; *Poor inquiry (D)*, p. 84. HC 1836, (36), xxxi, 1.
49 *Poor inquiry (D)*, p. 85.
50 *Report on agriculture III*, 1836, p. 330. HC 1836 (465), viii, 1.
51 *Poor inquiry (D)*, p. 87.
52 Dowdall, note 7 above; *Report on agriculture III*, 1836, pp 329-30 (see note 50).
53 *Irish Farmers' Journal*, 1845, p. 343.
54 Doyle, *Works of Martin Doyle*, p. 24 (see note 31).
55 *Irish Farmer's and Gardener's Magazine* (Dublin), 1838, p. 29.
56 *Poor inquiry (F)*, pp 372, 376, 383, 385. HC 1836 (38), xxxiii, 1.
57 Dubourdieu, *Statistical survey of Down*, p. 207.
58 (i) Townsend, *Statistical survey of Cork*, p. 654.
(ii) *Munster Farmers' Magazine* (Cork, 1811), pp 37, 70; 1812, p. 121.
59 *Poor inquiry (F)*, p. 227.
60 Ibid., p. 256.
61 *RDS Prize essays*, pp 44-5.
62 Townsend, *Statistical survey of Cork*, p. 228.
63 Cited in Davidson, 'The history of the potato and its progress in Ireland' in *JDA*, xxxiv (1937), pp 286-307 (p. 298).
64 *Drummond report*, 1837-8, App. B, no. 9. HC 1837-38 (145), xxxv, 449.
65 Lewis, *Topographical dictionary of Ireland*, i, 187.
66 Ibid., i, 244.
67 *Limerick Chronicle*, 30 July 1845.
68 Dubourdieu, *Statistical survey of Down*, p. 51.
69 G. Rye, *Considerations on agriculture* (Dublin, 1730).
70 *Thom's directory*, 1846, p. 173.
71 *Gardeners' Chronicle*, 1844, p. 270.
72 N. Gash, *Mr Secretary Peel: the life of Sir Robert Peel to 1830* (London, 1961), pp 220-2.
73 Constabulary reports, 1845, Londonderry, 21 Sept. Constabulary reports on the condition of the potato crop. Relief commission papers. PROI (National Archives), 1A.50.73.
74 *Limerick Chronicle*, 17 Sept. 1845.
75 *Cork Constitution*, 7 Oct. 1845.
76 P. M. A. Bourke, 'Emergence of potato blight, 1843-6' in *Nature*, cciii (1964), pp 805-8, above, chap. 7.
77 *Newry Commercial Telegraph*, 25 Sept. 1845.
78 13 Sept. 1845.
79 *Northern Whig*, 27 Sept. 1845; *Leinster Express*, 4 Oct.; *Southern Reporter*, 9 Oct.; *Dublin Mercantile Advertiser*, 10 Oct. 1845.
80 *Drogheda Conservative*, 11 Oct. 1845.
81 *Dublin Mercantile Advertiser*, 17 Oct. 1845.
82 *Cork Constitution*, 21 Oct. 1845.
83 *Nenagh Guardian*, 22 Oct. 1845.
84 T. P. O'Neill, 'Food problems during the great Irish famine' in *Journal of the Royal Society of Antiquaries of Ireland*, lxxxii, pt. ii (1952), pp 98-108 (p. 102).
85 Peel Papers (British Museum). Add. MSS. 40, 476, f. 500.
86 *Dublin Evening Post*, 8 Nov. 1845.
87 *Gardeners' Chronicle*, 1845, p. 783.
88 *Dublin Evening Herald*, 19 Nov. 1846.
89 *Limerick Chronicle*, 1 Nov. 1845.

90 *Journal of Agriculture* (Edinburgh), October 1845, p. 93.
91 Lewis, *Topographical dictionary*, ii, 437.
92 Ibid., ii, 146.
93 F. A. Pinkert, *Die Kartoffelnot unserer Zeit und ihre Abhülfe* (Weimar, 1843).
94 *Journal of Agriculture*, October 1845, p. 95.
95 W. Aitken, *The potato rescued from disease and restored to pristine vigour* (Edinburgh, 1837), p. 11.
96 McAdam, 'On the potato', p. 337 (see note 27).
97 A. Smee, *The potatoe plant, its uses and properties; together with the causes of the present malady* (London, 1846), p. 42.
98 K. H. Connell, 'Illicit distillation: an Irish peasant industry' in *Historical Studies III*, ed. J. Hogan (1961), pp 58-91 (p. 59, note 7).
99 Wilde, *The food of the Irish*, p. 133 (see note 22).
100 J. Rutty, *An essay towards a natural history of the county of Dublin*, 2 vols (Dublin, 1772), i, 82-3.
101 O'Neill, 'Food problems', p. 102 (see note 84).
102 *Limerick Chronicle*, 1 Nov. 1845.
103 Ibid., 22 Nov. 1845.
104 (i) *Thirteenth general report of the Ministry of Agriculture (Northern Ireland)*. Cmd. 348 (Belfast, 1956), pp 44, 98.
(ii) M. Neenan, 'Potato losses in storage' in *Biatas*, xx (1966), pp 257-9.
105 *Irish Farmers' and Gardeners' Magazine*, 1835, p. 202.
106 E. T. Craig, *An Irish commune: the history of Ralahine* (Dublin, 1920), pp 27, 85, 93, 135.
107 Constabulary returns, 1845 (see note 73).

Chapter 5

1 *Returns of agricultural produce in Ireland in the year 1847*. (Part 1) Tillage. HC 1847-8 (923), lvii, 1.
2 When Charles Trevelyan of the Treasury asked in September 1846 for information on the extent and yield of food crops in Ireland in normal years, Sir Randolph Routh, chairman of the relief commission, drew attention to the various estimates of crop yields given in evidence before the Devon commission, but added that 'it would cost a good deal of time to draw up a resumé'. *Correspondence from July 1846 to January 1847 relating to the measures adopted for the relief of distress in Ireland* (Commissariat series). HC 1847 (761), li, pp 56-7.
3 *Devon report*, 1845. Witness no. 729, question 17.
4 P. M. A. Bourke, 'Notes on some agricultural units of measurement in use in pre-famine Ireland' in *IHS*, xiv (1965), pp 236-45.
5 Dutton, *Statistical survey of Clare*, pp 186-7.
6 Simington, R. C. 'Tithe applotment books of 1834' in *JDA*, xxxviii (1941), pp 239-343.
7 W. N. Hancock, *On the alleged progressive decline of the prosperity of Ireland* (Dublin, 1863). p. 30, footnote.
8 Ibid., p. 41.
9 T. Barrington, 'The yields of Irish tillage crops since the year 1847' in *JDA*, xxi (1921), pp 205-29, 289-305. (This article was published anonymously. It is attributed to Barrington in *Agricultural statistics, 1847-1926* [Dublin, 1928], p. xxxvii.)
10 Ibid., pp 226, 216.
11 Ibid., p. 214.
12 T. Walsh, P. F. Ryan, and J. Kilroy, 'A half century of fertiliser and lime use in Ireland' in *JSSISI*, xix (1957), pp 104-36.
13 Barrington, 'Yields of Irish tillage crops', p. 209 (see note 9).
14 *Devon report*, 1845. Witness no. 395, q. 23.
15 Ibid., appendix no. 54.
16 Ibid., witness no. 278, q. 29.

17 Ibid., witness no. 800, q. 20.
18 *Poor inquiry (F)*, pp 1-31.
19 Ibid., p. 8.
20 *Dublin Evening Herald*, 5 Nov. 1846.
21 Ibid., 14 Nov. 1846.
22 *Quarterly Journal of Agriculture*, v (1834-5), pp 188-9.
23 *Report on agriculture III*. HC 1836 (465), viii, 1. pp 259, 260, 277, 279.
24 *RDS Prize essays*, p. 3.
25 *IFGM*, 1838, p. 102.
26 Ibid., 1838, p. 195.
27 R. Kane, *The industrial resources of Ireland*, 2nd edn (Dublin, 1845), p. 255.
28 *GC*, 1842, p. 221.
29 A. Young, *A tour in Ireland*, Bohn edn, 2 vols (London, 1892), ii, 39.
30 E. Wakefield, *An account of Ireland, statistical and political*, 2 vols (Dublin, 1812), i, 605.
31 *Quarterly Journal of Agriculture*, iv (1832-4), p. 297; *Report on agriculture II* p. 162; *Report on agriculture III*, pp 266, 277, 279.

Chapter 6

1 N. E. Stevens, 'Phytopathology – the dark ages in plant pathology in America: 1830-1870' in *Journal of the Washington Academy of Sciences*, xxiii (1933), pp 435-46.
2 Bourke, 'Emergence of potato blight, 1843-6' in *Nature*, cciii (1964), pp 805-8 (above, chap. 7).
3 C. P. Bosson, *Observations on the potatoe, and a remedy for the potatoe plague* (Boston, 1846).
4 *Report for 1845*, p. 514.
5 C. F. P. von Martius, *Die Kartoffel-Epidemie der letzten Jahre, oder die Stockfäule und Räude der Kartoffeln* (Munich, 1842).
6 Bourke, 'Emergence of potato blight', pp 805-8.
7 L. Peeters, *Guérison radicale de la maladie des pommes de terre et d'autres végétaux* (Namur, 1855).
8 J. Parkin, *The cause of the blight and pestilence in the animal kingdom* (London, 1846); *The prevention and treatment of disease in the potato and other crops* (London, 1847).
9 F. Zuppinger, *Die glücklich entdeckte Ursache der Kartoffelkrankheit* (Zürich, 1847).
10 D. Bain, *Observations upon the potatoe disease of 1845 and 1846* (Edinburgh, 1848).
11 J. Semal, P. Joly, and D. Lamy, 'L'épidémie de "maladie des pommes de terre" causée en Europe en 1845 par le *Phytophthora infestans* (Mont.) de Bary: les faits et les auteurs' in *Annales de Gembloux*, lxxxix (1983), pp 79-99.
12 C. Morren, *Instructions populaires sur les moyens de combattre et de détruire la maladie actuelle (gangrène humide) des pommes de terre* (Brussels, 1845).
13 C. Morren, *Nouvelles instructions populaires sur les moyens de combattre et de détruire la maladie actuelle (gangrène humide) des pommes de terre* (Paris, 1845).
14 C. Morren, 'Notice sur le Botrytis devastateur ou le champignon des pommes de terre' in *Annales de la Société Royale d'Agriculture et de Botanique de Gand*, i (1845), pp 287-92.
15 *Monthly Journal of Agriculture* (New York, 1845), p. 387.
16 Issue of 30 August.
17 Issue of 6 September.
18 2 September.
19 M. M. Dieudonné, *Rapport fait au conseil central de salubrité publique de Bruxelles sur la maladie des pommes de terre* (Brussels, 1845).
20 C. J. Boset, *Plantation des pommes de terre en 1846, d'après la théorie démontrée de leur maladie* (Liége, 1846).
21 Morren, *Instructions populaires*.
22 Morren, *Nouvelles instructions populaires*.

23 *L'Indépendance Belge*, 4 Sept. 1845.
24 C. Montagne, 'Observations sur la maladie des pommes de terre', *Bulletin de la Société Philomatique de Paris*, in *L'Institut*, xiii (1845), pp 312-14.
25 M. J. Decaisne, *Histoire de la maladie des pommes de terre* (Paris, 1846).
26 E. Roze, *Histoire de la pomme de terre* (Paris, 1898).
27 P. Duchartre, 'Sur la maladie des pommes de terre', *Revue Botanique*, i (1845), p. 177.
28 M. J. Berkeley, 'Observations, botanical and physiological, on the potato murrain' in *Journal of the Horticultural Society of London*, i (1846), pp 9-34.
29 *Gardeners' Chronicle* (1846), p. 531; E. C. Nelson, 'David Moore, Miles J. Berkeley and scientific studies of potato blight in Ireland, 1845-1847', *Archives of Natural History*, xi (1983), pp 249-61.
30 *The Plough* (1846), pp 516-19.
31 *Annals of Horticulture* (1847), p. 227.
32 *Journal d'Agriculture Pratique* (1845-6), p. 236.
33 R. McKay, *An anthology of the potato* (Dublin, 1961).
34 J. C. Morton, *A cyclopaedia of agriculture, practical and scientific* (London, 1855), ii, 667-94.
35 A. de Bary, *Die gegenwärtig herrschende Kartoffelkrankheit, ihre Ursache und ihre Verhütung* (Leipzig, 1861); 'Recherches sur le développement de quelques champignons parasites, etc.' in *Annals des Sciences Naturelles*, 4me sér. Bot., xx (1863), pp 1-148.
36 Duchartre, 'Sur la maladie des pommes de terre'.
37 P. Harting, *Recherches sur la nature et les causes de la maladie des pommes de terre en 1845* (Amsterdam, 1846).
38 Morren, 'Notice sur le Botrytis devastateur'.
39 Berkeley, 'Observations on the potato murrain'.
40 A. Puttemans, 'Reivindicação visando a denominação scientifica da doença da batateira' in *Rodriguésia*, ii (1938), pp 341-50.
41 Berkeley, 'Observations on the potato murrain'.
42 F. J. Graham, 'The potato disease' in *Journal of the Royal Agricultural Society of England*, vii (1847), pp 357-91.
43 Duchartre, 'Sur la maladie des pommes de terre'.
44 Roze, *Histoire de la pomme de terre*.
45 A. Prunet, 'Le mildiou de la pomme de terre' in *Revue de Viticulture*, xvii (1902), pp 663-6; xviii, pp 97-104.
46 L. R. Jones, N. J. Giddings, and B. J. Lutman, 'Investigations on the potato fungus, *Phytophthora infestans*' in *U.S. Department of Agriculture, Bureau of Plant Industry*, Bulletin no. 245 (Washington, 1912).

Chapter 7

1 N. E. Stevens, 'Phytopathology', in *Jn. Washington Acad. Sci.*, xxiii (1933), p. 435.
2 B. C. Dumortier, 'Observations sur la cloque des pommes de terre' in *Bull. Acad. Roy. Sci. et Belles-Lettres de Bruxelles*, xii (1845), pt. 2, p. 285.
3 M. Martens, 'Sur la maladie des pommes de terre' in *Bull. Acad. Roy. Sci. et Belles-Lettres de Bruxelles*, xii (1845), pt. 2, p. 356.
4 J. Bonjean, *Monographie de la pomme de terre* (Paris, 1846).
5 J. Muenter, *Die Krankheiten der Kartoffeln, insbesondere die im Jahre 1845 pandemisch herrschende nasse Fäule* (Berlin, 1846).
6 M. J. Decaisne, *Histoire de la maladie des pommes de terre en 1845* (Paris, 1846).
7 A. Payen, *Bull. Séances Soc. Roy. et Centrale d'Agric.*, ii (1846), p. 625.
8 J. F. W. Johnston (ed.), *The potato disease in Scotland, being results of investigations into its nature and origin.* Pamphlets nos. 1-6 (Edinburgh, 1845-6).
9 J. L. Jensen, in *Mém. Soc. Nationale de France*, cxxxi (1887), p. 131.
10 D. Milne, *Observations on the probable cause of the failure of the potato crop in 1845 and 1846* (Edinburgh and London, 1847).
11 C. Woodham-Smith, *The great hunger: Ireland, 1845-9* (London, 1962).

12 W. P. Alison, *Observations on the famine of 1846-7, in the highlands of Scotland and in Ireland* (Edinburgh and London, 1847).
13 D. Atanasoff, 'A study into the literature on stipple-streak and related diseases of the potato' in *Mededeelingen van de Landbouwhoogeschool*, Wageningen, no. 26 (1922).
14 C. F. P. von Martius, *Die Kartoffel-Epidemie der letzen Jahre* (Munich, 1842).
15 J. E. van der Plank, *Plant pathology*, ed. J. G. Horsfall and A. E. Dimond, iii (New York, 1960), p. 229.
16 D. Reddick, *Amer. Potato Jn.*, xx (1943), p. 118.
17 J. S. Niederhauser, *Trans. N. Y. Acad. Sci.*, 2nd ser., xix (1956), p. 55.
18 J. G. Hawkes, in *Euphytica*, vii (1958), p. 257.
19 See note 6.

Chapter 8

1 T. P. O'Neill, 'The scientific investigation of the failure of the potato crop in Ireland in 1845-6', in *IHS*, v (1946), pp 123-38.
2 *Limerick Chronicle*, 14 Mar. 1846.
3 O' Neill, loc. cit., p. 136.
4 *Poor inquiry (F)*, pp 232, 279.
5 *Gardeners' Chronicle*, 1845, p. 767 (15 Nov.).
6 *Prize essays on the potato, and the causes of the late partial failures* (Royal Dublin Society, 1835).
7 B. H. Hickey, 'On the potato' in *IFGM*, ii (1835), pp 18-19.
8 'Remarks on the recent failure of the potato crop' in *Quarterly Journal of Agriculture*, v (1834-5), pp 590-4.
9 Morren, C, *Instructions populaires sur les moyens de combattre et détruire la maladie actuelle des pommes de terre* (Brussels, 1845). English abstract in *Journal of Agriculture*, July 1846, pp 349-53.
10 *Gardeners' Chronicle*, 1845, p. 625.
11 Ibid., 1845.
12 Ibid., 1845, p. 639 (20 Sept.).
13 Ibid., 1846, p. 179 (21 Mar.).
14 *IFJ*, 1846, p. 650 (26 Aug.).
15 G. H. Pethybridge, 'Investigations on potato diseases (third report)' in *Department of Agriculture Bulletin*, xii (2) (1912), p. 340.
16 Id., 'Investigations on potato diseases (fourth report)' in *Department of Agriculture Bulletin*, xiii (3) (1913), p. 450.
17 *GC*, 1846, p. 582 (29 Aug.), p. 643 (26 Sept.).
18 Ibid., 1846, p. 598 (5 Sept.).
19 Ibid., 1847, p. 125 (20 Feb.); *Irish Farmers' Journal* (newspaper section), 1847 (24 Feb.).
20 *IFJ*, 1846, p. 656 (26 Aug.).
21 *GC*, 1846, p. 349 (23 May).
22 *IFJ*, 1846, p. 574 (29 July).
23 *GC*, 1846, p. 499 (25 July).
24 *Report of select committee of the house of commons on the potato crop, 1880*, HC, 1880, xii, 20.
25 E. C. Large, *The advance of the fungi* (London, 1940), chap. 17.

Chapter 9

1 O. Appel, 'Beiträge zur Kenntnis der Kartoffelpflanze und ihrer Krankheiten, 1' in *Arbeiten aus der Kaiserlichen Biologischen Anstalt für Land- und Forstwirtschaft*, Berlin, v (1907), pp 377-435.
2 Bourke, 'Emergence of potato blight, 1843-6', above, chap. 7; E. Roze, *Histoire de la pomme de terre* (Paris, 1898).

3 W. D. Davidson, 'A review of literature dealing with the degeneration of varieties of the potato' in *Economic Proceedings of the Royal Dublin Society*, ii (1928), pp 331-89.
4 Atanasoff, 'A study into the literature on stipple-streak and related diseases of the potato'.
5 J. K. Müller, 'Über die Ausartung der roten Kartoffeln' in *Rheinische Beiträge zur Gelehrtsamkeit*. Mannheim, i (1780), pp 444-50.
6 Atanasoff, 'A study into the literature on stipple-streak and related diseases of the potato'.
7 Davidson, 'A review of literature dealing with the degeneration of varieties of the potato', p. 332.
8 *GC*, p. 674.
9 There are two other independent sources of a similar error. One is a false identification of potato blight with earlier disease, as for example, in C. P. Bosson, *Observations on the potatoe, and a remedy for the potatoe plague* (Boston, 1846), pp 53-4, and A. Bush, 'Rot in potatoes' in *Trans. NY State Agric. Soc. for 1845*, v, pp 342-8. The second is a confusion of dates in the evidence of Mr H. Carruthers before the select committee on the potato crop (*Report*, HC 1880, xii, 309, pp 12-13, 17) in which he spoke of 1844 in referring to the events of 1845. This error was carried forward to the introduction written by Mr C. Whitehead to a later official document (*Report*, HC 1892, lxiv, 417, p. 10) and has been repeated and extended in J. G. Horsfall, 'The fight with the fungi' in *Am. Jn. Botany*, xliii (1956), pp 533, 535. Oddly, a similar confusion between the years 1842 and 1843 occurred in accounts of the first appearance of potato blight in the USA (N. E. Stevens, 'Phytopathology – the dark ages in plant pathology in America: 1830-1870' in *Jn. Washington Acad. Sci.*, xxiii (1933), pp 441-2.
10 M. C. Cooke, *Rust, smut, mildew and mould*, 2nd edn (London, 1870), p. 145.
11 J. L. Jensen, 'Moyens de combattre et de détruire la peronospora de la pomme de terre' in *Mémoires de la Société Nationale d'Agriculture de France* (Paris, 1887), cxxxi, pp 31-156, p. 148.
12 M. C. Cooke, 'Plant diseases and fungi' in *Essex Naturalist*, vi (1892), p. 22.
13 A. Prunet, 'Le mildiou de la pomme de terre' in *Revue de Viticulture* (Paris), xvii (1902), pp 663-6 (p. 664).
14 L. R. Jones, N. J. Giddings, and B. J. Lutman, 'Investigations of the potato fungus, *Phytophthora infestans*' in *United States Department of Agriculture, Bureau of Plant Industry*, Bulletin 245 (Washington, 1912).
15 Ibid., p. 21.
16 Stevens, 'Phytopathology – the dark ages in plant pathology in America; 1830-1870', p. 445.
17 Bourke, 'Emergence of potato blight, 1843-6', above, chap. 7.
18 W. R. Wilde, 'Table of cosmical phenomena, epizootics, famines and pestilences in Ireland', in *Census of 1851*, Part v, (i), HC 1856, (2087-1), xxix.
19 Bourke, 'The extent of the potato crop in Ireland at the time of the famine' in *JSSISI*, xx (1959-60), pp 1-19.
20 Bourke, 'Emergence of potato blight, 1843-6', above, chap. 7.
21 J. Townley, *The diseases, regeneration and culture of the potato* (London, 1847), pp 5-6.
22 N. Niven, *The potato epidemic and its probable consequences* (Dublin, 1846).
23 Ibid., pp 13-14.
24 e.g. M. Fjeldstrup, [Potato disease in Denmark] in *Tidsskrift for landoekonomi* (Copenhagen, 1844).
25 T. Whitehead, T. P. McIntosh, and W. M. Finlay, *The potato in health and disease*, 2nd edn (Edinburgh and London, 1945), p. 216.

Chapter 10

1 The relevant official summaries of grain traffic into and out of Ireland, which will hereafter be referred to as return (a), return (b), etc., are as follows:

(a) exports and imports for each of the ten calendar years 1839-48 in HC 1849 (588), l, 403
(b) exports for each of the three calendar years 1844-6 in HC 1847 (24), lix, 523
(c) exports for each month of 1846 in HC 1847 (32), lix, 493
(d) exports for each of the last two quarters of 1846 in HC 1847 (132), lix, 517
(e) exports for the first quarter of 1847 in HC 1847 (543), lix, 519
(f) exports for the second quarter of 1847 in HC 1847 (726), lix, 521
(g) exports in the calendar year 1846 in table 9 of HC 1847 (259), lix, 479
(h) imports totalled over the period 29 August 1846 to 3 July 1847 in HC 1847 (725), lvi, 291
(i) imports totalled over the eleven-month period ending 5 Dec. 1846 (table 9), exports in the same period (table 10), and a comparison of these exports with the annual exports in each of the years 1843-5 (table 11) in HC 1847 (1), lix, 469.

The amount of detail varies considerably from document to document. Table 9 in return (i) refers only to wheat, flour, maize and maize meal. At the other extreme, return (a) covers each individual grain, as well as peas, beans and malt which were at that time classified in the corn trade.

The fundamental document is clearly return (a), which is the basis of tables 2 and 3 in the present paper. The trade in peas, beans and malt has not been taken into account here. Figures for small quantities of buckwheat have been incorporated with wheat, buckwheat meal with flour, and bere with barley.

Table 10 of return (i) is important in that it shows that direct exports of grain from Ireland to foreign countries were negligible, and hence that statistics for the trade from Ireland to Great Britain may be accepted as total exports.

2 Compare the figures for July-September and October-December 1846 in return (d) with the totals for the corresponding months in return (c). Another inconsistency is that the exports of wheat and barley over the first eleven months of 1846 in table 10 of return (i) are shown as greater than those for the full year in return (c) and elsewhere. Further, there is a minor discrepancy between oatmeal exports in 1846 as recorded on the one hand in return (a) and on the other in returns (b) and (c). This carries over into a corresponding difference in the statistics for combined oats and oatmeal exports in 1846 as given in table 9 of return (g) and in return (b) respectively.

3 *Report on agriculture I*, p. 2, qq 16-18; p. 10, qq 155-7 (HC 1836 [79], viii, 1).

4 P. M. A. Bourke, 'The potato, blight, weather and the Irish famine' (Ph.D. thesis, NUI, 1967), App. 4.

5 *Distress correspondence*, 1847, p. 1, HC 1847 (761), li, 1.

6 P. M. A. Bourke, 'Notes on some agricultural units of measurement in use in pre-famine Ireland' in *IHS*, xiv (1965), pp 236-45.

7 *IFJ* (newspaper section), 1846, p. 391.

8 *GC*, 1846, p. 153.

9 *Distress correspondence*, 1847, p. 1.

10 *Distress correspondence*, 1846, pp 51, 53, HC 1846 (735), xxxvii, 41; *Report on agriculture II*, p. 81, qq 6003-5, HC 1836 (189), viii, 225; *Report on agriculture III*, p. 286, qq 14781-3, HC 1836 (465), viii, 1.

11 J. C. Drummond and A. Wilbraham, *The Englishman's food: a history of five centuries of English diet* (London, 1939), pp 350-1.

12 A Baker, *A vindication of the case of the corporation of bakers* (Dublin, 1756).

13 *The Patriot*, 10 Nov. 1814, market note.

14 *Poor inquiry (F)*, p. 284, HC 1836 (38), xxxiii, 1.

15 *GC*, 1844, p. 27; 1846, p. 606.

16 Approximate weights and measures 'as used in the public departments in England for purposes of conversion' and quoted in *Distress correspondence*, 1847, p. 1, include the following equations:

Quarter of wheat = 480 lb.
Hundredweight of flour = 137 lb. wheat
Quarter of oats = 320 lb.

The first two of these conversion rates, and also the following:

Quarter of oats = 308 lb.

Hundredweight of oatmeal = 196 lb. oats
are applied officially in returns (b) and (i).

17 *Report on agriculture III*, p. 309, q. 15276.
18 *Quarterly Journal of Agriculture*, iv (1832-4), pp 48-53.
19 *Poor inquiry (E)*, pp 2, 36, HC 1836 (37), xxxii, 1.
20 F. Dowdall in the *Dublin Evening Herald*, 10 Nov. 1846.
21 *Gardeners' Chronicle*, 1846, p. 606. A whole range of equivalents is given here, not only for grain meals but also for pea and bean meal.
22 *Distress correspondence*, 1846, pp 51, 63.
23 Ibid. In table 9, return (i) of note 1, a figure of 62,338 cwt of maize meal is equated with 18,182 qtr of maize. This is difficult to explain other than in terms of an error of calculation or a misprint.
24 M. Doyle, *A cyclopaedia of practical husbandry* (Dublin, 1839), p. 30.
25 This is an amended and expanded version of table 12 in App. 3 of P. M. A. Bourke, Ph.D. thesis.
26 *Census of 1851*, pt v, i, 360, HC 1856 (2087-1), xxix, 261.
27 *Report on agriculture II*, p. 82, q. 6037.
28 *Distress correspondence*, 1846, p. 218.
29 *Distress correspondence*, 1846, pp 92, 218-9; C. E. Trevelyan, *The Irish crisis* (London, 1848), p. 75 n.
30 *Distress correspondence*, 1846, p. 121.
31 See note 2. The difference arises according to whether the figures for the last quarter of 1846 are taken from return (c) or return (d) of note 1.
32 Return (h) of note 1.
33 *Distress correspondence*, 1847, p. 97.
34 C. Woodham-Smith, *The great hunger: Ireland 1845-9* (London, 1962), p. 123. The conversion rate of one-fifth as used here is valid only for maize grain (see table 1).
35 Return (c) of note 1.
36 Return (d) of note 1.
37 Table 9 of return (i) and return (a) of note 1.
38 T. P. O'Neill, 'Food problems during the great Irish famine', in *Journal of the Royal Society of Antiquaries of Ireland*, lxxxii, pt. ii (1952), pp 99-108.
39 P. M. A. Bourke, Ph.D. thesis, App. 4.
40 *Freeman's Journal*, 29 Oct. 1845.

Chapter 11

1 Peel's reactions to the onset and development of the potato disease are described in Lord Mahon and E. Cardwell (eds), *Memoirs by the Right Honourable Sir Robert Peel*, part iii (London, 1857).
2 The schoolboy Kettle's impressions are recorded in L. J. Kettle (ed.), *The material for victory, being the memoirs of Andrew J. Kettle* (Dublin, 1958).
3 Trevelyan's activities during Peel's premiership are dealt with in *Distress correspondence*, HC 1846 (735), xxxvii, 41.
4 Ibid., p. 149 (emphasis in original).
5 *IFJ*, 14 Oct. 1846 (p. 782).
6 Trevelyan's activities in the service of Russell are described in *Distress correspondence*, HC 1847 (761), li, 1.
7 A. Smee, *The potatoe plant, its uses and properties; together with the cause of the present malady* (London, 1846).
8 O'Connell to D. R. Pigot, 13 Aug. 1846, in *The correspondence of Daniel O'Connell*, ed. Maurice R. O'Connell (Dublin, 1980), viii, 83 (letter 3265). For O'Connell's rejection of the call to ban the export of Irish grain to England, see *FJ*, 29 Oct. 1845.
9 'Second letter to Archdeacon Singleton', in Sydney Smith, *Works*, 4 vols (London, 1839-40), iii, 113-4.

Chapter 12

1 *Distress correspondence*, HC 1847 (761), li, 1.

2 *New Blackfriars*, 1965, p. 60.

3 For Pim's comments, see Jonathan Pim, *The condition and prospects of Ireland* (Dublin, 1848).

4 For the work of the Quakers to combat famine, see Society of Friends, *Transactions of the central relief committee of the Society of Friends during the famine in Ireland* (Dublin, 1852).

5 R. Butler, *A memoir of the Very Reverend Richard Butler, dean of Clonmacnois and vicar of Trim* (Edinburgh, 1863), pp 232-3.

List of publications on the potato, blight, weather, the famine and related subjects by P. M. Austin Bourke

1953

'Potato blight and the weather: a fresh approach', *IMS Technical Note*, no. 12, Dublin, pp 1-11.

'The potato blight weather warning service in Ireland in 1952', *IMS Technical Note*, no. 13, Dublin, pp 1-45.

'Potato blight and weather in Ireland in 1953', *IMS Technical Note*, no. 15, Dublin, pp 1-37.

1955

'The forecasting from weather data of potato blight and other plant diseases and pests', *WMO Technical Note*, no. 10, Geneva, pp 1-48.

'El tizón de la papa en el clima de La Serena', in *Agricultura Téchnica*, Santiago de Chile, xv, 82-94.

1956

'Agricultural meteorology: a report prepared for the government of Chile', *UN Report*, no. TAA/CH1/2, New York, pp 1-90.

1957

'Weather and potato blight in Chile', in *WMO Bulletin*, Geneva, vi, 36-8.

'Meteorology and some problems of plant pathology', in *Indian Journal of Meteorology and Geophysics*, Poona, viii, 81-7.

'The use of synoptic weather maps in potato blight epidemiology', *IMS Technical Note*, no. 23, Dublin, pp 1-35.

1958

'Meteorology and crop protection', in *WMO Bulletin*, Geneva, vii, 14-17.

1959

'Modern meteorology and the epidemiology of plant diseases', in *Proceedings of the IV international congress of plant protection, Hamburg 1957*, Braunschweig, pp 169-74.

'Meteorology and the timing of fungicide applications against potato blight', in *International Journal of Biometeorology and Bioclimatology*, iii, part 2, section E, pp 1-8.

1960

'The extent of the potato crop in Ireland at the time of the famine'. With appendix on 'Uncertainties in the statistics of farm size in Ireland, 1841-51', in *JSSISI*, xx, part 3 (1959-60), 1-35.

1962

'Plant diseases and pests as influenced by weather', in *Biometeorology*, London, pp 153-61.

'The scientific investigation of the potato blight in 1845-6', in *IHS*, xiii, 26-32.
'J.K.L. and Jebb: pioneers in co-operation', in *The Irish Times*, 2 Jan. 1962, pp 7, 10.

1964
'Emergence of potato blight, 1843-6', in *Nature*, cciii, no. 4947, pp 805-8 (22 August 1964).

1965
'Notes on some agricultural units of measurement in use in pre-famine Ireland', in *IHS*, xiv, 236-45.
'The contribution of modern meteorology to plant disease forecasting', in *Phytopathology*, lv, 943-5.
'The agricultural statistics of the 1841 census of Ireland: a critical review', in *Economic History Review*, 2nd ser., xviii, 376-91.
'Meteorological studies in relation to plant diseases and pests', in S. Krishnamurti, (ed.), *Advances in agricultural sciences and their applications*, Madras, pp 504-14.

1966
'A contribution to the early history of the black leg disease of the potato', in *JDAF*, lxiii, 1-7.
'Reassessing the famine', in *The Irish Times*, 19-20 Oct. 1966.

1968
'The use of the potato crop in pre-famine Ireland', in *JSSISI*, xxi, part 6 (1967-8), 72-96.
'Some principles and methods in plant disease forecasting'; 'Meteorological influences on the epidemiology of potato blight'; 'The forecasting of apple scab and other plant diseases from weather factors'; 'Problems and prospects in plant disease forecasting', in *Proceedings of the WMO regional seminar on agrometeorology*, Wageningen, Netherlands, pp 21-33, 57-67, 129-43, 199-206.

1969
'Potato late blight in Canada in 1844-5', in *Canadian Plant Disease Survey*, Ottowa, xlix, 29-31.
'The average yields of food crops in Ireland on the eve of the great famine', in *JDAF*, lxvi, 3-16.
'Meteorological aspects of the earliest European epidemic of potato blight, 1845-6' (Abstract) in *Biometeorology*, Amsterdam, iv, part ii, p. 107.

1970
'The use of weather information in the production of plant disease epiphytotics', in *Annual Review of Phytopathology*, Altopalo, viii, 345-70.

1971
'Disease resistance of European potato varieties in the 1840s', in *Science*, Washington, clxxi, 955-6.
'Potato blight and the weather'; 'How potato blight came to Ireland', in *Biatas*, xxv, 112-5, 216-9.
'The potato in Ireland: a review of R. N. Salaman's *The history and social influence of the potato*', in *IHS*, xvii, 410-13.

1974
'The climate of Ireland as a natural resource', in *Administration*, Dublin, xxi, 365-83.

1976
'The Irish grain trade, 1839-48', in *IHS*, xx, 156-69.
'Meteorology and hydrology in aid of food production', in *Scientific lectures presented at the seventh world meteorological congress*, WMO no. 435, Geneva.

1977
'Apologia for a dead civil servant': Part 1: 'Trevelyan in the service of Peel', in *The Irish Times*, 5 May 1977, p. 8.
Part 2: 'Trevelyan in the service of Russell', in *The Irish Times*, 6 May 1977, p. 8.

1984
'Impact of climatic variations on European agriculture', in H. Flohn and R. Fantechi (eds), *The climate of Europe, past, present and future*, Dordrecht, pp 269-95 and 307-13.

1985
'Climate and the diseases and pests of agriculture', in M. J. Tooley and G. M. Sheail (eds), *The climatic scene*, London, pp 255-78.
(Jointly with Prof. H. H. Lamb)
'The spread of potato blight in Europe in 1845-6, and the accompanying wind and weather patterns', in *Commission of the European Communities: first R and D programme in the field of climatology, 1981-85*, Brussels, pp 265-71.

1987
'Half a lifetime with potato blight', in Lisa Shields (ed.), *The Irish Meteorological Service: the first fifty years 1936-86*, Dublin, pp 51-3.

1990
'Phytophthora and famine', in *Technology Ireland*, xxii, 42-4.

1991
'Potato blight in Europe in 1845: the scientific controversy', in J. Lucas *et al.* (eds), *British Mycological Symposium*, xvii, *Phytophthora*, Cambridge, pp 12-24.

UNPUBLISHED

1967
'The potato, blight, weather, and the Irish famine' (Ph.D. thesis, NUI).

General bibliography and abbreviations

Primary sources

Abstracts of blight returns, 1845-6. Parts 1 and 2. PROI (National Archives). Relief commission papers, bundles 1A.50.79 and 1A.50.80.

AG Armagh Guardian

Agricultural returns of 1847. Returns of agricultural produce in Ireland in the year 1847. Part i, Tillage. HC 1847-8 (923), lvii, 1. Part ii, HC 1847-8 (1000), lvii.

AH Annals of Horticulture, and Yearbook of Information on Practical Gardening for 1847. London, 1847.

Aitken, W. *The potato rescued from disease and restored to pristine vigour.* Edinburgh, 1837.

Anon. 'On Irish agriculture' in *Quarterly Journal of Agriculture*, iv (1832-4), 296-310.

Anon. *An essay on the potato blight and garden allotment system.* Oxford, 1846.

Anon. *The potato blight famine. Questions and replies between two travellers on its causes and results.* Dublin, 1847.

Atkinson, A. *Ireland in the nineteenth century.* Dublin, 1833.

Bain, D. *Observations upon the potatoe disease of 1845 and 1846.* Edinburgh, 1848.

Baker, A. *A vindication of the corporation of bakers.* Dublin, 1756. (Quoted in Swift, J. *History of the Dublin bakers and others.* Dublin, 1948, pp 149-52.)

Baker, T. H. *Records of seasons, prices of agricultural produce and phenomena observed in the British Isles.* London, 1883.

Balfour, J. H. *A manual of botany.* Edinburgh, 1860.

Barker, F. and Cheyne, J. *An account of the rise, progress and decline of the fever lately epidemical in Ireland*, i, Dublin, 1821.

Bartlett, G. *Solanumania, or the potato disease.* London, 1851.

de Bary, A. *Die gegenwärtig herrschende Kartoffelkrankheit, ihre Ursache und ihre Verhütung.* Leipzig, 1861.

– 'Recherches sur le développement de quelques champignons parasites' in *Annales des Sciences Naturelles*, Paris, 4me sér., xx (1863), 1-148.

Bascome, E. *A history of epidemic pestilences from the earliest ages.* London, 1851.

Beaumont, G. de. *L'Irlande sociale, politique et religieuse.* 2 vols. Paris, 1839.

Bellingham, Dr O'B. 'Observations upon the potato disease as it prevailed in Ireland this year'. (This paper was read to the Dublin Natural History Society on 14 November 1845, and reproduced in *Saunders' News-Letter*, supplement no. 32,424, 17 Nov. 1845. It was reprinted, with some additions, in the *Dublin Medical Press*, xiv [1845], 359-64, to which all quoted page numbers refer. It is copiously quoted in *Census of 1851*, pp 259-60.)

Bergsma, C. A. *De aardappel-epidemie in Nederland in den jare 1845.* Utrecht, 1845.

Berkeley, M. J. 'Observations, botanical and physiological, on the potato murrain' in *Journal of the Horticultural Society of London*, i (1846), 9-34.

BFM British Farmer's Magazine, London, new series.

Bicheno, J. E. *Ireland and its economy.* London, 1830.

Binns, J. *The miseries and beauties of Ireland*, ii, Dublin, 1837.

Blight progress returns. Returns showing progress of disease...in potato crop, 1846. PROI (National Archives). Relief commission papers, bundle 1A.50.85.

Boate, G. *A natural history of Ireland.* Dublin, 1755.

Bonjean, J. *Monographie de la pomme de terre envisagée dans ses rapports agricoles, scientifiques et industriels, et comprenant l'histoire générale de la maladie des pommes de terre en 1845*. Paris, 1846.

Boset, C. J. *Plantation des pommes de terre en 1846, d'après la théorie démontrée de leur maladie*. Liége, 1846.

Bosson, C. P. *Observations on the potatoe, and a remedy for the potatoe plague*. Boston, 1846.

Bourson, P. *Exposé analytique de diverses opinions sur les causes probables de la maladie des pommes de terre présenté à la commission institutée près du Ministère de l'intérieur*. Brussels, 1845. (Bourson was secretary of the Belgian commission of inquiry set up by King Leopold to report on the potato disease. The preparatory documentation contained in this informative pamphlet was, apart from some late material, printed in the *Moniteur Belge*, 15-18 November, 1845.)

British Association. *Report of the fifteenth meeting of the British Association for the Advancement of Science, held at Cambridge in June 1845*. London, 1846.

– *Report of the sixteenth meeting of the British Association for the Advancement of Science, held at Southampton in September 1846*. Notices and abstracts of communications. London, 1847.

BSSCRA Bulletin des Séances de la Société Royale et Centrale d'Agriculture, Compte Rendu Mensuel (Paris, 1845-7). 2me sér., i (1845-6), ii (1846-7).

BU Banner of Ulster, Belfast.

Buckman, J. *The potatoe blight, its causes and remedies*. Cheltenham, 1845.

Butler, Mrs R. *A memoir of the Very Reverend Richard Butler, dean of Clonmacnois and vicar of Trim*. Edinburgh, 1863.

Caird, J. *The plantation scheme, or the west of Ireland as a field of investment*. Edinburgh and London, 1850.

Carlyon, C. *Observations on the potato blight, its nature and appropriate antidote*. Truro, 1847.

Carroll, E. 'Observations on the conacre system' in *IFGM*, ii (1835), 9-12.

CC Cork Constitution

CE Cork Examiner

Census of 1841. Report of the commissioners appointed to take the census of Ireland for the year 1841. HC 1843 (504), xxiv.

Census of 1851. The census of Ireland for the year 1851. Part v, vol. i, table of deaths. HC 1856 (2087-1), xxix, 261.

CJ Clare Journal

Cobbett, W. *Rural rides*, ii, Everyman edn. London, 1830.

Constab. reports. Constabulary reports on the condition of the potato crop. Relief commission papers. PROI (National Archives) 1A.50.73. 1845.

– Constabulary reports (on the extent of the) potato crop 1846. Relief commission papers. PROI (National Archives) 1A.50.74-76. Antrim-Galway, Bundle 74. Kerry-Monaghan, Bundle 75. Queens-Wicklow, Bundle 76.

Cooper, E. J. 'Observations on the potato disease, with an inquiry into its possible connection with atmospheric phenomena'. (Presented, 29 October 1846. Read, 21 November 1846) *Proceedings of the Royal Dublin Society*, lxxxiii (1847), Appendix no. iv, pp xv-xxvii.

Couch, J. 'Observations on the disease which has injured the potatoe in the present year, 1845' in *Thirteenth Annual Report of the Royal Cornwall Polytechnic Society, 1845*, Falmouth, 1846, pp 9-21.

– 'Further enquiries into the nature and effects of the prevailing disease in potatoes' in *Fifteenth Annual Report of the Royal Cornwall Polytechnic Society, 1847*, Falmouth, 1848, pp 1-11.

Cox, H. 'On the potato disease' (Prize essay) in *Journal of the Royal Agricultural Society of England*, vii (1847), 486-98.

de Croeser de Berges, Le baron E. *Études sur l'histoire et la culture de la pomme de terre*. Bruges, 1860.

Croker, T. F. *Popular songs of Ireland* (1839). Morley's Universal Library edn. London, 1886.

Crum, W. 'Artificial production of the potato disease' in *British Farmer's Magazine*, new series, x (1846), 76-8.

CS Carlow Sentinel.

DA Drogheda Argus.

Decaisne, M. J. *Histoire de la maladie des pommes de terre en 1845*. Paris, 1846.

DEH Dublin Evening Herald.

DEP Dublin Evening Post.

DEM Dublin Evening Mail.

DE Packet Dublin Evening Packet

Devon report. Evidence taken before her majesty's commissioners of enquiry into the state of the law and practice in respect to the occupation of land in Ireland. HC 1845 (606), xix, 57; (616), xx, 1; (657), xxi, 1; (672), xxii, 1; (673), xxii, 225. (References are normally expressed in terms of witness and question numbers.)

Dieudonné, M. M. *Rapport fait au conseil central de salubrité publique de Bruxelles sur la maladie des pommes de terre*. Brussels, 1845.

Distress correspondence. Correspondence explanatory of the measures adopted by her majesty's government for the relief of distress arising from the failure of the potato crop in Ireland. HC 1846 (735), xxxvii, 41.

– *Correspondence from July, 1846 to January, 1847 relating to the measures adopted for the relief of distress in Ireland* (Commissariat series). HC 1847 (761), li, 1.

DMA Dublin Mercantile Advertiser.

DMP Dublin Medical Press. xiv, July-Dec. 1845; xv, Jan.-June 1846; xvi, July-Dec. 1846.

Dowdall, F. Series of anonymous articles on Irish agricultural statistics, in *Dublin Evening Herald* of 5, 10, 14, 19, 24, 26, November and 1, 8, December 1846. Summarised and attributed to Dowdall in *Thom's directory*, 1848, pp 165-7.

Doyle, M. 'Hints to small farmers' in *The works of Martin Doyle*. Dublin, 1830.

– 'Hints on roadmaking, etc.' in *The works of Martin Doyle*. Dublin, 1830.

– *A cyclopaedia of practical husbandry*. Dublin, 1839.

DR Downpatrick Recorder.

Drennan, W. *Glendalloch and other poems*. Dublin, 1859.

Drummond report. Second report of the commissioners appointed to consider and recommend a general system of railways for Ireland. HC 1837-38 (145), xxxv, 449.

Dubourdieu, J. *Statistical survey of the county of Down*. Dublin, 1802.

Duchartre, P. 'Maladie de la pomme de terre: resumé des travaux qui ont été publiés à ce sujet' in *Revue Botanique*, Paris, i (1845-6), 147-182, 223-9.

DUM Dublin University Magazine.

Dumortier, B. C. 'Observations sur la cloque des pommes de terre' in *Bulletin de l'Académie Royale des Sciences et Belles-Lettres de Bruxelles*, xii (pt. ii) (1845), 285-99.

Duncan, J. *Essays on the potato plant, its failure in 1845-6 and the remedy*. Wick, 1847.

Dutton, H. *Statistical survey of the county of Clare*. Dublin, 1808.

– *A statistical and agricultural survey of the county of Galway*. Dublin, 1824.

EC Enniskillen Chronicle.

Farmer's Guide The farmer's guide, compiled for the use of the small farmers and cottage tenantry of Ireland. Dublin, 1841.

Farran, C. *Letters on the origin of the disease in the potato*. Dublin, 1846.
FG Farmer's Gazette, Dublin.
FJ Freeman's Journal, Dublin.
Foster, T. C. *Letters on the condition of the people of Ireland*. London, 1846.
Fournet, J. 'Notice sur les orages et sur la pluie de terre de l'automne 1846' in *Annales de la Société d'Agriculture de Lyon*, ix (1846), 593-693.
FR Fermanagh Reporter, Enniskillen.
Gaskell, E. C. *The life of Charlotte Brontë*. London, 1924 edn.
de Gasparin. 'Sur la maladie des pommes de terre' in *Comptes rendus hebdomadaires des séances de l'Académie des Sciences*, Paris, xxi (1845), 1339-42.
GC Gardeners' Chronicle, London.
GM Galway Mercury.
Godard, P. *Histoire de la pomme de terre*. Paris, 1847.
Gooch, G. P. (ed.) *The later correspondence of Lord John Russell 1840-1878*, i, London, 1925.
Goodrich, C. E. 'An essay on the potato disease, mainly as it appeared in the year 1846' in *Transactions of the New York State Agricultural Society*, vii (1847), 425-60.
Graham, F. J. *The potato disease*. London, 1847. (This prize essay was originally published in *JRASE*, vii [1847], 357-91.)
GV Galway Vindicator
Hall, R. *Report on workhouse dietaries. Appendix (D), report no. 21 [pp 238-42] to sixth annual report of the poor law commissioners*. HC 1840 (253), xvii, 447.
Hall, Mr and Mrs S. C. *Ireland its scenery, character, etc.* 3 vols. London, 1843.
Hancock, W. N. *On the alleged progressive decline of the prosperity of Ireland*. Dublin, 1863.
Hardy, A. and son. *A treatise on the practical culture of the potato*. Maldon, 1853.
Harting, P. *Recherches sur la nature et les causes de la maladie des pommes de terre en 1845*. Amsterdam, 1846.
Hattersley, J. *The potato disease and its remedy*. Manchester, 1859.
Hawley, W. H. T. *Report on workhouse dietaries. Appendix (D), report no. 22 [pp 242-8] to sixth annual report of the poor law commissioners*. HC 1840 (253), xvii, 447.
Hill, G. (ed.) *The Montgomery manuscripts*. Belfast, 1869.
Hogan, W. 'A report of the result of experiments made in 1847, of M. Zander's method of propagating potatos [*sic*] from seed' in *Proceedings of the Royal Dublin Society*, lxxxiv (1847-8), Appendix no. iii, pp lxv-lxxiv.
– 'An analysis of the meteorological observations communicated by Mr G. Yeates' in *Proceedings of the Royal Irish Academy*, v (1850), 12-8.
IAM Irish Agricultural Magazine, Dublin.
IFGM Irish Farmer's and Gardener's Magazine, Dublin.
IFGR Irish Farmer's and Gardener's Register, Dublin.
IFJ Irish Farmers' Journal, Dublin.
ISB Irish Statistical Bulletin, Dublin.
JA Journal of Agriculture, Edinburgh.
Jackson, J. *A treatise on agriculture and dairy husbandry*. Edinburgh, 1840.
Jackson, W. H. R. *An address...on the landlord and tenant question*. Cork, 1848.
JAP Journal d'Agriculture Pratique et de Jardinage, Paris. 2me. sér., iii (June 1845-July 1846).
JD Journal des Débats, Paris.
Johnson, C. W. 'On the potato disease' in *British Farmer's Magazine*, new series, x (1846), 438-41.

Johnston, J. F. W. (ed.) *The potato disease in Scotland, being results of investigations into its nature and origin.* Pamphlets 1 to 6. Edinburgh, 1845-6.
– *Selection and preparation of the seed.* Edinburgh, 1846. (Quoted in *BFM*, x, 164.)
Jones, H. D. 'Daily observations on the weather, and on the rise and fall of the Shannon, during the years 1845, 1846, 1847 and 1848, made at Athlone by John Long, Esq.' in *Proceedings of the Royal Irish Academy*, iv (1849), Appendix no. vi.
JRASE Journal of the Royal Agricultural Society of England, London.
Kane, R. *The industrial resources of Ireland.* 2nd edn. Dublin, 1845.
– 'On the recent progress and the present state of industry in Ireland; and the Dublin international exhibition of 1865' in H. Parkinson and F. L. Simmonds (eds), *The illustrated record and descriptive catalogue of the Dublin international exhibition of 1865.* London, 1866, pp 52-9.
KCC King's County Chronicle, Parsonstown (Birr).
KE Kerry Examiner, Tralee.
KEP Kerry Evening Post, Tralee.
KJ Kilkenny Journal.
KM Kilkenny Moderator.
Kützing, F. T. 'Uber die Zellenfäule der Kartoffeln' in *Botanische Zeitung*, Berlin, iii (1845), col. 686-8.
LC Limerick Chronicle.
LE Leinster Express, Maryborough.
Lewis, S. *A topographical dictionary of Ireland.* 2nd edn. 2 vols. London, 1849.
LJ Londonderry Journal.
Long J Longford Journal.
Lortet, P. 'De la constitution atmosphérique des mois d'avril, juin, juillet, août, et septembre 1845, considerée comme cause déterminante de la maladie des pommes de terre' in *Annales de la Société Royale d'Agriculture de Lyon*, vii (1845), 473-81.
– 'Rapport sur les travaux de la commission hydrometrique en 1846' in *Annales de la Société Royale d'Agriculture de Lyon*, ix (1846), 714-9.
LSD Londonderry Standard.
LSL Londonderry Sentinel.
Lyon commission. La commission speciale nommée par la Société d'Agriculture de Lyon. 'Avis aux cultivateurs sur la renouvellement, la culture, la recolte et la conservation de la pomme de terre' in *Annales de la Société d'Agriculture de Lyon*, ix (1846), 710-3.
McAdam, R. S. 'On the potato' in *Quarterly Journal of Agriculture*, v (1834-5), 321-43.
McCulloch, J. R. *A dictionary of commerce and commercial navigation.* New edn. London, 1845.
M'Sweeny, J. 'An essay on the climate of Ireland' in *Transactions of the Royal Irish Academy*, xvii (1837).
Malam, J. *Facts and observations relative to the potato disease, its probable cause and cure.* Hull, 1855.
Mareska, J. and Kickx, J. *Rapport sur l'épidémie actuelle des pommes de terre.* Gand, 1845.
Martens, M. 'Sur la maladie des pommes de terre' in *Bulletin de l'Académie Royale des Sciences et Belles Lettres de Bruxelles*, xii, part ii (1845), pp 356-72.
Maule, A. J. *The potato, what is it?* Bristol, 1876.
Maunsell, W. *On the culture of potatoes from the shoots.* Dublin, 1794.
Maxwell, R. *The practical husbandman, being a collection of miscellaneous papers on husbandry, etc.* Edinburgh, 1757.

Mayhew, H. *London labour and the London poor*, iii, London, 1861.
Mayo T Mayo Telegraph.
MB Le Moniteur Belge, Brussels.
MC Mayo Constitution, Castlebar.
MFM Munster Farmers' Magazine, Cork.
MHC Report. Report of the Mansion House Committee on the potato disease. Dublin, 1846.
Michot, l'Abbé. 'Opinion de M. l'abbé Michot sur la maladie de la solanée tubéreuse' in *Le Moniteur Belge*, Brussels, 7-8 September 1845.
Milne, D. *Observations on the probable cause of the failure of the potato crop in 1845 and 1846.* Edinburgh and London, 1847.
Ministère de l'Agriculture et du Commerce. *Altération des pommes de terre en 1845.* Paris, 1845.
Mitchell, C. *The newspaper press directory for the year 1846.* London, 1846.
MJA Monthly Journal of Agriculture, New York.
MLE Mark Lane Express, London.
Morewood, S. *A philosophical and statistical history of...inebriating liquors.* Dublin, 1838.
Morren, C. *Instructions populaires sur les moyens de combattre et de détruire la maladie actuelle (gangrène humide) des pommes de terre, et sur les moyens d'obtenir pendant l'hiver des récoltes de ces tubercules, suivies de renseignements sur la culture et l'usage du topinambour.* Brussels, 1845. (Note: A second edition of this pamphlet, with some changes, was published later in the same year in Paris, under the title *Nouvelles instructions populaires...*).
Morris, W. O'Connor. *Memories and thoughts of a life.* London, 1895.
Morton, J. C. *A cyclopaedia of agriculture, practical and scientific*, ii; article on the potato. London, 1855, pp 667-94.
Mounier, M. 'Sur la maladie des pommes de terre' in *L'Echo du monde savant.* Paris, 1845, cols. 1167-8.
MT Medical Times, London.
Muenter, J. *Die Krankheiten der Kartoffeln, insbesondere die im Jahre 1845 pandemisch herrschende nasse Fäule.* Berlin, 1846.
Murray, A. *The book of the Royal Horticultural Society.* London, 1863.
NCT Newry Commercial Telegraph.
New Blackfriars, London.
Newenham, C. B. *Good news: potatoes grown from peels.* Cork, 1848.
Newman, E. *Notes on Irish natural history.* London, 1840.
NG Nenagh Guardian.
Niven, N. *The potato epidemic and its probable consequences.* Dublin, 1846.
Norton, J. P. 'The potato disease in Scotland' in *Transactions of the New York State Agricultural Society for 1845*, Albany, New York, v (1846), 349-79.
NS Northern Standard, Monaghan.
NW Northern Whig, Belfast.
NWC North Wales Chronicle.
O'Connell, D. *The correspondence of Daniel O'Connell*, ed. Maurice R. O'Connell. 8 vols. Dublin, 1972-80.
Ordnance survey met. returns. Meteorological observations taken during the years 1829 to 1852 at the Ordnance Survey Office, Phoenix Park, Dublin; to which is added a series of similar observations made at the principal trigonometrical stations, and at other places in Ireland. Dublin, 1856.
O'Rourke, J. *The history of the great Irish famine of 1847.* Dublin, 1875.
Parkin, J. *On the remote cause of epidemic diseases.* London, 1841.

– *The cause of blight and pestilence in the animal kingdom*. London, 1846.
– *The prevention and treatment of disease in the potato and other crops*. London, 1847.
– *The remote cause of epidemic diseases; or the influence of volcanic action in the production of general pestilences*, part ii. London, 1853.
Payen, A. and Chevallier, A. *Traité de la pomme de terre*. Paris, 1826.
Peel memoirs. *Memoirs by the Right Honourable Sir Robert Peel*. Ed. Lord Mahon and E. Cardwell, part iii. *The repeal of the corn laws, 1845-6*. London, 1857.
Peeters, L. *Guérison radicale de la maladie des pommes de terre et d'autres végétaux*. Namur, 1855.
Philanthropist. *A cure for the potatoe disease*. London, 1848.
Phillips, G. 'On the nature and cause of the potato disease' (Prize essay) in *Journal of the Royal Agricultural Society of England*, vii (1847), 300-33.
Pim, J. *The condition and prospects of Ireland*. Dublin, 1848.
Pinkert, F. A. *Die Kartoffelnot unserer Zeit und ihre Abhülfe*. Weimar, 1843.
Playfair, L. 'On the nature and cause of the decay in potatoes' in *Journal of the Royal Agricultural Society of England*, vi (1846), 532-65.
PLC report. *Twelfth annual report of the poor law commissioners, with appendices*. HC 1846 (704) (745), xix, 1, 33, 1846.
– *Thirteenth annual report of the poor law commissioners, with appendices*. HC 1847 (816) (873), xxviii, 1, 35.
– *First annual report of the commissioners for administering the laws for relief of the poor in Ireland, with appendices*. Dublin, 1848. This document was also issued as HC 1847-8 (963), xxxiii, 377.
Plough The Plough, London.
Poor inquiry (A). *Appendix (A) to the first report of inquiry into the condition of the poor in Ireland*. HC 1835 (369), xxxii, pt. i, 1.
Poor inquiry (D). *Appendix (D) to the first report of inquiry into the condition of the poor in Ireland*. HC 1836 (36), xxxi, 1.
Poor inquiry (E). *Appendix (E) to the first report of inquiry into the condition of the poor in Ireland*. HC 1836 (37), xxxii, 1.
Poor inquiry (F). *Appendix (F) to the first report of inquiry into the condition of the poor in Ireland*. HC 1836 (38), xxxiii, 1.
Poor inquiry (H). *Appendix (H) to the first report of inquiry into the condition of the poor in Ireland*. Part i. HC 1836 (41), xxxiv, 643. Part ii. HC 1836 (42), xxxiv, 657.
QJA Quarterly Journal of Agriculture, London and Edinburgh.
Quetelet, A. 'Observations météorologiques des mois de mai, juin, juillet, août et septembre 1845, faites à l'Observatoire Royale de Bruxelles' in *Bulletin de l'Académie Royale des Sciences et Belles Lettres de Bruxelles*, iii (1845), part ii, 205-23.
Radcliff, T. *A report of the agriculture and live stock of the county of Wicklow*. Dublin, 1812.
Rawstorne, L. *The cause of the potato disease ascertained by proofs*. London, 1847.
RDS Prize essays. *Prize essays on the potato, and the causes of the late partial failures*. Dublin, 1835.
Report of Belgian commission. 'Troisième rapport présenté à M. le Ministre de l'intérieur par la commission chargé de l'examen des questions relatives à la maladie des pommes de terre' *MB*, 15 November 1845.
Report of Playfair and Lindley. *Copy of the report of Dr Playfair and Mr Lindley on the present state of the Irish potato crop and on the prospect of approaching scarcity* (dated 15 Nov. 1845). HC 1846 (28), xxxvii, 33.
Report on agriculture I. *First report from the select committee appointed to inquire into the state of agriculture*. HC 1836 (79), viii, 1.

Report on agriculture II. Second report from the select committee appointed to inquire into the state of agriculture. HC 1836 (189), viii, 225.

Report on agriculture III. Third report from the select committee appointed to inquire into the state of agriculture. HC 1836 (465), viii, 1.

Report on bogs I. First report of commissioners on the nature and extent of bogs in Ireland. HC 1810 (365), x, 389.

Report on bogs II. Second report of commissioners on the nature and extent of bogs in Ireland. HC 1810-11 (96), vi, 579.

Report on bogs III. Third report of commissioners on the nature and extent of bogs in Ireland. HC 1813-14 (130), vi, pt. i.

Report on bogs IV. Fourth report of commissioners on the nature and extent of bogs in Ireland. HC 1813-14 (131), vi, pt. ii, 167.

Report on the potato crop. Report from the select committee appointed to inquire into means of diminishing the frequency, etc., of failures in the potato crop. HC 1880 (274), xii, 309.

Returns of grain, flour, etc. Returns of the quantities of grain and flour of all sorts imported into Ireland from 1 January 1839 to 1 January 1849...HC 1849 (588), 1, 403.

RJ Roscommon Journal

Rothwell, W. 'Potato disease' in *The British Cultivator and Agricultural Review*. London, 1845, i, 334-5.

Rutty, J. *An essay towards a natural history of the county of Dublin*. 2 vols. Dublin, 1772.

Ryan, R. *Prize essay upon the following subject of inquiry, 'What are the best means of rendering the national sources of wealth possessed by Ireland effectual for the employment of the population?' proposed by the Royal Irish Academy, 1822*. London, 1824.

Rye, G. *Considerations on agriculture*. Dublin, 1730.

Sampson, G. V. *Statistical survey of the county of Londonderry*. Dublin, 1802.

Savoureux. *Nouveau procédé de culture des pommes de terre*. Rouen, 1847.

SC Sligo Champion

Scarcity reports. Weekly reports of the scarcity commission, showing the progress of the disease in the potatoes, the complaints which have been made and the applications for relief, in the course of the month of March 1846...HC 1846 (213), xxxvii, 459.

Senior, N. W. *Journals, conversations and essays relating to Ireland*. 2 vols. London, 1868.

Shea, T. 'The minute book of the Ballineen Agricultural Society, 1845-47: a famine document', in *Cork Hist. Arch. Soc. Jn.* 2nd ser., i (1946), 52-60.

Sinclair, J. *On the culture and uses of the potato*. Edinburgh, 1828.

SJ Sligo Journal.

Smee, A. *The potatoe plant, its uses and properties; together with the cause of the present malady*. London, 1846.

SNL Saunders' News-Letter, Dublin.

Society of Friends. *Transactions of the central relief committee of the Society of Friends during the famine in Ireland*. Dublin, 1852.

Solly, E. 'On the influence of electricity on vegetation' in *Journal of the Horticultural Society of London*, i (1846), 81-109.

– 'Further observations on the influence of electricity on vegetation', ibid., ii (1847), 42-5.

SR Southern Reporter, Cork.

SRCA Bulletin des séances de la Société Royale et Centrale d'Agriculture. Paris. In A. Payen (ed.), *Compte Rendu Mensuel*, 2me sér., i (1845-6); ii (1846-7).

Survey of Londonderry. Ordnance survey of the county of Londonderry, i. *Memoir of the city and north western liberties of Londonderry*. Dublin, 1837.

TC Tipperary Constitution and Munster and Leinster Advertiser, Clonmel.
TCD met. returns. Observations made at the magnetical and meteorological observatory at Trinity College, Dublin, ii (1844-1850). Dublin, 1869.
TFP Tipperary Free Post, Clonmel.
TH Tyrawly Herald, Ballina.
Thompson, H. S. *Ireland in 1839 and 1869*. London, 1870.
Thompson, R. 'Observations and experiments made in the garden of the society in 1846 relative to the potato disease' in *Journal of the Horticultural Society of London*, ii (1847), 179-82.
Thom's directory. Thom's Irish almanac and official directory. Dublin.
Threlkeld, C. *Synopsis stirpium Hibernicarum alphabetice dispositarum...being a short treatise of native plants, especially such as grow spontaneously in the vicinity of Dublin*. Dublin, 1727. (Note: This work is not paginated. References to the potato are under the heading 'solanum tuberosum esculentum').
Tighe, W. *Statistical observations relative to the county of Kilkenny*. Dublin, 1802.
Townley, J. *The diseases, regeneration and culture of the potato*. London, 1847.
Townsend, H. *Statistical survey of the county of Cork*. Dublin, 1810.
TRC Tralee Chronicle.
Trench, W. Steuart. *Realities of Irish life*. Dublin, 1868.
Trevelyan, C. E. *The Irish crisis*. London, 1848.
Trimmer, J. K. *A brief inquiry into the present state of agriculture in the southern part of Ireland*. London, 1809.
Tuam H Tuam Herald.
TV Tipperary Vindicator, Nenagh.
TYC Tyrone Constitution, Omagh.
UC Ulster Conservative, Belfast.
UG Ulster Gazette.
US Patents report. Report of the commissioner of patents for the year 1845. Appendix no. 6. Washington, 1845.
Van den Hecke. 'Maladie des pommes de terre' in *L'Organe des Flandres*, Gand, 31 July, 1 August 1845. (Reproduced in the following days, with acknowledgment, in *L'Impartial* [Bruges]. The article was published anonymously, the author was named by Bourson [1845, pp 38-9]).
Vissering, S. *Eenige opmerkingen ter zake der aardappelziekte*. Amsterdam, 1845.
Von Martius, C. F. P. *Die Kartoffel-Epidemie der letzten Jahre, oder die Stockfäule und Räude der Kartoffeln*. Munich, 1842.
Wakefield, E. *An account of Ireland, statistical and political*. 2 vols. Dublin, 1812.
Walford, C. 'The famines of the world: past and present' in *Journal of the Royal Statistical Society* (London), xli (1878), pt. iii, 433-535 and xlii (1879), 79-265.
Walkinshaw, Clotworthy. *Prevention of the decay in potatoes, with numerous experiments*. 2nd edn. Belfast, 1856.
WC Wexford Conservative.
WCH Waterford Chronicle.
Weighman, G. *A treatise on the true nature and cause of the present destructive disease of potatoes, with the means of cure*. London and Nottingham, 1846.
WF Waterford Freeman.
WI Wexford Independent.
Wiggins, J. *The monster misery of Ireland*. London, 1844.
Wilde, W. R. 'The food of the Irish' in *Dublin University Magazine*, xliii (1854), 127-46.
– 'On the introduction and time of the general use of the potato in Ireland' in *Proceedings of the Royal Irish Academy*, vi (1853-7), 356-72.

Williams, J. 'The late mild winter' in *Journal of the Horticultural Society of London*, i (1846), 186-8.
Wilmot, C. *An Irish peer on the continent (1801-1803): the tour of Stephen, 2nd Earl Mount Cashell, through France, Italy, etc.* ed. T.U. Sadleir. London, 1920.
Wilson, J. M. *The potato: an essay on its constitution, diseases, varieties, cultivation and uses*. Edinburgh, 1850.
WM Waterford Mail.
Wolseley, J. *The 'difficulty' met: a letter to the labouring poor of Ireland*. Dublin, 1846.
Young, A. *A tour in Ireland*. Bohn edn. 2 vols. London, 1892.
Zuppinger, F. *Die glücklich entdeckte Ursache der Kartoffelkrankheit*. Zürich, 1847.

Secondary sources

Adams, W. F. *Ireland and Irish emigration to the New World*. New Haven, 1932.
Ambirajan, S. 'Malthusian population theory and Indian famine policy in the nineteenth century' in *Population Studies*, xxx (1976), 5-14.
Andrews, J. H. 'Road planning in Ireland before the railway age' in *Irish Geography*, v (1964), 17-41.
Appel, O. 'Beiträge zur Kenntnis der Kartoffelpflanze und ihrer Krankheiten, I' in *Arbeiten aus der Kaiserlichen Biologischen Anstalt für Land- und Forstwirtschaft*, Berlin, v (1907), 377-435.
Atanasoff, D. 'A study into the literature on stipple-streak and related diseases of the potato' in *Mededeelingen van de Landbouwhoogeschool*, Wageningen, no. 26, 1922.
Attwood, E. A. and Heavey, J. F. 'Determination of grazing livestock units' in *Irish Journal of Agricultural Research*, iii (1964), 249-51.
Barrington, T. 'The yields of Irish tillage food crops since the year 1847' in *Journal of the Department of Agriculture*, Dublin, xxi (1921), 205-29, 289-305. (This article was published anonymously. It is attributed to Barrington in *Agricultural statistics, 1847-1926*, Dublin, 1928, p. xxxviii.)
Bergman, M. 'The potato blight in the Netherlands and its social consequences (1845-1847)' in *International Review of Social History*, xii (1967), 390-431.
Black, R. D. C. *Economic thought and the Irish question 1817-70*. Cambridge, 1960.
Bowen, F. C. *A century of Atlantic travel*. London (n.d., apparently 1932).
Boyle, P. P. and Ó Gráda, C. 'Fertility trends, excess mortality and the great Irish famine' in *Demography*, xxiii (1986), 542-62.
British Mycological Symposium, xvii, *Phytophthora*. Ed. J. Lucas *et al.* Cambridge, 1991.
Britten, J. and Boulger, G. S. *A biographical index of British and Irish botanists*. London, 1893.
Budget inquiry. Household budget inquiry, 1951-2. Central Statistics Office, Dublin, 1954.
Burton, W. C. *The potato*. London, 1948.
Butler, E. J. and Jones, S. G. *Plant pathology*. London, 1949.
Cathcart, Earl. 'On the cultivated potato' in *Journal of the Royal Agricultural Society of England*, xx (1884), 266-300.
Charbonneau, Hubert and Larose, André (eds). *The great mortalities: methodological studies of demographic crises in the past*. Liège, 1981.
Chart, D. A. *Ireland from the union to Catholic emancipation. A study of social, economic and administrative conditions, 1800-1829*. London, 1910.
– *An economic history of Ireland*. Dublin, 1920.
Chavée-Leroy. *La maladie des pommes de terre*. Paris, 1883.

Connell, K. H. *The population of Ireland, 1750-1845*. Oxford, 1950.
– 'The history of the potato' in *Economic History Review*, 2nd ser., iii (1951), 388-95.
– 'Illicit distillation: an Irish peasant industry' in *Historical Studies III*, ed. J. Hogan (1961), pp 58-91.
– *Irish peasant society*. Oxford, 1968.
Connolly, J. *Labour in Irish history*. London, 1922 edn.
Cork Hist. Arch. Soc. Jn. Journal of the Cork Historical and Archaeological Society.
Cousens, S. H. 'The regional variation in mortality during the great Irish famine' in *RIA Proc.*, Section C, lxiii (1963), 127-49.
– 'Regional death rates in Ireland during the great famine from 1846 to 1851' in *Population Studies*, xiv (1960), 55-74.
Cox, A. E. and Large, E. C. 'Potato blight epidemics throughout the world' in *Agricultural Handbook*, no. 174. Agricultural Research Service, US Department of Agriculture. Washington, 1960.
Craig, E. T. *An Irish commune: the history of Ralahine*. Dublin (n.d., *c.* 1920.)
Crawford, E. M. 'Indian meal and pellagra in nineteenth century Ireland' in Goldstrom and Clarkson (eds), *Irish population*, pp 113-33.
– 'Dearth, diet, and disease in Ireland, 1850: a case study of nutritional deficiency' in *Medical History*, xxviii (1984), 151-61.
– 'Scurvy in Ireland during the great famine' in *Journal of the Social History of Medicine*, i (1988), 281-300.
– (ed.) *Famine: the Irish experience 900-1900: subsistence crises and famines in Ireland*. Edinburgh, 1989.
Crosier, W. *Studies in the biology of Phytophthora infestans (Mont.) de Bary*. Cornell University Agricultural Experiment Station, Memoir no. 155, 1934.
Cullen, L. M. 'Irish history without the potato' in *Past and Present*, no. 40 (1968), 72-83.
Daly, M. *The great famine in Ireland*. Dublin, 1986.
Davidson, W. D. 'A review of literature dealing with the degeneration of varieties of the potato' in *Economic Proceedings, Royal Dublin Society*, ii (1928), 331-89.
– 'History of potato varieties' in *Journal of the Department of Agriculture*, Dublin, xxxiii (1935), 57-81.
– 'The history of the potato and its progress in Ireland' in *Journal of the Department of Agriculture*, Dublin, xxxiv (1937), 286-307.
Department of Health. *National nutritional survey*. Part vi. Dublin, 1950.
Devine, T. *The great highland famine*. Edinburgh, 1988.
– 'Why the highlands did not starve' in S. Connolly, R. Houston, and R. J. Morris (eds), *Proceedings of the 4th conference of Irish and Scottish economic and social historians* (forthcoming).
Dickson, D. 'The gap in famines [1745-1815]: a useful myth?' in Crawford (ed.), *Famine*, pp 96-111.
Dineen, P. S. *An Irish-English dictionary*. Dublin, 1927.
Doberck, W. 'On the rainfall and temperature of Markree, Co. Sligo' in *Quarterly Journal of the Royal Meteorological Society*, London, x (1884), 158-61.
Dodds, J. W. *The age of paradox: a biography of England, 1841-1851*. London, 1953.
Doncaster, J. P. and Gregory, P. A. 'The spread of virus diseases in the potato crop' in *Agricultural Research Council Report Series*, no. 7. HMSO, London, 1948.
Donnelly, J. S. Chaps. xii-xix in W. E. Vaughan (ed.), *A new history of Ireland, v. Ireland under the union 1 (1801-70)*. Oxford, 1989.
Drake, M. 'Marriage and population growth in Ireland, 1750-1845' in *Economic History Review*. 2nd ser., xvi (1963), 301-13.
Drummond, J. C. and Wilbraham, A. *The Englishman's food: a history of five centuries*

of English diet. London, 1939.
Dun, Finlay. *Landlords and tenants in Ireland*. London, 1881.
Dwyer, G. P. and Lindsay, C. M. 'Robert Giffen and the Irish potato' in *American Economic Review*, lxxiv (1984), 1988-92.
Edwards, R. D. and Williams, T. D. (eds). *The great famine: studies in Irish history, 1845-52*. Dublin, 1956.
EHR English Historical Review.
Evans, E. Estyn. *Irish heritage*. Dundalk, 1942.
– *Irish folk ways*. London, 1957.
Fitzpatrick, D. 'The disappearance of the Irish agricultural labourer, 1841-1912' in *Ir. Econ. and Soc. Hist.*, vii (1980), 66-92.
– *Irish emigration 1801-1921*. Dublin, 1984.
Foley, K. 'The Killarney poor law guardians and the famine 1845-52'. MA thesis, NUI, 1987.
Freeman, T. W. *Pre-famine Ireland*. Manchester, 1957.
Froggatt, P. 'The demographic work of Sir William Wilde' in *Irish Journal of Medical Science*, Dublin, 1965, pp 213-30.
– 'The response of the medical profession to the great famine' in E. M. Crawford (ed.), *Famine*, pp 134-56.
Garner, E. *To die by inches: the famine in north east Cork*. Fermoy, 1986.
Gash, N. *Mr Secretary Peel: the life of Sir Robert Peel to 1830*. London, 1961.
– *Sir Robert Peel: the life of Sir Robert Peel after 1830*. London, 1972.
Gibbon, P. 'Colonialism and the great starvation in Ireland 1845-9' in *Race and Class*, xvii (1975), 131-9.
Glazier, I. (ed.) *The famine immigrants: lists of Irish immigrants arriving at the port of New York, 1846-1851*. 7 vols. Baltimore, 1983-5.
Glazier, I., Mageean, D., and Okeke, B. 'Socio-demographic characteristics of Irish immigrants 1846-1851' in Klaus Friedland (ed.), *Maritime aspects of migration*. Cologne, 1989.
Goldstrom, J. M. 'Irish agriculture and the great famine' in Goldstrom and Clarkson (eds), *Irish population*, pp 155-71.
Goldstrom, J. M. and Clarkson, L. A. (eds). *Irish population, economy and society*. Oxford, 1981.
Grant, J. 'The great famine in the province of Ulster 1845-9: the mechanism of relief'. Ph.D. thesis, QUB, 1986.
– 'The great famine and the poor law in Ulster: the rate-in-aid issue of 1849' in *IHS*, xxvii (1990), 30-47.
Gray, Asa. *Scientific papers of Asa Gray*, ii. London, 1889. (Biographical sketch of John Lindley), pp 333-6.
Green, E. R. R. *The Lagan valley, 1800-1850*. London, 1949.
Grew, S. 'Meteorology at Armagh Observatory' in *Irish Astronomical Journal*, i (1951), 230-7.
Griffiths, A. R. G. 'The Irish Board of Works in the famine years' in *Historical Journal*, xiii (1970), 634-52.
Grigg, D. B. *Population growth and agrarian change: a historical perspective*. London, 1980.
Grimshaw, T. W. *Facts and figures about Ireland*. Dublin, 1893.
Handley, J. E. *The Irish in Scotland: 1798-1845*. 2nd edn. Cork, 1945.
Hart, J. 'Sir Charles Trevelyan at the Treasury' in *English Historical Review*, lxxv (1960), 92-110.
Hawkes, J. G. 'Significance of wild species and primitive forms for potato breeding' in *Euphytica*, Wageningen, vii (1958), 257-70.

Hayter, A. *A sultry month*. London, 1965.
Hickey, P. 'A study of four peninsular parishes in west Cork 1796-1855'. Ph.D. thesis, NUI, 1980.
Holt, J. H. 'The Quakers in the great Irish famine'. M. Litt., TCD, 1967.
Hurst, M. *Maria Edgeworth and the public scene*. London, 1969.
Ir. Econ. and Soc. Hist. Journal of the Irish Economic and Social History Society of Ireland.
IHS Irish Historical Studies.
Ivins, J. D. and Milthorpe, F. L. (eds). *The growth of the potato. Proceedings of the tenth Easter school in agricultural science, University of Nottingham, 1963*. London, 1963.
JDA Journal of the Department of Agriculture, Dublin.
JDAF Journal of the Department of Agriculture and Fisheries (successor of *JDA* from 1965, vol. lxii).
Jn. Econ. Hist. Journal of Economic History.
Johnson, T. and Boyle, C. 'The industrial and nutritive value of the potato in Ireland' in *Journal of the Department of Agriculture*, Dublin, xviii (1918), 443-71.
Jones, E. L. *Seasons and prices: the role of the weather in English agricultural history*. London, 1964.
Jones, L. R., Giddings, N. J. and Lutman, B. J. 'Investigations on the potato fungus, *Phytophthora infestans*' in *US Department of Agriculture, Bureau of Plant Industry*, Bulletin no. 245. Washington, 1912.
Joyce, P. W. (ed.) *Old Irish folk music and songs*. Dublin, 1909.
JRSS Journal of the Royal Statistical Society.
JSSISI Journal of the Statistical and Social Inquiry Society of Ireland.
Kaukiainen, Y. 'Harvest fluctuations and mortality in agrarian Finland, 1810-1870' in T. Bengtsson *et al.* (eds), *Pre-industrial population change*. Stockholm, 1986.
Keane, T. *Weather and potato blight*. Irish Meteorological Service, agrometeorological memorandum no. 8. Dublin, 1982.
Kennedy, L. and Ollerenshaw, P. (eds). *An economic history of Ulster 1820-1939*. Manchester, 1985.
Kettle, L. J. (ed.) *Material for victory: the memoirs of Andrew J. Kettle*. Dublin, 1958.
Kiely, B. *Poor scholar: a study of the works and days of William Carleton (1794-1869)*. London, 1947.
Kierse, S. *The famine years in the parish of Killaloe 1845-1851*. Killaloe, 1984.
Lamb, H. H. *The English climate*. London, 1964.
Large, E. C. *The advance of the fungi*. London, 1940.
– 'The interpretation of progress curves for potato blight and other plant diseases' in *Plant Pathology*, i (1952), 109-17.
Lee, D. H. K. *Climate and economic development in the tropics*. New York, 1957.
Little, G. A. *Malachi Horan remembers*. Dublin, 1943.
Ludlum, D. M. *Early American hurricanes: 1492-1870*. Massachusetts, 1963.
MacArthur, W. A. 'Famines in Britain and Ireland' in *Journal of the British Archaeological Association*, 3rd ser., ix (1944), 66-71.
McArthur, M. 'Some factors involved in estimating calorie requirements, with special reference to persons engaged in agricultural labour in Asian countries' in *Journal of the Royal Statistical Society*, ser. A, cxxvii (1964), 392-408.
McDowell, R. B. *Public opinion and government policy in Ireland, 1800-1847*. London, 1952.
McGregor, P. 'The impact of the blight upon the pre-famine rural economy in Ireland' in *Economic and Social Review*, xv (1984), 289-393.
– 'Demographic pressure and the Irish famine: Malthus after Mokyr' in *Land Economics*, lxv (1989), 228-38.

McHale, E. 'The famine in Mayo' in *North Mayo Historical and Archaeological Society: Bliainiris*, 1 (v) (1986-7), 9-23.
McHugh, N. 'Famine and distress in Drogheda during 1847' in *Louth Arch. Soc. Jn.*, xxi (1986), 157-78.
Macintyre, A. *The liberator: Daniel O'Connell and the Irish party, 1830-1847*. London, 1965.
McKay, R. 'Pioneer workers in the field of plant pathology in Ireland; and a list of papers on plant disease' in *Journal of the Department of Agriculture*, Dublin, xlviii (1951-2), 5-31.
– *Potato diseases*. Dublin, 1955.
– *An anthology of the potato*. Dublin, 1961.
MacNeill, M. *The festival of Lughnasa*. London, 1962.
MAFF Leaflet 218. Advisory leaflet 218: *Dry rot of potatoes*. Ministry of Agriculture, Fisheries and Food. London, 1956.
Manley, G. 'Early meteorological journals: some further notes' in *Quarterly Journal of the Royal Meteorological Society*, London, lxxiv (1958), 75-7.
Mansergh, N. *The Irish question, 1840-1921*. London, 1965.
Marshall, W. A. L. *A century of London weather*. London, 1952.
Merry, A. *The hunger: being realities of the famine years in Ireland, 1845 to 1848*. London, 1910.
Meunier, L. J. E. *Du sulfatage systématique de la pomme de terre*. Auxerre, 1904.
Miller, K. *Emigrants and exiles*. New York, 1985.
Ministry of Agriculture (NI). *Thirteenth general report of the Ministry of Agriculture (Northern Ireland)*. Cmd. 348. Belfast, 1956.
Mitchison, R. *Agricultural Sir John: the life of Sir John Sinclair of Ulbster, 1754-1835*. London, 1962.
Mogey, J. M. *Rural life in Northern Ireland*. London, 1947.
Mokyr, J. 'The deadly fungus: an econometric investigation into the short-term demographic impact of the Irish famine, 1846-1851' in *Research in Population Economics*, ii (1980), 237-77.
– 'Irish history with the potato' in *Ir. Econ. and Soc. Hist.*, viii (1981), 8-29.
– *Why Ireland starved: a quantitative and analytical history of the Irish economy, 1800-1845*. London, 1983; revised edn, 1985.
Montague, R. J. 'Relief and reconstruction: public policy in Ireland, 1845-9'. D.Phil. thesis, Oxford, 1976.
Morash, C. *The hungry voice: the poetry of the Irish famine*. Dublin, 1989.
Morgan, W. A. *Summers in Dublin*. Irish Meteorological Service, internal memorandum 44/65, 1965.
Morineau, M. 'La pomme de terre au 19e siècle' in *Annales ESC*, xxv (1970), trans. in R. Forster and O. Ranum (eds), *Food and drink in history*. Baltimore, 1979, pp 17-36.
Murphy, P. A. 'A study of the seasonal development of the potato plant in relation to blight attack and spraying' in *Scientific Proceedings of the Royal Dublin Society*, new ser., xxii (1939), 69-83.
Murphy, P. A. and McKay, R. 'Further experiments on the sources and development of blight infection in potato tubers' in *Journal of the Department of Lands and Agriculture*, Dublin, xxv (1925), 10-21.
NAAS. National Agricultural Advisory Service. Terrington: *Fourth annual review*. Ministry of Agriculture, Fisheries and Food. London, 1963.
Neenan, M. 'Effect of premature haulm destruction on yield, tuber size and dry matter content of potatoes' in *Irish Journal of Agricultural Research*, iv (1965), 67-79.

Nelson, E. C. 'David Moore, Miles J. Berkeley and scientific studies of potato blight in Ireland, 1845-7' in *Archives of Natural History*, xi (1983), 249-61.
Nelson, M. C. *Bitter bread: the famine in Norrboten 1867-1868*. Uppsala, 1988.
Nowlan, K. B. *The politics of repeal. A study of the relations between Great Britain and Ireland, 1841-50*. London and Toronto, 1965.
O'Brien, G. 'Workhouse management in pre-famine Ireland' in *R.I.A. Proc.*, lxxxvi, section C (1985), 113-34.
O'Brien, R. Barry. *Thomas Drummond: life and letters*. London, 1889.
Ó Cíosáin, M. *Cnoc an Fhomhair*. Maynooth, 1988.
O'Donovan, J. *The economic history of live stock in Ireland*. Cork, 1940.
Ó Gráda, C. *Ireland before and after the famine*. Manchester, 1988.
– *The great Irish famine*. London and Dublin, 1989.
O'Herlihy, T. *The famine 1845-1847: ravages and causes*. Drogheda, 1947.
O'Neill, T. P. 'The organisation and administration of relief during the great famine'. M.A. thesis, NUI, 1946.
– 'The scientific investigation of the potato crop in Ireland, 1845-6' in *IHS*, v (1946), 123-38.
– 'Food problems during the great Irish famine' in *RSAI Jn.*, lxxxii, pt. ii (1952), 99-108.
– 'The queen and the famine' in *Threshold*, i (1957), 60-3.
– 'The Society of Friends and the great famine' in *Studies*, xxxix (1950), 203-13.
O'Neill, Timothy. 'The famine of 1822'. MA thesis, NUI, 1966.
– 'Fever and public health in pre-famine Ireland', in *RSAI Jn.*, ciii (1973), 1-34.
– 'The state, poverty and distress in Ireland, 1815-45'. Ph.D. thesis, NUI, 1971.
– 'Poverty in Ireland 1815-1845' in *Folk Life*, xi (1973), 22-33.
Ó Raghallaigh, D. *Sir Robert Kane*. Cork, 1942.
O'Rourke, K. 'Agricultural change and rural depopulation: Ireland 1845-1876'. Ph.D. thesis, Harvard University, 1989.
– 'Did the great famine matter?' in *Jn. Econ. Hist.*, li (1991), 1-22.
Ó Tuathaigh, G. *Ireland before the famine 1798-1848*. Dublin, 1972.
Passmore, R. 'Estimation of food requirements' in *Journal of the Royal Statistical Society*, ser. A, cxxv (1962), 387-97.
Percival, J. *Wheat in Great Britain*. 2nd edn. London, 1948.
Pethybridge, G. H. and Lafferty, H. A. 'Further observations on the cause of the common dry-rot of the potato tuber in the British Isles' in *Scientific Proceedings of the Royal Dublin Society*, new ser., xv (1917), 193-222.
Populer, C. *Le comportement des épidémies de mildiou du tabac*. Gembloux, Belgium, 1964.
Post, J. *The last great subsistence crisis in the western world*. Baltimore, 1977.
Prebble, J. *The highland clearances*. London, 1963.
Prunet, A. 'Le mildiou de la pomme de terre' in *Revue de Viticulture*, Paris, xvii (1902), 663-6; xviii, 97-104.
Puttemans, A. 'Reivindicação visando a denominação scientifica da doença da Batateira (Phytophthora infestans [Mont.] de Bary.)' in *Rodriguésia*, ii (1937), 341-50.
Rashid, S. 'The policy of laissez-faire during scarcities' in *Economic Journal*, xc (1980), 493-503.
Ravaillon, M. *Markets and famines*. Oxford, 1987.
Rayner, R. W. and Hopkins, J. C. F. *Blue mould of tobacco; a review of current information*. Miscellaneous publication no. 16 of the Commonwealth Mycological Institute, London, 1962.
Reddick, D. 'Whence came Phytophthora infestans?' in *Chronica Botanica*, Leiden,

v (1939), 410–2.
Reid, T. W. *Life of the Right Honourable William Edward Forster*. London, 1889.
RIA Proc. Proceedings of the Royal Irish Academy.
Royle, S. A. 'Irish famine relief in the early nineteenth century: the 1822 famine on the Aran Islands' in *Ir. Econ. and Soc. Hist.* xi (1984), 44–59.
Roze, E. 'Sur des bactériacées de la pomme de terre' in *Bulletin de la Société Mycologique de France*, xii (1896), 55–63.
– *Histoire de la pomme de terre*. Paris, 1898.
RSAI Jn. Journal of the Royal Society of Antiquaries of Ireland.
Safford, W. E. 'The potato of romance and of reality' in *Journal of Heredity*, xvi (1925), 113–26; 175–84; 217–30.
Salaman, R. N. *The influence of the potato on the course of Irish history* (Finlay Memorial Lecture). Dublin, 1943.
– *The history and social influence of the potato*. Cambridge, 1949; revised edn, 1985.
Semal, J., Joly, P. and Lamy, D. 'L'épidémie de "maladie des pommes de terre" causée en Europe en 1845 par le *Phytophthora infestans* (Mont.) de Bary: les faits et les auteurs' in *Annales de Gembloux*, lxxxix (1983), 79–99.
Sen, A. K. *Poverty and famines*. Oxford, 1981.
Simington, R. C. 'Tithe applotment books of 1834' in *Journal of the Department of Agriculture*, Dublin, xxxviii (1941), 239–343.
Solar, P. M. 'Why Ireland starved: a critical review of the econometric results' in *Ir. Econ. and Soc. Hist.*, xi (1984), 107–15.
– 'The great famine was no ordinary subsistence crisis', in Crawford (ed.), *Famine*, pp 112–33.
Steers, J. A. (ed.) *Field studies in the British Isles*. London, 1964.
Steinhauser, F., Eckel, O. and Sauberer, F. *Klima und Bioklima von Wien*. Vienna, 1955.
Stevens, N. E. 'Phytopathology – the dark ages in plant pathology in America: 1830–1870' in *Journal of the Washington Academy of Sciences*, xxiii (1933), 435–46.
Stevens, N. E. and Stevens, R. B. *Disease in plants. An introduction to agricultural phytopathology*. Walton, Mass., 1952.
Sukhatme, P. V. 'The world's hunger and future needs in food supplies' in *Journal of the Royal Statistical Society*, ser. A, cxxiv (1961), 463–508.
Terlouw, Frieda. 'De aardappelziekte in Nederland in 1845 en volgende jaren' in *Economisch en Sociaal-Historisch Jaarboek*, xxxiv (1971), 263–308.
Todd, F. A. 'The occurrence of the blue mold of tobacco in West Germany, Switzerland, France and other European countries' in *Plant Disease Reporter*, xlv (1961), 319–26.
Van der Plank, J. E. *Plant diseases: epidemics and control*. New York and London, 1963.
Waidson, H. M. *Jeremias Gotthelf: an introduction to the Swiss novelist*. Oxford, 1953.
Walsh, T., Ryan, P. F. and Kilroy, J. 'A half century of fertiliser and lime use in Ireland' in *Journal of the Statistical and Social Inquiry Society of Ireland*, xix (1957), 104–36.
Watkins, S. C. and Menken, J. 'Famines in historical perspective' in *Population and Development Review*, xi (1985), 647–75.
Whetzel, H. H. *An outline of the history of phytopathology*. Philadelphia and London, 1918.
Woodham-Smith, C. *The great hunger: Ireland, 1845-9*. London, 1962.
Wood-Martin, W. G. *History of Sligo*. Dublin, 1892.
Woods, C. J. 'American travellers in Ireland before and during the great famine: a case of culture-shock', in W. Zach and H. Kosok (eds), *Literary interrelations: Ireland, England and the world*. Tübingen: Narr, 1987, iii, 77–84.

Index

INDEX